AFFILIATION
— IN THE —
WORKPLACE

AFFILIATION
— IN THE —
WORKPLACE

Value Creation in the
New Organization

RON ELSDON

Westport, Connecticut
London

Library of Congress Cataloging-in-Publication Data

Elsdon, Ron, 1950–
    Affiliation in the workplace : value creation in the new organization / Ron Elsdon.
      p. cm.
    Includes bibliographical references and index.
    ISBN 1–56720–436–8 (alk. paper)
    1. Organizational behavior.   2. Business networks.   3. Interpersonal relations.   I. Title.
HD58.7.E427   2003
    658.3'145—dc21   2002069695

British Library Cataloguing in Publication Data is available.

Library of Congress Catalog Card Number: 2002069695
ISBN: 1–56720–436–8

First published in 2003

Praeger Publishers, 88 Post Road West, Westport, CT 06881
An imprint of Greenwood Publishing Group, Inc.
www.praeger.com

Printed in the United States of America

The paper used in this book complies with the
Permanent Paper Standard issued by the National
Information Standards Organization (Z39.48–1984).

10 9 8 7 6 5 4 3 2 1

Copyright Acknowledgment

The author and publisher gratefully acknowledge permission for the use of the following material:
Ron Elsdon and Seema Iyer, "Creating Value and Enhancing Retention Through Employee
Development: The Sun Microsystems Experience." Reprinted with permission from *Human
Resource Planning*, Vol. 22, No. 2 (1999). Copyright 1999 by The Human Resource Planning
Society, 317 Madison Avenue, Suite 1509, New York, NY 10017, Phone: (212) 490-6387, Fax:
(212) 682-6851.

This book is for my family

Kindness in words creates confidence
Kindness in thinking creates profoundness
Kindness in giving creates love
Lao-tzu (about 600 B.C.)

Contents

CONTENTS

Illustrations

ILLUSTRATIONS

Preface

This book is about people, about us, about our hopes and fears, our dreams and aspirations. The real stuff that inspires. It is about the divine within us; in the words of the Roman poet Horace (23 B.C.) it is about "Awakening the music sleeping on the strings." I first heard these words on U.S. National Public Radio about a year after starting this book. They capture the essence of this story.

This is a time of transformation in our working lives and in the relationship of individuals to organizations. The working environment is shifting from a manufacturing base within national boundaries to service and information provision on an international scale delivered by a wide range of organizational structures. The workforce, which at one time was mainly permanent employees recruited from a large resource pool, now includes many contingent and contract employees, whose talents in many cases are in short supply. Visions of the future that have been offered range from the apocalyptic (Rifkin 1995) to a technology-induced nirvana of prosperity (Rubin 2001). It is not surprising that there is much confusion about a path forward.

In most sectors of the economy, the paternalistic organization of the past is gone. However, we are struggling to find a replacement. This struggle affects us deeply as individuals, in our ability to "Let the beauty we love be what we do" as the thirteenth-century poet Rumi so acutely observed (Moyers 1995). It affects our organizations in their ability to create value. It fundamentally affects each organizational leader and human resources (HR) in defining roles and enabling organizations and the individuals within them to manage change for the benefit of all. We are in many ways at a fork in the road. In one direction lie the seeds of destruction in a bifurcated society of those having great resources and those barely subsisting. In another direction is a path that leads to new relationships between organizations and individuals that energizes working lives, propels organizations to growth and prosperity and invigorates communities. At the core of this path is affiliation between individuals and organizations, and that is the subject of this book.

As in any time of fundamental change, it is difficult to see clearly where to find calm waters, prosperity and enhanced individual meaning. It is hard to know which signals are mere perturbations and which represent a permanent change. Prominent among these signals is the availability of people to staff organizations. Leaders and HR are in the eye of this particular storm. People in organizations are the primary source of value creation, and they leave at the end of each day. We will examine pointers for distinguishing the transitory signals from those that are leading indicators of permanent change.

During the 1980s, 1990s and early 2000s organizations sent a strong message that loyalty is dead and that message was well heard by employees. In the late 1990s and in the early 2000s we saw the consequences. Rapidly spiraling attrition rates, little sense of community in organizations, growth constrained by lack of people, not lack of capital. While softening of the economy in many developed countries mitigated these issues in the short term, they remain as major structural issues for the long term. This book examines new ways to think about the connection between the organization and each person in it. New ways to think about and practice affiliation, so that we are no longer nomads in a strange land.

Organizational leaders and HR face several dilemmas today. There is a desperate need to create a new relationship with employees that strengthens connections and a sense of community, but it is also necessary to devise approaches that recognize, create and adapt to changing business needs. We must meet our needs for fulfillment as individuals and create dynamic organizations. We must link the need for business performance with the need to meet individual aspirations. We must create meaning and substance, so that all in our organizations can commit and engage. Employment is not a one-night stand, although that is the message so often sent. How do we create a more enduring relationship, a relationship that builds meaning and continuity?

These are the ideas that are explored in the book. We explore how to build affiliation in the organization of the future, and how this differs from the traditional model of retention as one of limiting choices. We examine the dilemmas that leaders and human resource professionals face in engaging the workforce of the future. We explore changing models of organizations, changing roles and approaches to consider in the future. We explore new roles for leaders and human resource professionals to help build affiliation and community within the organization so that people elect to stay and organizations survive and thrive.

Central to this process is the need to support individual development. There are many reactions possible to a focus on individual development as a means to increase the connection of individuals to organizations. At one extreme is an acceptance on faith that this benefits the individual and the organization. The other extreme would view individual development as a waste of time and money. We explore measurement approaches that can help address this dilemma by guiding the commitment of resources so that they are used most effectively. We explore how to determine an optimum resource level. We look at how to bridge the organization of the past to that of the future and the challenges this represents. We look at approaches for the future and how inclusion is at their core.

On one level the journey that led to this book began with a conversation about the relationship of individuals to organizations. It took place in an office at the Career Action Center, a nonprofit organization that specialized in careers. Several of us were discussing workforce challenges that organizations face. Being fresh into the career field I was fired with idealistic notions in this area, which I admit have strengthened rather than diminished in the intervening years. We questioned how to show a bottom-line benefit to an organization investing in individual fulfillment and development. We questioned whether there is an optimum attrition level for an organization. I remember sketching a chart that showed this. But we had no idea how to move from these ideas to reality, as the only data that seemed to be available was anecdotal rather than quantitative. The whole subject might have lain dormant if it weren't for a fortunate association between the Career Action Center and Sun Microsystems. The Career Action Center was providing on-site career counseling at a number of Sun's locations to help employees in their development. Still fired by this naïve idealism I was struck by the opportunity to explore the questions in some depth based on the ongoing work at Sun.

There were also some other pieces of the jigsaw. They came from an unlikely source, the world of technology and business planning. In the early 1980s I was working for Amoco Chemical Company in a business planning capacity, fresh from life as a research engineer. In those days Amoco Chemical was a vibrant organization, not long formed. The planning group included engineers and MBAs who were given freedom to experiment with new analytical approaches. This is a dangerous step with a naïve idealist like me. I was exploring the application of some rather arcane mathematical techniques to business planning and looking into factors that link and characterize economic performance. Some had application at the time, some remained curiosities and it turns out that others have application to today's analysis of workforce dynamics. I then found myself in a series of leadership positions responsible for growing businesses or for functional areas responsible for new business growth. These experiences taught me, firsthand, the complex and fragile nature of the relationship between individuals and organizations. They taught me that leaders build this relationship one person at a time.

Which brings us back to Sun Microsystems, the Career Action Center and individual career counseling. Continuing the naïve idealist thread, I approached Sun with the notion of exploring the organizational benefits of supporting individuals in their career development and individual fulfillment. Sun in the late 1990s had a similar vibrancy to Amoco in the early 1980s. Instead of dismissing the idea as unworkable, which was the reaction of one external advisor, Sun offered it to one of their staff members, Seema Iyer, as an interesting collaborative project. The potential benefits to Sun were the opportunities to quantify and optimize the use of resources and the potential to further strengthen links with the workforce. Seema being a demographer, and displaying a sense of irrepressible curiosity coupled with a much greater dose of realism than I possessed, accepted the opportunity. So Seema and I set out to create a protocol to address this area. We drew on Seema's ability to access data from the Sun system and my background in defining key business elements and performing the needed analyses. We started gradually, not sure of the outcome, quickly concluding that the approach offered value and insights, and dived in more deeply (Elsdon and Iyer 2000). The resulting study, which is reviewed in Chapter 7, provides an approach and factual data linking investment in enhanced individual fulfillment to a bottom-line benefit for the organization.

At the same time my naïve idealism was being further fueled by studies in career development at John F. Kennedy University, where learning occurs in a marvelous, open and inquiring environment. This led me into the world of individual career counseling and ultimately to a private practice. In doing career counseling and coaching I was given the rare gift of being present with people in their hopes, dreams, disappointments and aspirations. I was able to bring learnings from my organizational work to individuals and vice versa.

Then I joined Drake Beam Morin (DBM), helping support organizations in their evolving workforce needs. In 2000, finding and keeping employees was a dominant theme. It was a chance discussion with Susan Kaminski, then of Applied Materials, that led to the next phase. Susan has a profound understanding of organizational dynamics and a deep respect for the people in the organization. She is a brilliant human resource strategist. We were discussing how to better understand and quantify employee losses and movement, and develop approaches that would strengthen future employee commitment. Drawing on the attrition demographic approaches developed at Sun and interviewing approaches developed at DBM, we created a protocol to understand the what and why of employee attrition. It has been used successfully with a number of organizations, each a leader in its field, and each committed to excellence in the workplace. In addition to Applied Materials, some other examples are Kaiser Permanente in healthcare and Boeing in aerospace. Results from these and other studies with individual organizations provide some of the raw material for this book. In addition the content is based on contacts with more than 1,000 organizations and more than 2,000 people on the subject of employee affiliation in 2000, 2001 and 2002. Interwoven with this organizational experience are the learnings gained from many individual career counseling sessions. Thoughts and ideas developed over several years based on reflections about individual and organizational relationships are also included. Some of these ideas have been presented to professional societies, individual organizations and other gatherings of interested parties. I am deeply grateful to DBM for encouraging me to write this book and spend time on it where needed. However, the content contained here reflects my own opinions, it is not the expressed opinion of DBM or any other organization. Any errors are solely my responsibility.

There is debate about the applicability of the best practices approach in the human resource arena. This approach is based on the assumption that human resource practices can be identified in one organization and universally translated to other organizations. While Delery and Doty (1996) find some support for this approach with certain practices they also identify other views that suggest either the practices need to be specific to a given organization, or that it is the sum total of a pattern of interventions that is the key. In the area of employee affiliation I am mindful of the pitfalls that can emerge from a best practices approach. I am often asked if there are organizations whose practices should be emulated in the area of employee affiliation. My response is that some organizations have developed interventions that are effective for their culture but they may or may not transplant. Indeed there are examples in the literature of organizations cited for excellence in human resource practices (Michaels 2001) that are subsequently found to be sorely lacking, Enron being a case in point. So I suggest using great caution and not simply seeking to copy others in this area. The process of building affiliation with the workforce is a personal process for each organization, requiring the investment of time and resources in its construction. It is not about pulling a simple checklist off the shelf and following it. By investing in understanding the characteristics and needs of the workforce, it is possible for any organization to step ahead of its peers. This is a more effective approach than simply attempting to emulate past practices from a different cultural context that may be fading in relevance.

In providing reference information for Internet sources, the website name, and if it is not too lengthy, the Universal Source Locator (URL) are included in the body of the text, with full information in the references. While this URL information was confirmed at the time the book was prepared, it is possible that some URLs will change over time. The source information for all text references is included alphabetically in the References section. The term leader is used throughout the book for anyone in the organization with the ability to materially influence future direction. In some organizations this may mean the entire workforce, in others it may mean only a small group of people, with many organizations between these two extremes. The term HR is also used throughout the book referring to anyone in the human resources function.

Acknowledgments

This book grew out of many acts of kindness, gifts from others. It gave me much pleasure to recall those moments. I hope that in some small way this book is an acknowledgment to those people for their acts of kindness. My first exposure to an academic world that was accepting and encouraging came at Leeds University in England. Had it not been for the openness and support of the staff in the department of Chemical Engineering I would have lost interest in the world of the mind. It was a revelation to find an environment that looked not to judge but to support, that looked not to constrain but to encourage. Then at Cambridge University in England, I found a world that prized the pursuit of knowledge, unfettered and unbounded. I was not an easy student and I still appreciate my advisors, Charlie Shearer and Ron Nedderman, giving me the freedom to grapple with the greatest intellectual challenges of my life. With their guidance I began to touch the edge of human knowledge in one tiny area, and realized that the wonder is not how much we know, but how little we know and understand even less. I learned about the strength of the research process propelled by our curiosity. For some the new frontier is physical, for others, including me, it is conceptual.

But there is another world, the world of the person, the team and the organization. I am grateful for my years at Amoco Chemical Company and Amoco Fabric and Fibers, and the many fine people I met there for awakening this awareness in me. They opened the eyes of a people-challenged nerd like me. Here was an environment that valued conducting business with the highest standards of integrity. There were towering figures such as Bob Cadieux, whose brilliant mind and humility were inspirational to many others and to me. There were friends, co-workers and managers whose small acts of kindness and flashes of inspiration made those years exciting and sowed the seeds of ideas that are surfacing in this book. People such as Benny Benjamin, Hans Pohlmann, Ron Carlson and Pete Thornley. Most of all at Amoco I am grateful to the members of the teams I led in the southern United States and in the midwest, who managed to inspire me as their leader. The world of the organization is becoming daily more culturally diverse and I am grateful to those at Air Liquide such as Jim Redmond and Wayne Swafford, who helped me appreciate this and the value of operational excellence. I also learned at Air Liquide the importance of being true to yourself, and began a new journey.

John F. Kennedy University manages to combine a deep sense of social responsibility with an abiding care for the individual. It was a revelation for me to learn more of the beauty of the human spirit in that environment. Wonderful and supportive staff such as Sue Aiken, David Cherner, Joan Sullivan, Mark Guterman and Bob Gardner opened a whole new horizon for me. My fellow students were a constant source of inspiration and support. This experience recharged the sense of wonder in me and formed a bridge to the Career Action Center. These were the best of times and the worst of times. Diane Saign and Betsy Collard were the best. Their support and tremendous intellectual depth were primary catalysts in starting the thinking that led to this book. There were many others whose lives touched and enriched mine, such as Stephanie Moore, Joanne Martens and many in the teams I led.

Others along this path with their kindness and thoughtfulness left me a better person and opened new horizons of thinking. Teri Quatman opened a door to the world of teaching, for which I will always be grateful. Many students at Santa Clara University brought life to my classes and a freshness of ideas and thinking. Roy Blitzer has been a good friend and mentor. Pearl Sims and Carter Andrews are good friends who show by their example how to bring hope to many lives lived without it.

I would like to give special mention to my friends and colleagues Seema Iyer and Deborah Warner. It was Seema's willingness to follow a new path that led to some of the key initial steps described in this book, and Seema's insights helped shape that initial path. Deborah has stayed true to her path and been a wise and valued friend.

Acknowledgments

I have been fortunate to work with many in organizations whose quiet devotion to their cause and great depth of knowledge have been key to shaping the ideas in this book. These heroic figures include Ross Schraeder, formerly of Texas Instruments; Steve Leven of Texas Instruments; Susan Solat, Gloria Debs, Lora Colflesh and Carole Guterman, who were in the world of Sun Microsystems when we met; Dottie Moser and Barbara Lewis of Easter Seals; Marian Spitzberg of Belo, Ken Johnson of Spectra Physics, Monique Breault of Hewlett-Packard, Jim Dagnon of Boeing, Bob Sachs and Pat Finnegan of Kaiser Permanente, Bill Huffaker of Providian, and Susan Kaminski and Debra Scates of Applied Materials. To all I owe a great debt of gratitude.

This book would not have happened without the support of many friends, colleagues and leaders at DBM. It has been a pleasure to work for this organization of the heart that embodies a mission of helping improve people's lives. I owe a debt of deep gratitude to many, including Sherry Cadorette, who has demonstrated the principles developed in this book by example; to Tom Silveri, Craig Sawin and Bob Petisi, who demonstrated servant leadership at its finest; to John Brock, whose faith in this work has meant a great deal to me; to Cathy Farrell and John Miller for leading in just the right way; to Barbara Langham my colleague and friend for always encouraging and setting an outstanding example; to Ken Kneisel and many members of his delivery team for supporting new areas when it would have been much easier to stay with the status quo; and to many account executives in DBM who bring this work to life, such as Brad Burgess, Kierstin Frey, Lisa Just, Shari Krueger, John Matchette, Mindy Mazer, Nancy Paris, Mel Ruiz, Kirsten Sorensen, Brad Smith, Carl Weisiger and many others. The DBM marketing team Gerald Purgay, Shari Fryer and Nicci Rinaldi have been a source of energy, enthusiasm and creativity and contributed the description of the Applied Materials study in Chapter 6. Finally I owe a deep debt of gratitude to the retention services team, Julie Allan, Joe Bruccoleri, Michele DeRosa, Mary Ann Dolan, Joan Luciano, Abby Price, Karen Yetman and many consultants working with the practice in the United States for their outstanding work in creating and building a vibrant practice and in exemplifying the ideas that are central to this book. In particular Julie Allan's tremendous data analysis skills were central to the creation of meaning from many individual projects, in pooling the individual project data and in creating the generations chart in the Introduction. The international team in DBM has been an ongoing source of encouragement, with Bob Critchley, Jacques Eliard, Celia Nicholson, Rod Watson, Day Merrill and Nurit Berman bringing special and valued perspectives to this work. Meanwhile Dick Snowden's depth of insight into the consultative process enabled the conversion of theory to reality. Others whose inputs I have valued greatly, bringing new thinking to the area of social capital, are Wayne and Cheryl Baker of Humax and Steve Flannes and Charlie Grantham.

There are others whose contributions are at the foundation of this book. These are the clients I have worked with in my private career counseling practice, at John F. Kennedy University, at the Career Action Center and while doing executive coaching for DBM. Their willingness to share their lives with me has been deeply moving. It has confirmed for me the beauty and resilience of the human spirit walking with God. The examples in the book reflect the learning I have gained from working with these clients. The descriptions are given in such a way that they respect individual confidentiality.

I am very grateful to my editor at Greenwood, Hilary Claggett, for having the faith to propose the development of this book. Hilary was always available as a source of encouragement as the book progressed and to answer my countless questions as we shaped the final form. Hilary has been a pleasure to work with.

I am so thankful to my family whom I love deeply. For the support from my mother Barbara and father Frank over many years. Our children Mark and Anna's lives are a blessing to all of us as they show kindness and compassion to those around them. Our daughter-in-law Erica has been a new light in our family, as has our friend Andy Domek. All have endured my absence, while hunched over a computer screen creating this book, with good humor and much support. Finally I am very grateful to my wife Linda, whom I love deeply. Linda has been a source of deep support; encouraging me where needed and keeping me grounded where needed. This, during the long hours of preparation of the book. The book exists in its current form due to Linda's support, compassion and caring.

Introduction

Two weeks, two calls, two lost jobs and two new lives. These calls came from colleagues, leaving their organizations after many years. I could hear the loss and concern in their voices, and also the sense of opportunity. Ironically, one person was working on a retention program for her organization when she decided to leave. Another was exploring how to develop people in his company. Less than two weeks later, a manager of human resources said to me, "I am dying over this," as we talked about her challenges to recruit and retain new employees. As I met with groups of managers and human resource professionals over the coming weeks and months, this theme of loss was repeated with growing intensity. My clients in career counseling voiced their sense of loss and concern about being disconnected from their work. But they also voiced an emerging sense of new opportunity, opportunity crafted from a growing sense of self-awareness. From a growing realization that they can choose places to work that match their needs, rather than conform to an organizational stereotype.

At the same time that many people feel an increasing sense of disconnect around fulfillment in their traditional work, they are beginning to exercise a basic right to work in an environment that supports their development. Meanwhile, organizations are struggling to find the right people to carry forward the creation of growth and value. Today our organizations are limited not by the traditional economic resources, such

Figure I-1
Recent U.S. Generations (Birth Years)

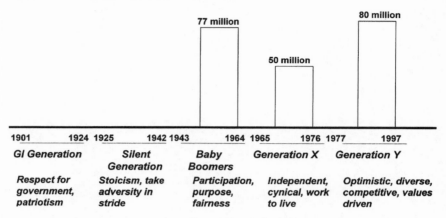

1901	1924	1925	1942	1943	1964	1965	1976	1977	1997
GI Generation		*Silent Generation*		*Baby Boomers*		*Generation X*		*Generation Y*	
Respect for government, patriotism		*Stoicism, take adversity in stride*		*Participation, purpose, fairness*		*Independent, cynical, work to live*		*Optimistic, diverse, competitive, values driven*	

as land, equipment and capital, but by the resources of human ingenuity, creativity and innovation. These resources are scarce and unpredictable. They are subject not only to the call of intellect and reason but also to the call of affect and emotion. And today, for the first time on a broad scale since the beginning of the Industrial Revolution, that emotion can seek direct expression through each person's decision to affiliate or not.

In industrialized nations, population demographics are such that a slower growth of entrants into the workforce will exacerbate the difficulty of finding employees in the future. This is not a short-term perturbation that will go away so that life returns to business as usual. It is the beginning of a fundamental restructuring in the relationship between individuals and organizations. Recognizing and responding effectively to this change is a matter of survival for organizations. And for individuals it means fully expressing who they are in their work lives. The revolutionary changes occurring in the workforce reflect many aspects:

• Generational differences with different perspectives on the relationship of work and personal life as shown in Figure I-1, which includes estimates of the number of people in the United States who are part of the three most recent generations.

While there are various perspectives on the specific years that distinguish the generational cohorts and their characteristics (Halstead 1999, SHRM 2001, Zemke 2001), and there are substantial individual differences within a given generational cohort, the overarching perspectives shown here underline the tensions that can develop in the workforce due to different generational core values.

Figure I-2
U.S. Labor Force Annual Growth Rates Showing 10-year Moving Average

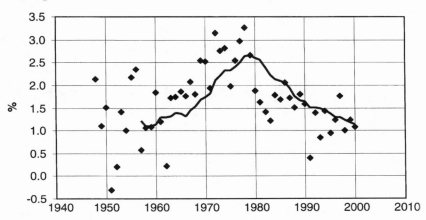

- An aging population, with the 60+ cohort expected to grow by almost 50% over the next 20 years in the United States based on the U.S. Census Bureau middle series projections (U.S. Census Bureau: http://www.census.gov/).
- Growing ethnic diversity with today's minorities projected to account for almost 40% of the U.S. workforce by 2025, up from less than 20% in 1980 (Fullerton 1999).
- Slowing growth rate of the U.S. workforce as shown in Figure I-2 (Bureau of Labor Statistics [U.S.]: www.bls.gov).

The diamonds show the annual growth in the U.S. workforce each year from 1947 to 2000. The solid line is the ten-year moving average, which is the average of the prior ten years of data. The growth rate of the workforce increased steadily from the mid-1950s through the end of the 1970s, in part due to accelerated entry of women into the workforce. However, since 1980 there has been a steady decline in the growth rate of the workforce. The difficulties of finding people in the late 1990s, as GDP growth was accelerating and workforce growth was slowing, are not surprising. A key question is, what will happen to future growth rates? One of the interesting aspects of population and workforce demographic projections, unlike most other projections, is that barring a catastrophic event, they have a high probability of occurring. Figure I-3 shows the past and projected U.S. workforce and workforce growth rate.

These projections are based on the U.S. Census Bureau middle series (Fullerton 1999). The bars show the number of people in the U.S. work-

Figure I-3
U.S. Labor Force Growth Through 2025

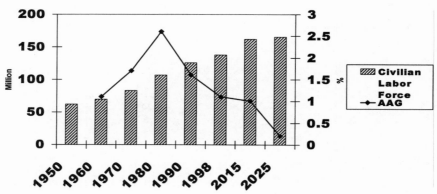

force in millions referring to the left axis. The line shows the average annual growth rate (AAG) of the workforce between each of the years shown on the horizontal axis. The growth rates refer to the right axis. The growth rate of the U.S. workforce is projected to decline to almost zero by 2025. It is clear that employee scarcity will become a more pressing issue in the years ahead. Employee scarcity is here to stay, and with it the balance of power is shifting away from organizations.

Employment choices in the future world, which were not as readily available to prior generations, include an ongoing decision about whether to stay engaged with an organization, and, if so, in what capacity. They include the choice to participate in the contingent workforce. They include the choice to change organizations or career directions when priorities and lifestyle needs change. These choices introduce tensions into our organizations and into our individual lives. The evolution of thinking in the field of career development provides a perspective on these changes.

Much of the foundation of career development began with the Trait and Factor approach of Parsons (1909), focused on measuring individual capabilities (traits) and relating these to organizational need (factors). Reviews of Parsons' work are given for example by Sharf (1992) and Zunker (1998). In parallel with the evolution of career development processes is the evolution of thinking about career counseling, which is focused on the individual. The introduction by Carl Rogers (1942) of client-centered approaches to counseling profoundly influenced the field of career counseling, providing a counterpoint to other more directive approaches (Williamson 1939). Rogers' framing of the counseling process as one of mutual respect, focused on helping individuals integrate various aspects of themselves in determining their own destiny, was a landmark. Since then advances and development in theory and practice have reinforced a framework that provides each person with a basis for taking control of their work lives.

On an organizational level career development evolved with the growth of corporations and an emphasis on training to mold individuals to fit organizational demands. Implicit in this fit was an understanding that the organization would provide a safe haven for each employee. In the 1980s and early 1990s we saw this implied contract severed, as organizations sought to increase short-term efficiencies. The organizational emphasis switched to self-reliance based on individuals taking ownership of their careers, with organizations providing support for their development, but not long-term commitment. Employment became a one-night stand or, euphemistically, employment-at-will. Those unable to function in this environment were left with depleted resources and options. However, changing population demographics created a scarcity of critical skills by the late 1990s and, as a result, some organizations could not reach their growth potential. Many organizations began to experience increased attrition rates and difficulty recruiting. Most organizations began to critically evaluate their relationship with their employees, recognizing the need for a major transformation, but unclear about the direction of this transformation. While the slowing economy of the early 2000s mitigated employee scarcity temporarily in some sectors of the economy, workforce demographics will drive employee scarcity as a central issue in the years to come. It is the purpose of this book to offer ideas about the organizational transformation needed to succeed in this emerging world. For it is in this transformation that the seeds for future individual fulfillment and growing organizational prosperity reside.

This journey begins with some fundamental questions about the relationship of individuals to organizations. Why would a person choose to connect, and remain with, an organization since by doing so he or she relinquishes some freedom of choice? Conversely, why would an organization seek any but a transactional relationship with its members, since such a relationship maximizes organizational flexibility and freedom of choice?

Let us first examine the choice faced by an individual considering joining or remaining with an organization. If this decision were purely economic then financial return would be the only criterion for deciding. This is not the case. In studies described in Chapter 4 financial return is well down the list of individual priorities. Instead career development, recognition, and work environment are higher in priority. For the decision to connect, at its core, is an emotional decision. Seeking this sense of affection or affiliation is a fundamental human need that drives the formation of organizations, in spite of the difficulties, tensions and ambiguities that such affiliation can create. The decision to affiliate is complex, intimately connected to finding fulfillment, and unique for each of us.

Now let us examine the driving forces for the organization, or more accurately for key individual decision makers in organizations. This leads to the concept of value creation. There are many proven techniques for calculating the economic value of organizations, for example the discounted value of projected future cash flows. In all cases the organization must engage in a conversion process that generates economic value. In times past these processes were largely physical, for example iron ore into steel, or natural fibers into yarn, fabric and garments. Today processes that create and deliver information or components of a knowledge system, for example visual images, computer software, or new designs for clothing drive much of our economic growth. In some cases they are intangibles, for example processes to strengthen leadership. These processes require a growing body of knowledge and frequently involve complex internal and external relationships. People gain in effectiveness in these areas with time and experience by extended affiliation. So economic value is enhanced through extended rather than transient relationships. Affiliation both enhances individual fulfillment and organizational value creation.

What is meant by affiliation? Affiliation is defined as becoming closely connected or associated. It is from a medieval Latin word meaning to adopt. This mutual adoption of an organization by an individual and vice versa requires tenacity, commitment, shared values and common goals. It is most likely to occur in an environment of open communication. It is unlikely to occur where this openness is missing. The traditional approach connecting individuals to organizations more closely mirrors the definition of retention, which is: to hold back, keep, restrain or to keep in one's pay or service. It implies a one-way bond. What are the problems with the golden handcuffs approach? Aside from ethical considerations, in today's world and the world of the future it is impractical. People have real choices, and these choices will multiply in the future. The work world begins to resemble the formation of a giant guild (Rosenfeld 2001), in which all are potential members. And those members are becoming a scarce resource.

What does this mean for the future? The approach to retention as one of constraining and limiting options needs to be replaced with an approach that fosters openness and development. This may seem counterintuitive. The bond of affiliation is stronger when the bonds of tethering are weaker? Affiliation at its core is a two-way relationship, supported by both the individual and the organization. Retention at its core is a one-way relationship, done by the organization to the individual. In the emerging world of work both parties have an equal say. Such a two-way relationship is strong only when both parties willingly participate without one being coerced by the other. So the new approach contains the following elements:

- Understand individual needs
- Provide options and choices
- Foster learning
- Support breadth in development
- Engage individuals as free agents

Let us examine each of these elements. Since a strong relationship of individuals to organizations is two-way, it must reflect each person's individual needs. It is no longer sufficient to present a relationship as a "take it or leave it" proposition that is rolled off an organizational assembly line. Instead the nature of the relationship and engagement needs to be crafted to each individual. This is a one-to-one relationship, not one to many. It requires significantly enhanced interpersonal skills for those in the organization chartered with building these relationships. Furthermore, it requires deep knowledge of organizational direction and opportunities as the relationship is built and grows around the provision of options and choices. These choices include practical aspects such as time flexibility, structural aspects such as the nature of management relationships and content aspects such as project areas of interest. I still well remember a co-worker early in my career who lived a nocturnal existence. It worked for him and, since his primary contact was with the computer, it worked for the organization. He eventually moved on to become a dentist, so hopefully he has some nocturnal patients.

It used to be said that the half-life of technical knowledge is about five years. No more, today it is measured in months rather than years in many fields. This extends beyond highly technical fields to the tools that we use for analysis and communication. In this environment, survival requires constant learning. Recently I heard a vice president of HR describe her company's management planning process. One year previously the organization reviewed the required competencies of its top managers and repeated the exercise a year later. The second review led to the conclusion that in that one year, half of the positions became obsolete. This is our pace of change. In this environment it is essential to provide ongoing learning for employees so that organizations remain competitive and employees maintain their currency. This means supporting development in a broad sense in areas that interest and engage people, whether these areas are technical, interpersonal or business. The organizational challenge is to harness this wealth of individual enthusiasm, which changes over time, so that the business needs of the organization are served. This is a very different challenge from one of requiring conformity to a predetermined organizational norm.

These aspects all support Drucker's idea that we engage individuals as volunteers. Affiliation is a daily choice. This places a much greater responsibility on the organization to foster the relationship than the past traditional approach. But it offers the possibility of engaging people in a much deeper and more productive relationship.

This leads to the fundamental principles of affiliation to be explored throughout this book:

- Organizations to prosper and grow in the world of the future will create a strong sense of affiliation for their members.
- Affiliation is a voluntary relationship that succeeds only when all parties benefit.
- Affiliation occurs on multiple levels.
- Affiliation at its core is an emotional connection.
- Enabling individuals to seek their path of greatest fulfillment through affiliation will create economic prosperity and cultural richness.
- Affiliation means inclusion.
- Affiliation extends from the organization to the broader community.

The single most critical resource for a successful organization in the future will be its employees. Here is how Eric Benhamou, the chairman and CEO of 3Com, a $6 billion high-tech organization headquartered in Silicon Valley, expresses it: "I'm much less worried about one of our competitors stealing the designs of our latest product than I am about one of our competitors stealing one of our best minds" (Benhamou 1998). In this environment, securing, strengthening and building a workforce becomes a pre-eminent business task. This means creating a strong sense of affiliation for individuals. This relationship is voluntary and two-way, requiring that each party contributes and that each party benefits. It is a multilevel relationship involving many points of contact and multiple aspects of human experience whether these relate to survival issues, financial issues or self-actualization. At its core affiliation is an emotional connection that extends well beyond intellectual commitment. The strength of emotions that surface when that bond is severed is a testament to this.

Practitioners in the career field take it as an item of faith that enabling each person to find greater fulfillment in their work also benefits their organization. There is a growing body of evidence to support this contention and we will examine it in this book. Inclusion is central to affiliation. That means inclusion to support breadth of viewpoint, breadth of perspective and breadth of experience. The engine of intellectual capital generation is stimulated by the fuel of diversity and by the mechanism of inclusion, which leads to the broader community. Individual connections to many groups and organizations form our communities. It is through the growth of these connections and the development of broader organizational cooperation to address changing workforce needs that much opportunity exists. We will explore this area further in this book.

What about the role of leaders and HR in the new organization? How will these roles change? Let us examine the role of the leader first. I remember well sitting in a meeting of the top management group of a multibillion dollar organization a number of years ago. The president was expressing his frustration at the decision-making processes in the organization and the expectations of individuals within it. With a flick of cigar ash (these were less enlightened times), he complained about how everyone wanted to be a part of the decision-making process, whereas in his opinion it belonged with the top management team (or person). The rest of the organization just needed to get busy implementing. It is not surprising that this organization no longer exists but has been acquired. This approach of command and control, where the top tells the middle what to do to the bottom, will not work in our future work world. It lacks mutuality, it lacks respect for the individual and it is anathema to affiliation.

In marked contrast is the relatively recent elevation of self-awareness as a key management skill. Self-awareness is a critical first step needed to relate to and understand others, which in turn will be essential to foster the two-way relationship that will characterize successful organizations in the future. So the role of the leader is evolving into one of providing a framework in which each person can best express his or her natural talents and abilities. This means fostering open communication, creating business opportunities and translating these into individual opportunities, it means supporting inclusion of different viewpoints, it means taking a leadership role in relation to workforce development issues as they affect all members of the community. DePree (1992) relates the story of the owner of a small business who also composed for the local orchestra, and asks the question, was he an amateur composer and a professional businessman, or was he a professional composer who ran a business for the love of it. Asking such questions and helping members of organizations discover their own answers are central to the role of leadership in the new organization. I remember a situation several years ago when the CEO of a successful organization I was working with was discussing a problem that occurred in a remote location. While he was concerned about what happened, a greater concern was the fact that within the organization, prior to the event, someone knew about the problem and could have provided the information that would have prevented it. But there was no mechanism to bring forward what could be controversial information. This leader encouraged his organization to greater openness. It is not surprising that this organization remains a leader in its field.

How about the role of HR? I was talking with an HR group recently about the challenges of building a workforce today. One person in the group was struggling with managers in her organization asking that she bring anyone in to fill their open positions. She knew well that securing the first willing candidate would likely lead to their early departure if there was not a good fit. Her role became one of bringing fundamental strategic issues of workforce development to the organization. Issues such as: What is the profile of those who will fit well with the organization? How does the organization adapt to changing workforce demographics and what does that mean for hiring practices? What can be offered to attract and connect people strongly with the organization? What is needed from the workforce to secure business objectives? What is required to balance, prioritize and build a business case for needed people resources? How is a clear set of values developed and communicated within an organization that consists of many contingent workers? By asking and guiding the organization to answer such questions, HR plays a central role in the organization's survival and growth. It is in evolving to this role that HR will add its greatest value. This book explores the implications for leaders and HR of the new relationship between organizations and individuals.

The book builds a foundation in Part I, by framing the environment and issues. The focus is on the interface between the individual and the organization and the implications for leaders and HR. It begins with an exploration in Chapter 1 of the central dilemma in the natural tension between the need for individuation and the need for community. This chapter will pose this dilemma and examine it in the context of today's work world from the perspective of the leader and HR. It will look at alignment and success for individuals and organizations and important dimensions of leadership. It will pose questions of leaders and HR that will be addressed in the remainder of the book.

Chapter 2 continues this theme by exploring the emerging world of work. Since the onset of the Industrial Revolution, management has focused primarily on increased efficiency of capital utilization through economies of scale in the use of hard assets such as equipment and land. In many ways people were considered a cost of production to be minimized. The world of work is changing rapidly to one in which flexibility to drive change and intellectual capital to spur growth are the primary elements needed to succeed. In this emerging world, people become the main source of value creation, and people leave at the end of each workday. This chapter will highlight what these changes mean for the leader and HR and their impact on the individual, the organization and the community. It will develop approaches to characterizing the workforce that are a needed foundation for moving to action.

The engines of value creation are shifting from economies of scale or scope to economies of ingenuity and innovation. This is explored in Chapter 3 along with the implications for organizational structure, organizational dynamics and measurement. The driving forces that led to the structure of large, mature organizations are contrasted with the approaches used by small, emerging units. The meaning of each, their strengths and weaknesses, are examined for the leader and HR.

Part I is completed with a discussion of the concept of listening to the organization and the forms that such listening can take. Examples include input from people in a broad cross-section of organizations, and pooled input from in-depth studies with individual organizations. The findings from such listening lay the groundwork for modeling approaches in the next section.

Part II is focused on creating models of the future workforce. The approaches to quantitative modeling introduced here can pave the way for making predictions about future workforce dynamics and prescribing steps that lead in preferred directions. The techniques in this area are in their infancy and the material presented here is intended to stimulate thinking about approaches that could be further developed. Chapter 5 introduces the section by examining different approaches to modeling and suggests a preferred framework.

In Chapter 6 modeling techniques are applied at the community, organizational and individual level. One of the challenges facing the leader and HR is identifying appropriate measures to link human resource initiatives to affiliation and value creation. Chapter 6 introduces some approaches to such linkages through modeling. This chapter of necessity contains mathematical content that may be new to those unfamiliar with calculus. The conclusions from the chapter are summarized so that the content is accessible to all readers regardless of mathematical background. A Nomenclature section included at the end of the book lists the symbols used in the equations developed in Chapter 6. Part II concludes with Chapter 7, which contains a case study illustrating the linkage between individual development and organizational value creation.

Part III focuses on developing a path forward and the fundamental changes in leadership approaches that will be needed in the future. The changing roles of leaders and HR in the emerging organization are discussed in Chapter 8. In their role as developers of the organization's primary asset, its people, leaders and HR are challenged to adopt expanded roles with changed priorities. These priorities include guiding values and overall direction, acting as change agents and providing coaching and development to enhance affiliation. They require new behaviors supporting all aspects of employee engagement from recruiting through integration, development and transition. This chapter examines what these changes mean in terms of affiliation to the organization and what they mean for value creation, namely opportunities to enhance it and barriers that may be inhibitors.

The fundamental changes that are described will be hard won. They challenge the basic political and social fabric of organizations. Chapter 9 explores the practical aspects of instituting such major change, drawing on past examples and proposing approaches to implementation. This includes examining some existing myths about employee affiliation and how to overcome these myths.

One basic change proposed for the future is a shift from organizations as separate islands to organizations as partners. This shift is more advanced on a business level; it has barely begun from a workforce perspective. Chapter 10 explores the meaning of organizational partnership in workforce development, the opportunities and challenges that it presents.

Chapter 11 completes Part III and the book by examining paths to resolve the central dilemma of aligning individual and organizational needs. This chapter examines the purpose of organizations and alternative forms of relationship with individuals. Moving into the future the ability to be inclusive will be a key differentiator. The chapter explores what this means from the perspective of internal inclusion (workforce diversity), external inclusion (partnerships), community inclusion (philanthropy) and global inclusion (greater good). It concludes with a discussion of the meaning for leaders and HR and how to awaken the music for all within our organizations. This is not an easy journey with simple solutions and a checklist to follow. It is as much a journey of the heart as it is a journey of the head, for affiliation at its core is an emotional connection.

— PART I —

FRAMING THE ENVIRONMENT AND ISSUES

May you live all the days of your life.

Jonathan Swift

— 1 —

The Central Dilemma

We worked together for almost a year, my client, a vice president in financial services and I. We will call her Karen. It began when Karen sensed problems with her current organization, which was recently acquired by a regional competitor. Her extensive experience and knowledge of the industry meant little in the political mayhem that followed the acquisition. It was no surprise when she lost her job about two months after we met. There followed a time of introspection, some self-recrimination, and some depression. We explored Karen's aspirations in depth and she began to realize that a new life could come out of the ashes of this loss. This new life could offer Karen the expression of her natural gifts in her work, the opportunity to join an organization that matched her values and relocation to a place that she and her husband desired. In short, it could provide alignment of who she was with how she worked and lived. Or as Brewi and Brennan (1989, 96) describe it, "the spirit within us, found in the core of our own Selves . . . slowly and painfully weaves its way through anxiety, confusion, tension and conflict to hear the rhythm of our own personal tune made up of choices and values that are truly our own. This becomes our great contribution to the world."

So with growing elation and some anxiety, over the following months, Karen gradually developed a finely tuned sense of who she was and where she could best express this. It was no surprise when she located an organization that valued her innovative and slightly irreverent style. It was in the location she wanted and it needed her knowledge and expertise. So they came together, Karen and the organization, and they crafted a path forward that was better for both of them. They crafted a path forward that was fulfilling for Karen and that generated value for the organization. They crafted a path forward based on mutual affiliation.

Now, what is unusual about this story? Certainly not her job loss. In the 1980s, 90s and 2000s downsizing has been a corporate mantra. Not the roller coaster of emotions that Karen felt as time passed. These are natural responses to this traumatic event. The unusual aspect is the extent to which Karen was able to completely redefine her life and find alignment where there was little previously. Part of this alignment was affiliation with an organization, a community, which shared her values. Part of it was a rebalancing of her life to meet her spiritual, psychological and practical needs. This was a transforming experience, which led to a fundamental re-expression of her humanity. And for the organization that was fortunate to employ her? Here we see the seeds of transformation due to the infusion of her new ideas expressed through her engagement and commitment.

Will this transformation last for Karen and for the organization? We now confront a dilemma facing each of us as individuals and facing organizations today. We can now make choices about our lives and our work that do not require extended relationships with any one organization. In the future there will be more jobs than people to fill them, and the gap will grow. Our organizations are struggling with the challenge of growing while recruiting from a shrinking labor pool. The approach of hiring for convenience, which seemed so appealing in the late 1980s and 90s, is losing its appeal as employees vote with their feet for transitory connections. How does Karen make sense of her organizational affiliation and what framework should her organization adopt to strengthen its affiliation with her?

This leads to the central dilemma of how to integrate the drive for organizational performance with the search for individual fulfillment. At an individual level there is a natural tension between the need for individuation and the need for community. This is reflected in our ambivalence toward organizations, and it is reflected in the great disparities we observe in our global community. At an organizational level it raises questions as to how to balance communal responsibility with individual drive, and how to enhance the infusion of new ideas that is part of growth and renewal with the wisdom that builds from experience.

This chapter addresses the central dilemma from the perspectives of:

- Differing forms of relationship of individuals to organizations
- Individual and organizational values
- Alignment and success
- Driving forces for affiliation and separation
- Implications for leaders and HR

DIFFERING FORMS OF RELATIONSHIP OF INDIVIDUALS TO ORGANIZATIONS

Exploring examples of the relationship of individuals to organizations from both the individual and the organizational perspective provides insights into an appropriate framework for the future. Two example forms of relationship are that of a free agent and that observed in the traditional organization. A free agent is employed by an organization for a given project with no implied longevity of relationship, although it may extend in practice for several years. The traditional organization, on the other hand, maintained an implied contract with employees of continued employment in exchange for observance of corporate policies, being a loyal corporate citizen, being present and working hard. Here is how these two relationships can look to the individual:

Factors Important to the Individual	Free Agent	Traditional
Financial stability	Low	High, but subject to at-will employment
Support for personal growth	Defined by individual	Defined by organization
Flexibility	High	Low
Sense of community in organization	Low	May be high
Commitment to organization purpose	Individual purpose	May be high
Organizational affiliation	Low	High
Career development responsibility	Individual	Organization
Relationship with management	Contractual	Performance based
Clarity of expectations	Defined by individual	Determined by management capability

Opportunity to do best work	High	Organizationally dependent
Recognition	Self-generated	Political
Individual opinions count	High	Depends on organization

While it is clear that free agency offers benefits (flexibility, clarity, self-determination and opportunity to do best work) it suffers from major drawbacks (instability and a low sense of organizational affiliation). On the other hand, the traditional organization, which once offered the possibility of enhanced stability, is often replete with political frustration and bureaucracy. Stability is also in question after the experience of the 1980s, 90s and early 2000s. Neither of these extremes is a sound approach for the future.

This is how the two relationships can look from the organizational perspective:

Factors Important to the Organization	Free Agent	Traditional
Workforce flexibility	High, but depends on labor market	Low
Creation of common purpose	Difficult	Management determined
Growth in intellectual capital	Low	Difficult to infuse new ideas
Ability to create growth	Uncertain	May be constrained by existing views
Builds affiliation	Low	Subservient role

Workforce flexibility may be high with the free agency relationship although that depends on prevailing labor market conditions. Workforce flexibility is low with the traditional approach. A free agent relationship makes creation of a common purpose difficult and contributes in only a limited way to organization intellectual capital. The traditional approach may constrain the infusion of new ideas and growth. From the organizational perspective neither relationship works well. And both relationships limit affiliation. In the free agency case there is little affiliation, whereas in the case of the traditional organization it is a subservient relationship built around the negative consequences of separation.

INDIVIDUAL AND ORGANIZATIONAL VALUES

This presents a dilemma in that neither free agency nor the traditional relationship are likely to meet future needs. It also raises the question as to what framework exists to guide the choices made by individuals for themselves and for their organizations. Is it a simple matter of individuals selling their services to the highest bidder? Is it a simple matter of organizations maximizing shareholder value by focusing on short-term cash flow? In both cases this would suggest a Darwinian survival of the fittest perspective. Probably not, as Izzo and Withers indicate (2000, 79) that "when 1,000 working adults were asked whether they would rather earn high salaries or earn 'enough' doing work that makes the world a better place, 86% chose the latter." Selling (out) to the highest bidder was not acceptable. Izzo and Withers (2000, 89) also quote David Packard, the co-founder of Hewlett-Packard, as saying "I think people assume, wrongly, that a company exists solely to make money. Money is an important part of a company's existence, if the company is any good. But a result is not a cause. We have to go deeper and find the real reason for our being. . . .[A] group of people get together and exist as an institution that we call a company, so that they are able to accomplish something collectively that they could not accomplish separately—they make a contribution to society." So it is not just about money for the organization either.

Put another way, how can we avoid an ethical lobotomy in establishing an organizational perspective? Lynn Rhodes, from the Pacific School of Religion in Berkeley, California (Rhodes 1999), poses three questions that get to the heart of the individual, organizational and community issues. These questions challenge us to consider fundamental values in wrestling with the tensions inherent in the relationships between individuals, organizations and communities. The questions are as follows:

• How do we as a community honor work that sustains and supports our lives?
• How do we support each person in expressing the unique gifts they have to offer?
• How do we integrate meeting our individual aspirations with seeking the common good?

An examination of the evolution of work over the past century and a half in the context of Rhodes' questions provides a perspective on the balance of individual and organizational control. "During the 1870s in the U.S., over one-third of the workforce was self-employed, largely as farmers. Even among wage earners, about 32% were agricultural laborers or domestic workers, over 80% of the wage earning population was male, and child labor was common" (International Survey Research 2000). While progress was made in terms of limiting child labor and the length of the work week, by the early years of the twentieth century safety was viewed as an employee responsibility, "there was no minimum wage, very few limits on working hours . . . no job security by law or custom nor was there a government provided social security net" (International Survey Research 2000). It is not surprising that membership in American labor unions grew during this time. One hundred years ago, many were employed like indentured servants, with little control over their conditions of work. In some cases organizations acted as benevolent dictators, providing amenities such as housing in exchange for fealty, as in the textile industry. In other cases organizations exploited their workforce, resorting to violence to achieve conformity as in the incidents of the 1930s. Out of this mistrust and confrontation organized labor gained strength and the opportunity for people to affiliate with their union as opposed to their organization. While the three questions posed by Lynn Rhodes may have been in the minds of a small number of leaders they were not central to the relationship of individuals to organizations. Indeed, it was with some surprise that Elton Mayo's experiments at the Western Electric Hawthorne Works in Chicago from 1927 to 1932 demonstrated the power of paying attention to people. By creating an environment that led to a strong social connection and team commitment, productivity soared (Accel-team: www.accel-team.com).

By the 1950s, 60s and 70s we had reached the era of the organization man, with gender equality in the workplace still in its early stages. The relationship between people and organizations was based on people providing their time and knowledge in return for stability and security. People were viewed as a necessary cost from which to extract value largely from the more traditional sources of economic prosperity, namely land, equipment and capital. Again, the questions posed by Lynn Rhodes were not central to the corporate perspective.

By the 1980s and mid-1990s the organizational view of people as a disposable asset was evident as demonstrated by extensive layoffs designed to reduce costs. The questions posed by Lynn Rhodes were irrelevant in the headlong rush for immediate profits. And then, prompted by the growing scarcity of people, a slow organizational awakening began that in the emerging information and service-based economy, people were the central element of value creation and they were hard to find.

By the early 2000s leaders in organizations were struggling with how to define their relationship with their employees. They were forced, out of self-interest and the scarcity of people, to begin confronting difficult issues of meaning and purpose in work. Organizations began moving into unfamiliar territory and confronting questions such as those posed by Rhodes about the reasons people affiliate. Some answers were cosmetic, such as the provision of concierge services or pet days. Others were more profound, such as supporting individuals in their development. A slowing economy mitigated these pressures in some sectors in the short term, but employee scarcity remains a fundamental long-term issue. Most organizations are cast adrift in an unfamiliar sea, unsure about how to respond in this emerging world. This is illustrated by the struggle to be proactive in human resource practices. In this information from an issue of *Fast Company* (2001a) citing a McKinsey study, each item is an opportunity for organizations to be proactive in their human resource capabilities and practices. Few saw the need to be.

- Our company has enough talented managers to pursue all or most of its promising opportunities: Only 7% strongly agree
- Our company has enough talented managers to substantially increase our performance relative to competitors: Only 11% strongly agree
- Our company is always looking for talented people, even if we are not trying to fill a specific position: Only 8% strongly agree
- Our company pays whatever it takes to prevent losing our high performers to other companies: Only 6% strongly agree

Is this reticence due to indifference to these workforce development issues or uncertainty about how to respond to them? It leads to another aspect of the central dilemma, namely defining alignment and success from an individual and organizational perspective.

ALIGNMENT AND SUCCESS

Individual View

Pamela was a vice president in a technology-based organization. She was outwardly successful and well compensated for her business unit responsibility. But there was something missing. She questioned the connection of her contributions at work to her aspirations. She wondered about her ability to communicate effectively with her peers. She wondered about her future with the organization and how to both experience greater meaning and contribute more effectively at a senior level. On Maslow's hierarchy of needs (Sharf 1992, 262):

1. Physiological
2. Safety
3. Belongingness and Love
4. Esteem
5. Information
6. Understanding
7. Beauty
8. Self-actualization

she was searching for self-actualization. In Pamela's case she was seeking to satisfy a need at the apex of the Maslow hierarchy. Success in her case was exploring and finding the means for self-actualization. Through an expansion of her role and a re-evaluation of her priorities she was able to find greater alignment with her needs, while delivering greater value to her organization.

Viewed from another perspective, that of our expectations from our work, Brewer (1996) framed the question of why we work in the context of the interior processes of discovering meaning (what), being (who) and doing (how), and identified four work relationships to the external world:

• A job: based on material rewards, a transaction
• An occupation: involving greater meaning, but doing dominates
• A career: requiring personal initiative, but needing collective approval
• A vocation: calling in the service of a greater good

I frequently ask clients in career counseling where they wish to be in this continuum and invariably it is the search for a vocation or call in the service of a greater good. This is the search that confronted Pamela. Success, then, is complex and highly individual. Increasingly throughout our lives it involves movement from taking and receiving external approval, to giving and expressing internal preferences. This is the generativity of Erikson (Levinson 1978, 29), and it represents a wealth of human potential. For as Goethe said, "Treat people as if they were what they ought to be and you help them become what they are capable of being" (Peter 1979, 409).

But there is a dilemma for people in organizations when there is a dearth of the unconditional positive regard of Carl Rogers (1995). It is no wonder that contradictory parts of our nature arise as Whyte observed (1996): "Our love of creative fire, its warmth and its intensity and at the same time our fear of being burned." Realizing our full potential means claiming our aspirations and expressing who we are. In a DBM study of the hard-boiled world of Silicon Valley, employees of one leading high-tech organization were clear about why they were leaving: it was because of lack of meaningful work and a feeling that they were not adding value. It was not for compensation or benefits. Success is about expression of individual human potential that in turn brings value to organizations.

Organizational View

On the surface, organizational success is easy to define. In the non-profit world it is about achieving a vision. In the for-profit world it can be measured by the discounted value of future cash flows, which translates into stock price for the shareholders of publicly held companies or asset valuation for those that are privately held. However, future cash flows and appropriate discount rates are highly uncertain. Cash flows are dependent on current and past decisions that precariously balance short-term benefits and longer-term value creation. In today's information- and service-based economy value creation is linked more to workforce creativity, ingenuity and productivity than to hard assets. This linkage is created by leadership.

Leadership models range from the paranoid (Andy Grove of Intel), to the structured (Jack Welch of GE), to the tyrannical (Al Dunlap of Sunbeam), and the humble (Max DePree of Herman Miller). Each presents a different approach to bringing out maximum value from the organization. And yet the extent of the differences speaks to the uncertainty about leadership and measurement of results. When is the Jack Welch model appropriate, and when the Max DePree approach? What are the consequences for the workforce and for value creation? Compound this with the stirring rhetoric of *In Search of Excellence* (1982), or the studied analysis of *First Break All the Rules* (1999), and their different implied approaches for linking individuals to organizations. Characterizing leadership and organizational success is complex. The opportunity exists to develop models that clearly link individual fulfillment to organizational value creation, expressing the former in terms of achieving aspirations and the latter in tangible financial terms.

Overlaying the individual-organizational relationship is the greater community. Here a metaphor that comes to mind from the world of architecture is that of moving from individual dwellings to villages then to towns and cities. In the world of architecture patterns have been identified (Alexander et al. 1977) that speak to successful aesthetic and practical designs. Such patterns likely exist, but have yet to be uncovered in our organizational world, as we move from the individual to the organization and the community. These patterns represent approaches that meld our needs as individuals with organizational imperatives and community ideals.

A tension that challenges organizations is the balance between meeting short-term objectives and long-term value creation. It is intimately linked to decisions about the workforce. The tension arises when looking at decisions to invest or not, to downsize or not. Such decisions can depress (capital investment) or elevate (downsizing) near-term cash flow or financial profitability. However, longer-term consequences may reverse the immediate impact. Decisions about the workforce have long-term implications that reverberate for years throughout an organization. For example, recent exit interviews of employees leaving one organization revealed the catastrophic impact of a strike one year previously on morale a year later. Settlement of the strike did not settle the emotional concerns of employees and the lack of trust the strike engendered. The consequences of this strike will reverberate for many years. At a community level the consequences can extend much further than forty years, the average life of a company in the United States. Today's ghost towns were vibrant communities yesterday. Success in the organization is a complex tapestry that addresses future value creation capability, with a key component being the connection with the workforce.

DRIVING FORCES FOR AFFILIATION AND SEPARATION

In thriving organizations the decisions and directions of individuals reinforce each other to create clear, positive outcomes. On the other hand, where there is mistrust and contradiction, the source and commonality of objectives is extinguished. Building trust, shared direction and the capability to fully express individual capabilities takes time. With time and experience the potential to create organizational value grows. Reichheld (1996, 124) shows individual productivity, as measured by revenue per employee, increasing for stockbrokers, truck drivers and insurance agents with the same general pattern, as tenure with the organization increases. The productivity increase with tenure is dramatic in these very different situations. While the shape and steepness of the curve varies according to sector, the pattern does not. So the opportunity is to secure the productivity improvements that come from the growing wisdom and generativity of the workforce, while not compromising creativity and innovation.

This leads to an exploration of the driving forces for affiliation at any given instant, remembering that affiliation is a two-way relationship between the individual and the organization. In this relationship both the bonds of connection and the tug of separation need to be considered. But what constitutes this bond of connection? In studies I have guided at DBM, those leaving organizations repeatedly say that their main losses are their co-workers and their organizational community. This is true even when the overall environment is perceived as dysfunctional. So there is a sense of harmony, of connectedness with fellow employees that develops. The bonds between individuals are strong and enduring. The bonds to the organization, on the other hand, are weak and tenuous in the absence of individual fulfillment and creation of an inspiring purpose.

Separation is promoted by practices that limit development (barriers to movement), that limit commitment (at-will employment clauses), that speak to impermanence (downsizing) and that seek to evaluate rather than encourage (ordinal performance ranking). Separation is encouraged by manager reward systems that stress immediate and parochial results. It is cemented by leadership practices that ignore individual needs and foster disproportionate rewards at higher organizational levels. So it is not surprising that the fabric of the organization tears when stress builds for an individual. The tug of separation is stronger than the bonds of connection in this case. And the tug of separation is created largely by the organization, not by the outside world. The results of exit interviews, described in Chapter 4, show that most people leave organizations due to dissatisfaction rather than for external opportunities. This is a cost of nonconformance in the language of quality and it demands an investment of resources, a cost of conformance, to reduce the tug of separation. Much of this dissatisfaction is a direct result of management and leadership practices.

IMPLICATIONS FOR LEADERS AND HR

A major component of leadership is creating a common and uplifting view that inspires, and in so doing minimizes the tug of separation and maximizes the bond of connection. Leaders face particular challenges as they seek to build one bridge from their functional expertise to business needs, and a further bridge to interpersonal interactions. Each bridge must cross a major chasm. There are a number of dimensions to leadership that enable leaders to cross these chasms. They can be examined in light of employee affiliation and the balancing forces of connection and separation. These leadership dimensions are as follows:

- Inspirational vs. Judgmental
- Participative vs. Directive
- Reflective vs. Reactive
- Self-Effacing vs. Self-Promoting
- Open vs. Contained
- Process Oriented vs. Outcome Oriented
- One-to-one Orientation vs. One-to-many Orientation
- Employee Development Focused vs. Employee Performance Focused

The first two dimensions relate to leadership behaviors that address the ability to create an inspiring purpose and the extent to which leaders create a participative vs. directive decision-making environment. The creation of an inspiring environment coupled with a participative decision-making style maximizes the sense of employee connection and minimizes the tug of separation. As the sense of inspiration is lost so the sense of connection declines. As the degree of participation in decisions declines, so the tug of separation increases, culminating in a high likelihood of employee separation when both the sense of inspiration is low and the degree of participation is low. The interplay of these two dimensions is shown in Figure 1-1.

A similar chart can be constructed for the following three pairs of leadership dimensions.

- The reflective/reactive and self-effacing/self-promoting dimensions address the perspective the leader brings to his interpersonal interactions.
- The open/contained and process-oriented/outcome-oriented dimensions address the leader's business perspectives.
- The one-to-one orientation/one-to-many orientation and employee development–focused/employee performance–focused orientation address the leader's primary orientation to employees.

We can now summarize the forces of connection and separation for each of these dimensions as shown in Table 1-1.

The strongest bond of connection and the weakest tug of separation are generated by leaders who:

Figure 1-1
Leadership Dimensions

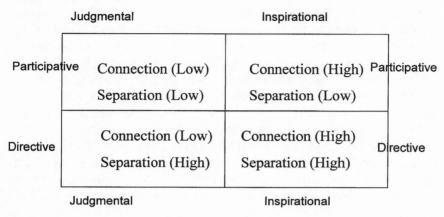

	Judgmental	Inspirational	
Participative	Connection (Low) Separation (Low)	Connection (High) Separation (Low)	Participative
Directive	Connection (Low) Separation (High)	Connection (High) Separation (High)	Directive
	Judgmental	Inspirational	

Table 1-1
Impact of Leadership on Connection and Separation

Leadership Perspective	Dimensions	Connection High	Separation High
Environment created	Inspirational/Judgmental Participative/Directive	Inspirational Participative	Judgmental Directive
Interpersonal interactions	Reflective/Reactive Self-Effacing/Self-Promoting	Reflective Self-Effacing	Reactive Self-Promoting
Business framework	Open/Contained Process Oriented/Outcome Oriented	Open Process/ Individual Outcome	Contained Only Financial Outcome
Orientation to employees	One-to-One/One-to-Many Development/Performance	One-to-One Development	One-to-Many Ordinal Performance

- Create an inspiring sense of purpose and a participative decision-making environment
- Are reflective in building self-understanding and are self-effacing to facilitate recognition of their employees
- Are open with information and focus on individual outcomes and the process by which they are attained
- Encourage a one-to-one relationship between the individual and the organization, which emphasizes individual development.

With these dimensions in mind, one question that arises is, what is controllable and what is beyond the control of the leader? The issues and interactions internal to the organization are within the leader's sphere of influence, specifically the dimensions identified above. Many of the organization's interactions with the external community are within the leader's control, whereas most of the factors driving the global business environment are outside the leader's direct control. However, the organization's responses to these factors are within the leader's sphere of influence. For example, the DuPont Company has reinvented itself about every thirty years since the early 1800s as successive leaders negotiated the changing business and technical environment. In so doing, the organization provided employment for many, and introduced new products such as nylon and many pharmaceuticals that have improved lives and communities. So the leader's role is pivotal in setting the tone within the organization and in sustaining a relationship with the outside world that respects the ever-changing external environment.

Where does the HR professional fit into this picture? With the workforce now a central element in value creation, HR is poised to assume a major role that addresses the following aspects:

- Identifying and nurturing critical leadership skills that enhance employee affiliation and enable attainment of business objectives
- Sponsoring and implementing a framework for employee development linked to business direction
- Providing a framework that enables each person to identify his or her path of personal fulfillment and linking this to organizational direction
- Providing approaches that enable leaders to understand the impact of workforce development on value creation
- Enabling the organization to optimize the contribution of each person in the organization

For leaders and HR considering the central dilemma of blending the needs of the individual and the organization, it will be important to address the following questions:

- What is the nature of the relationship that should be built with people in the organization? Is it based on growing capabilities and accomplishments over time, or is it based on short-term transactions?
- How can an environment be crafted that enables each person to reach his or her full potential?

The Central Dilemma

- How is the creation of value in the organization maximized while respecting the needs of each person in it?
- What is the appropriate role of the organization in supporting community well-being?
- How is success measured both individually and for the organization?
- How can we ensure that our own life is an expression of who we are?

The answers to these questions touch deeply the humanity in us. The answers are not simple or static. They embody the ability to create organizational communities built on respect for each person, which ennoble each of us and, in so doing, create great organizational value. The opportunity is to close some of the huge gap between each person's potential and their expressed reality. This will be explored further in the remainder of the book.

— 2 —

The Emerging World of Work

The first time I saw an at-will clause was in a job offer letter from a nonprofit organization. It read as follows: "In accepting this offer please understand that your employment relationship with . . . is voluntary, for no specified period, and based on your mutual consent and that of. . . . Notwithstanding the above, you are free to resign at any time for any reason or for no reason, as you deem appropriate. Of course, . . . will have a similar right and may conclude your employment at any time, with or without cause." It captures well the spirit of the organizational climate in the 1990s, that the employment relationship is one of convenience, not of commitment. It is expressed in the doublespeak of the 1990s organization world. *1984* revisited. It is our world today.

In moving to the future world of employee scarcity, what kind of relationship is appropriate between organizations and individuals? Is the 1990s approach of mutual convenience appropriate? Should we strive for a transactional relationship offering the greatest short-term flexibility to terminate people, or should we strive for a deeper sense of affiliation where the focus is on development and value creation? How do these questions fit with the ethical issues raised in the last chapter? Answers to the ethical questions transcend organizational boundaries and can provide a framework within which organizations operate. Answers to many other questions will vary by organization and by employee constituency within an organization. These answers need to be crafted to match the values and goals of each organization. They provide a framework within which to create an inspiring organizational purpose and develop human resource strategies. This chapter will address the implications of the emerging world of work in the context of these issues and their meaning for individuals and organizations.

Sam was wrestling with finding a fulfilling work experience when he first came for career counseling. After recent organizational changes he felt trapped and was unsure of his path forward. Sam began his work life in an individual contributor capacity and was now at a senior management level. He doubted his ability to work at this level in spite of his accomplishments. Over time we worked on exploring his aspirations and how he might achieve them. Soon after we started working together, Sam was promoted and began to spread his wings, building confidence in his leadership abilities by turning a struggling organization around. Then, suddenly, the organization was sold to a new management team that valued control and intimidation, in exchange for good pay. It was no surprise when Sam left three months later, for a competitor that was building its business model on cooperation, integrity and commitment. It was also no surprise when Sam's former operation went into steep decline, losing market position and employees.

Many aspects of the emerging world of work are mirrored in Sam's experiences. They include the major impact of losing a talented employee on business results, the disconnect between a control-oriented management culture and the expectations of today's employees, the inability of money to bridge disconnects around integrity, and the instability of the working environment. At a basic level the relationships that two management teams chose to foster with individuals in their organizations are a distinguishing characteristic of organizational survival. The team that chose control and intimidation put the organization's survival at risk. Clarifying this relationship is not easy for either organizational leadership or individuals. Let us explore some characteristics of our emerging world of work and what they mean for the relationship.

THE EMERGING WORLD OF WORK

Traditional economic models focused on land, equipment and capital as the fundamental drivers of wealth creation. People in organizations were stewards of these assets and their role was to develop efficient systems for their disposition. This meant installing complex decision-making processes and centralized control systems designed to minimize the risk of mistakes. This was a world of slow change built on economic value creation from tangible assets. This is not the emerging world. To-day processes that create value from tangible assets have largely been mastered. We are just beginning to master the processes that create value from human ingenuity. This is true whether in the more esoteric world of scientific research or the ambiguous world of interpersonal interactions. The relative predictability of physical processes is replaced with the uncertainty that is part of the creative process. Three factors are converging to impact the relationship of individuals to organizations:

- Growing scarcity of people
- Decreased sense of individual affiliation
- Value creation centered on people rather than hard assets

As shown in the Introduction, changing population demographics and the aging population are driving the growing scarcity of people. A complementary perspective from Hudson/Walker (Drizin 2000) suggests that by the year 2012, for the first time in the United States there will be fewer people entering the workforce than leaving it. It will be much more difficult to attract and retain people in the future. This is compounded by the decreased sense of affiliation individuals feel with organizations, driven partly by generational differences and partly by a natural response to the downsizings of the 1980s, 90s and the early 2000s. It is further compounded by value creation in today's information- and service-based economy being all about people rather than hard assets. These three factors are converging and creating substantial tension. This is occurring in a work world subject to the following transitions:

- Stability to change
- Constant skills to constant learning
- Lifelong commitment to engagement for mutual benefit
- Paternalism to self-reliance
- Local to global
- Hierarchy to fluidity
- Abundance to scarcity of skilled people
- Internal to external

Stability to change. John Chambers, the CEO of Cisco Systems, one of the largest of the new technology companies, was quoted as saying (Brandt 1998, 124): "I believe you have to change your company almost every two years. . . . In fact, we don't plan financially beyond three years." This was remarkably prescient as Cisco suffered in the Internet economy meltdown of 2001 with Chambers declaring it has been like a "100-year flood. It's something you don't expect to see in your lifetime." (Anders 2001, 102). Speeds of communication and reaction have eliminated many of the attenuating factors that dampened system responses in the past. We are more closely approaching the ideal of a perfect market, where information is widely available instantaneously and decisions are made in that light. Consequently, the world is evolving from one of relative stability to one of rapid change. The systems and the connection between employees and organizations will need to reflect this shift and recognize that individuals increasingly can access information about internal organization culture, about compensation levels and about other opportunities. Choice abounds and the information needed to make choices is close at hand.

Constant skills to constant learning. Here are some statistics from Tapscott, Lowy and Ticoll (1998, 181):

• 45% of U.S. college students are 25 and over
• Students 35 and older outnumber those who are 18 and 19

A world in which life stages occurred linearly and sequentially, with education as a single activity, equipping us for life, is gone. This is due to two factors. The first factor, driven by changing internal perspectives over the course of our lives and an abundance of work opportunities, is our willingness to recalibrate our lives multiple times seeking closer alignment of who we are with our work. The second factor is the rapidly changing skill needs of the workplace. In the 1960s through the 80s technical knowledge had a half-life of about four to five years. Today the half-life of technical knowledge is measured in months rather than years. And this extends beyond technical areas. With this ferocious pace of change organizations must provide constant development and re-skilling opportunities for employees. The expectation of employees is shared responsibility for employability with career development driven by the individual but supported by the organization.

Lifelong commitment to engagement for mutual benefit. Research that will be reviewed in more depth in Chapter 4, from more than 400 organizations in North America, showed the following:

• On average respondents had been employed with at least four different organizations since college or high school
• 47% expect to be with their current organization for no longer than three years

Time horizons are short and engagement is a precarious state. In fact the average attrition rate for organizations in this same study was 20%. This is a world of disposable organizations and it raises a major question for the future as to how we wish our organizations to be viewed.

Local to global. Daniels and Mathers (1997, 24) refer to an early 1995 *Newsweek* magazine cover, which "featured a photograph of a Samburu tribesman in Africa. Wearing a red plaid robe, he stood barefoot in front of the cattle corral, with a spear in his left hand. In his right hand pressed to his ear, was a cellular phone." This image captures the essence of the global community where boundaries to communication are vanishing even though social and political boundaries are strong. The now defunct telecommunications company, Iridium, ran an advertisement with a view of the Earth and a byline: "Welcome to your new office, it measures 197 million square miles." Again, this emphasizes the elimination of boundaries to communication.

Today, customers, competitors, suppliers and employees may come from any part of the globe. As employee scarcity grows in developed nations there is an opportunity to reach out to developing nations for the enhanced prosperity of both groups. For a bifurcated world of haves and have-nots is no more stable than a bifurcated country, town or village. If the entire world were a village of 100 people, today only 2 people would have a college education, only 4 would own a computer and 20 people would earn 89% of the world's wealth (*Fast Company* 2001b). The challenge and opportunity is to translate emerging economic prosperity into benefits for all, and, in so doing, stimulate the engines of growth.

Hierarchy to fluidity. The traditional approach to organizational structure is built on a military model with divisions into well-defined cells and a command and control approach to decision making. It is designed to concentrate decision making in the hands of a few individuals. It assumes the primary purpose of many people in the organization is to implement decisions made elsewhere, by contributing physical labor or repetitive activity with limited creative contribution. That is not the world that we now inhabit. Today's work world demands broad-based creative and intellectual contributions, and organization structures need to mirror that. For example, fluid work groups are emerging where people bring their skills and knowledge and contribute them as needed according to changing business conditions. AT&T established a group based not on defined jobs, but on the creation of a large, skilled assemblage of people. The model is one of Brownian motion in the organization, where each person moves independently while connected to the whole.

Abundance to scarcity of skilled people. The demographic trends described in the Introduction are driving to a world of scarcity of skilled people in developed nations. While there is some short-term mitigation when an economy slows, the long-term trend of scarcity is clear. This not only affects large organizations with hundreds or thousands of openings, it also affects small organizations. For example, after I spoke at a local chamber of commerce event the owner of a body shop came up afterward, concerned that he could not grow his small business because of lack of people. The scarcity of people crosses geographies, industry sectors, and organizations. It is with us for the foreseeable future in the developing countries and it fundamentally redefines the nature of the relationship between individuals and organizations.

Internal to external. In the world of the past driven by natural resources and tangible products, the internal means of production and internal efficiencies readily became a primary focus. In the world of the future driven by relationships and information flow external interfaces become paramount. Craig Barrett, the CEO of Intel, predicted (Donlon 1998) that there would be one billion connected computers by the first decade of this century. Focus shifts to the external, bringing with it a requirement to embrace diversity and difference. What does this translate to in terms of our workforce? Recently, at a U.S. briefing I was giving on the emerging world of work, one of the participants highlighted her enthusiasm for bringing in new employees from different cultures. However, she also expressed concerns about the challenges this represented, in particular about expectations of immediate integration. One major issue that we will revisit later in the book is how to build a culture of inclusion for our increasingly diverse workforce.

In total these changes speak to a world of ambiguity and uncertainty. This is a world in which people continuously recalibrate their direction as organizations also recalibrate their path. This is a world with vanishing boundaries to information flow, but one that struggles with political, social and ethnic boundaries. It is a world placing increasing demands on corporate community responsibility, and a world that places much greater burdens on leadership and HR in organizations to build and develop relationships internally and externally. Let us examine the implications of these workforce transitions first for organizations, then for individuals.

ORGANIZATIONAL IMPLICATIONS

What do these transitions mean for organizations? Tom was a top-ranked engineer in a multibillion-dollar, high-tech organization. He readily mastered the skills needed to function in the first division he joined and reached a point where he was ready to move to new challenges. He enthusiastically approached his manager with a request to transfer to a sister division where he could apply his knowledge to new product areas. However, rather than supporting the transfer, his manager tried to persuade Tom not to move. Tom then approached the next level in the corporate hierarchy, his director. The director greeted his request the same way, trying to persuade Tom why he should not move. Tom was exasperated. By fortunate coincidence, the following week, the organization's CEO was holding a breakfast meeting with a small group of employees to take the pulse of the organization. Tom was in this group. He had the audacity to ask the CEO about the opportunity to transfer. The CEO's reaction was very different from the earlier managers. He was pleased about Tom's request and agreed to help him secure a transfer. By sheer serendipity the organization saved Tom. If it had not been for the CEO's intervention Tom would have left. This underlines some of the critical issues for organizations in the emerging world of work:

• People are the key source of value creation
• It is essential to create a highly efficient internal job market
• Intellectual capital is a cornerstone of growth

People are the key source of value creation. The ability to identify opportunities, marshal resources and create value is inherently a people process. Through it, individuals impact the top and the bottom line of the profit and loss statement in a for-profit organization and in a non-profit the ability of the organization to achieve its purpose. Attrition simultaneously affects the organization's ability to achieve its purpose, generate revenue and operate efficiently. Indeed, there are organizations where the cumulative impact of attrition over a five-year planning period is in the billions of dollars. The ability of the organization to keep its key employees is fundamental to its wealth creation capability; it is not a peripheral issue.

Given the characteristics of the emerging world of work, what does this imply about the perspective the organization's leaders adopt about the employees? One reality, introduced earlier, is Drucker's concept of employees as volunteers. For that is the new world of work, since each person has the opportunity to leave the organization at the end of each day. The idea of treating employees as volunteers has fundamental implications for the way we value people, recognize each other, engage people in decision making, and interface with their non-work lives. The traditional concept of work life separate from other aspects of life does not match people's expectations in the emerging world of work. The various aspects of people's lives are tightly interlinked and organizational practices need to recognize this. People are volunteers in their work lives as in their personal lives.

It is essential to create a highly efficient internal job market. We saw in Tom's example earlier the dramatic benefits of removing internal barriers to movement and development. In fact it is essential that an organization's internal job market be more efficient than the external job market, and it is often the reverse. By eliminating barriers to movement people can find their best fit, which in turn benefits the organization. The relationship becomes a one-to-one relationship and not a one-to-many relationship driven by standard policies.

Intellectual capital is a cornerstone of growth. In an agricultural economy, fertile land is a cornerstone of growth; in an industrial economy it is access to resources and the efficient configuration of production systems. In an information- and service-based economy, growth stems from knowledge and relationships, and their development by people in an ever-changing environment. The contribution of individuals to an organization builds with time and experience. One implication is the importance of developing leaders who lead by example, lead by service not by command, lead in uncharted territories and guide the organization through the resulting ambiguity. This requires that the organization provide leaders with support in development of their interpersonal and other skills.

INDIVIDUAL IMPLICATIONS

What do these transitions in the workforce mean for individuals? There are five major aspects that individuals need to consider in building a path to the future. Leaders and HR need an awareness of these factors on a personal level, and to support the employee population in these five areas:

• Know yourself
• Keep learning
• Stay flexible

- Champion change while searching the horizon
- Dare to dream

Know yourself. Isaac Newton has fascinated me for some time. I was fortunate to attend the same university as Newton. In spite of my aging appearance we did miss each other by a few years. While Newton was at Cambridge his head supposedly had an encounter with an apple, which led to his formulating the theory of universal gravitation. This, along with many other scientific discoveries, was the precursor of our high-technology world today. And so I offer the apple as a bridge into our world, and ask the question, how many different ways in today's world could we work with an apple? They include transport it, measure it, draw it, teach about it, sell it, count it. Each of these draws on a different set of skills, and each of these to varying degrees uses technology. For example, we now have sophisticated genetic engineering techniques that improve the taste and appearance of apples. We have new instruments that enable us to count and measure apples. And each person could potentially work in any of these areas. But it is highly unlikely that they would all be equally appealing. It is important to know ourselves well enough to understand where we can find fulfillment in work at any point in life. It is just as true for leaders and HR as for the newest employee in an organization. This inner search comes first and organizations need to provide the tools and resources to support this search.

Keep learning. I wonder how many people know what a slide rule is today. This hardy instrument used to do math calculations before the days of electronic calculators. Companies built businesses around making slide rules. Where are those companies today, giants in the calculator business? No. They are not even players. I still have my slide rule from college. How about the valuable skill of using a slide rule? Is it valuable today? About the only thing that I can use it for is giving one of my lectures, which are completely ignored, to my adult children, about how hard it was in the old days, and how we used to get up before we went to bed and other assorted distortions of the past. So there is an important learning here. The skills developed at one point in our lives do not necessarily last, and we have to continually develop new skills. It is an organizational responsibility to provide a framework that supports each person in pursuing such development.

Stay flexible. It would have been difficult to imagine in the days of the slide rule that there would be computers sitting on desks, interconnected around the globe. It would have seemed totally implausible. This leads to the third learning, that it is difficult to anticipate the nature of revolutionary change, as by definition it stands the world on its head. But it is possible to stay flexible, to look out for the signs of such change, and to build the new skills that it demands. In fact it is essential for survival. Today we can no more predict what the world twenty-five years in the future will look like, and what skills will be needed, than we could twenty-five years ago. The world will likely be radically different. It is the ability to constantly move with change that will be the key to survival and prosperity for each individual. This will be needed regardless of whether people are genetically engineering the apple, counting it or selling it. Because in every case the relentless march of technology will fundamentally change work. It is an organizational responsibility to help equip people with the mindset and skills that enable such personal flexibility.

Champion change while searching the horizon. It was not surprising when I heard Scott McNealy, the chairman and CEO of Sun Microsystems, telling new college hires that a main message was bring the new ideas in, but be ready to fight a system that will likely reject them. As will be explored more in Chapter 9, there is a huge inertia in our systems that will resist even the most positive change and in the emerging work world people will need the ability to champion change while looking to the horizon to anticipate unfolding needs. It is an organizational responsibility to create an environment that supports innovation and access to information that helps people read the emerging signals.

Dare to dream. The final area is one of holding an individual dream and letting it build and shine, whatever form it takes. I recently worked with a client who at 71 was entering a new phase of his life, writing and creating new seminars, and was engrossed in it. I also worked with a 27-year-old client whose eyes were lighting up at the prospect of making a major shift into physical therapy. She found her passion and was ready to live it. Discovering a vocation is possible at any point in life. We can only fully engage people when they connect their individual passion with an inspiring organizational purpose. It is an organizational responsibility to provide an environment that encourages this to happen.

CHARACTERIZING THE WORKFORCE AND THE RELATIONSHIP WITH INDIVIDUALS

The needs of the individual and the organization converge in the emerging world of work around the need for individual expression translated into organizational value creation. However, the nature of the relationship between the individual and the organization will change significantly according to individual aspirations and the expectations of the organization for different workforce constituencies. Examining two dimensions of this relationship provides an example of how to characterize the workforce.

The first dimension is that of a transactional vs. an extended relationship. A transactional relationship means that the individual contracts to complete a certain task in a defined time period in return for financial compensation. It is characterized by limited interaction beyond the defined project, a short time frame and no commitment on the part of the organization to provide development for the individual beyond the immediate project learning. An example of this would be an independent contractor who is hired to complete a particular project. There is limited opportunity to develop synergy with staff in the organization, but there is a great deal of flexibility around the relationship following project completion. At that point either party may sever the relationship without obligation to the other.

Contrast this with an extended relationship. Here the engagement is longer term, not limited to a single project. The organization sponsors learning for the individual with the expectation that it will garner the benefits from this learning in the form of increased productivity. Individuals also experience greater fulfillment in their work lives. There is an implied obligation on the part of both the individual and the organization that extends beyond a purely financial transaction.

An analogy for these two forms of relationship comes from the area of negotiating. The purchase of a car is typically a single transaction with the objective of both parties being to maximize their immediate economic return. This is the transactional relationship. Alternatively in negotiating a long-term contract for the supply of services such as tutorial support for children, expectations are for an extended relationship and many factors beyond simply the financial will enter into this negotiation.

The second dimension is the organizational view of the relationship with employees, whether it is a one-to-one relationship, recognizing the needs of each individual, or a one-to-many relationship where collective policies dominate. In the former case there is no requirement for equity in the agreement with each person, in the latter case there is little flexibility to adjust systems to meet individual needs. An example that approaches the former case is given by these statements from Nordstrom's employee handbook (Tushman 1993):

Rule No. 1: Use your good judgment in all situations
There will be no additional rules

Figure 2-1
Organization/Individual Relationships

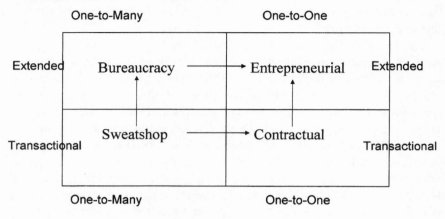

An example that approaches the latter case would be the requirements established by military units for the relationship with their personnel. We can now examine the implications of these two dimensions as shown in Figure 2-1. The four quadrants represent four possible forms of relationship between an organization and its employees. In the lower left corner is the transactional, one-to-many relationship. In a situation of limited alternatives for individuals this can lead to exploitation, as in a sweatshop. For example, migrant farm workers or textile workers engaged in piece work may unfortunately be located here. This implies an unequal distribution of power with the organization as the dominant party. The upper left corner is the situation of an extended relationship in which organizational policies are defined at the collective level. This is the traditional corporate approach. The lower right corner applies to the transactional relationship negotiated on a one-to-one basis. An example of this would be an agreement between an organization and an independent contractor. In the upper right corner is the combination of an extended relationship developed on a one-to-one basis. This implies an equal division of power between the individual and the organization. Entrepreneurial relationships can reside here. The arrows on the chart represent a possible dynamic over time, showing movement from the lower left quadrant to either greater independence in the lower right or greater collectivism in the upper left, and then in both cases to the entrepreneurial situation in the upper right.

Leaders and HR in each organization need to decide where they wish to operate with respect to their employee populations. These decisions need to reflect the values and principles of the organization as well as business objectives. For example, the sweatshop model fails the test of all three ethical principles raised in Chapter 1, regardless of its business implications. A critical strategic step for organizations is to map the workforce and segment it in such a way that there is clarity about the nature of the relationship sought with each group. This can then be clearly communicated to individuals so that people can select the environment and relationship principles that match their individual needs. Additional dimensions can be added to the initial two.

The third dimension, voluntary vs. controlled, is an indication of the degree to which the organization seeks to encourage individual expression and action in contrast to containing action within prescribed limits. This is functionally dependent; for example, a research function will typically need a high degree of creativity and autonomy for individuals. A manufacturing operation using hazardous materials or complex processes will typically need tightly defined operating principles, although it too can operate on a continuum regarding receptivity to new ideas.

The fourth dimension is that of entitled vs. serving. We have heard much in the past about employee entitlement. This is the sense that a person has a right to certain benefits regardless of his or her contribution. It contrasts with an attitude of serving that is based on the principle of meeting the needs of others, including the organization. Organizations too can, on occasion, adopt an attitude of entitlement. That is to assume that employees will come and stay simply because of past achievements and the established name of the organization. As with individual entitlement, it is in direct contrast to the perspective of serving. Serving from an organizational viewpoint means meeting the needs of stakeholders, including employees.

The fifth dimension is that of development vs. performance. Both aspects can coexist. Development means supporting growth, marketability and employability of individuals. A colleague in a Silicon Valley high-tech organization included learning objectives in her plans for the prior year. One of these objectives was to take a particular course for her development. By the end of the year she had not taken this course. Her annual bonus was reduced as a result of this because the organization placed high value on individual development. This is in contrast to a performance focus, where the entire emphasis is on meeting business goals regardless of individual development. To some degree this is trading the long-term benefits of building individual competencies for short-term performance benefits. An important issue for leadership and HR is how to effectively integrate both developmental and performance elements.

The sixth dimension is that of proactive vs. reactive. In the context of workforce dynamics this means putting support mechanisms in place that enable managers and leaders to stay close to employee issues and concerns. These practices may entail listening to the organization (which will be discussed in Chapter 4), new employee integration, maintaining competitive compensation levels, attracting top performers regardless of current business conditions and supporting the workforce during downturns. Contrast this to a reactive environment where the organization responds only to changing business dynamics with a view to maximizing short-term profitability regardless of long-term consequences. Examples of proactive and reactive workforce practices are given by O'Malley (2000, 149). "In late 1995, textile producer Malden Mills burned down. Owner Aaron Feurstein kept his 1,000 employees on the payroll while the factory was rebuilt. It cost him $15 million to do that. Contrast that with a restaurant chain that lays off workers, without pay, for two to four weeks while restaurants are refurbished. Seriously, for whom would you rather work? The turnover rate at Malden Mills is about 5 percent and over a 14-year span, revenues tripled (in constant dollars) and the workforce doubled. The restaurant chain experiences from 200 to 300 percent turnover."

In summary the dimensions of the organization/individual relationship are as follows:

- Transactional vs. extended
- One-to-one vs. one-to-many
- Voluntary vs. controlled
- Entitled vs. serving
- Developmental vs. performance
- Proactive vs. reactive

An example of the workforce characterization process applied to an organization and the implications for operating practices follow. While, in practice, each of the six dimensions should be examined, this example illustrates the approach by focusing on the first two dimensions.

Organization focus: Human resource consulting
Workforce segments: Contract delivery staff: 500
                      Permanent delivery staff: 400

Figure 2-2
Workforce Characterization

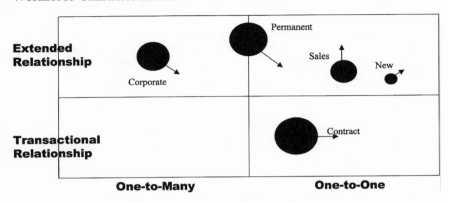

Permanent sales staff: 200
Permanent corporate staff: 300
New business venture staff: 50

Figure 2-2 shows the first two workforce dimensions. The size of each bubble is proportional to the number of people in that segment of the organization. The arrow on each bubble shows the direction the organization wishes to move each workforce segment. This is based on analyzing the key value-contributing component of each area as shown in Table 2-1.

The preferred relationship for four of the five groups is Extended. This framework can be translated into specific operating practices as shown in Table 2-2.

IMPLICATIONS FOR LEADERS AND HR

Organizational leaders and HR play two key roles in navigating through this emerging workplace. The first is to ensure that critical external factors and strategic issues are incorporated in decision making. This means addressing issues and questions such as the following:

- Values regarding relationships with employees and other stakeholders
  - What are the ethical principles the organization will adopt in establishing and maintaining its relationships?
- Rapidity of change: cyclicality/stability and the need for flexibility
  - What does the pace of external change mean for the changing composition and capabilities of the workforce?

Table 2-1
Workforce Characterization: Value Contribution

Workforce segment	Primary value contribution	Key value-contributing component	Need for extended vs. transactional relationship	Need for one-to-one vs. one-to-many relationship
Corporate	Efficiency	Functional knowledge	Extended	One-to-many
Permanent delivery	Customer satisfaction/ new content	Delivery expertise	Extended	One-to-many
Contract delivery	Customer satisfaction	Delivery expertise	Transactional	One-to-one
Sales	Revenue	Customer relationships	Extended	One-to-one
New Business	Learning, revenue	Innovation	Extended	One-to-one

- Importance of accumulated learning
  - How significant is accumulated learning in driving organizational effectiveness? What does this mean for knowledge generation processes?
- Availability of key skills
  - What are skill needs for the future and how will they be acquired?
- Opportunities for individual development
  - What are the opportunities for, and limitations of, development available for individuals? How will deficiencies be addressed?
- Leadership capabilities
  - What competencies are available, or need to be developed in leadership to execute workforce strategies?

The second key role of the organization's leaders and HR is to characterize the workforce and define the form of relationship needed with each employee segment, recognizing that this may change over time. The process for doing this will be specific to each organization, reflecting the culture and operating practices. The following overall framework can be modified as needed for a given situation:

Table 2-2
Workforce Characterization: Operating Practices

Workforce segment	Career development	Communication	Performance management	Compensation	Decision-making	Management style
Corporate	Internal organization framework	Hierarchical	Objectives driven	Base, small variable	Consensus	Functional/ consensus
Permanent Delivery	External professional organization affiliations	Centralized	Driven by client satisfaction criteria	Base, bonus linked to metrics	Centralized	Focus on defined standards
Contract Delivery	Individual responsibility	Local	Project based	Project based	Flexible within operating parameters	Informal
Sales	Internal organization framework	Local and central	Quota driven	High variable component tied to quota	Individual autonomy	Hands off
New Business	Learning through business experience	Business unit	Driven by business penetration	Individual, bonus linked to business performance	Autonomous	Encourages risk taking

- Establish organizational objectives driving the relationship with individuals
- Ensure that top leaders engage as owners of the workforce characterization process
- Conduct workforce characterization to identify key employee segments
- Develop a protocol for the relationship definition process for each segment
- Assemble teams representing key employee segments
- Conduct relationship definition sessions with representatives from each segment
- Ratify the results with organizational leaders
- Define behaviors and principles associated with the identified relationships
- Communicate behaviors and principles to the organization and to new recruits

Leaders and HR need to adjust the approach to meet the needs of different organizational cultures. In some cases leaders will take a primary role in guiding the process. In others this role will be the responsibility of HR and line management jointly. Regardless of the details of the process, it is a powerful tool for establishing consensus on a strong and vital relationship between the organization and its employees. As such it provides a foundation that can guide workforce development, clarify and enhance relationships with individuals and strengthen the organization's ability to create value.

In the next chapter we explore issues related to value creation. This begins with an overview of what is meant by value creation, the importance of the individual, and the importance of affiliation. It continues with an exploration of community implications, the impact of affiliation in different industry sectors, and the changing workforce needs as an organization evolves. Measurement concepts are then introduced along with organization structure issues. The chapter concludes with implications for leaders and HR in guiding value creation built from the relationship of individuals and organizations.

— 3 —

The Organization of the Future:
Value Creation

Picture a multinational, mega-organization with one central control room. In it sits the CEO, reading the *Wall Street Journal*, occasionally checking on his automated operation. No other people are involved in this operation. This is a company of one. That is the response, pushed to the extreme, of one natural resource company to the potential shortage of people in the future. Unfortunately, it doesn't work well when confronted with the ambiguities of our changing world, and the realities of our information- and service-based economy. So we must explore other alternatives that embrace rather than exclude people, for people are at the core of value creation in the emerging economy.

VALUE CREATION LINKED TO AFFILIATION

What do we mean by value creation? Organizational value is the sum total of the organization's knowledge, capabilities, operating practices, connections inside and outside, how they fit together, and the ability to marshal these to meet customers' needs. This value is created one person at a time. Securing this value means unlocking the potential of the workforce. It means liberating people to do what they can do best. It means relinquishing control and opening up opportunity. This is equally true in a nonprofit where value creation is all about the organization achieving its purpose and a for-profit where value creation can be expressed in tangible financial terms.

Traditional financial measures look at return on capital, expressed in different ways, for example return on assets or return on capital employed. They measure past, rather than future potential. In today's world, future potential comes from pooled knowledge. Pooled knowledge comes from the skills and expertise that we each bring. Like a giant snowball where each tiny, beautiful snowflake bonds together, our individual contributions add together to create the value of the whole organization. So the key becomes identifying and maximizing value contribution from each person, and that, as we will show in a later chapter, is directly linked to individual fulfillment.

Affiliation

Gwen needed help. When she came for career counseling she was lost, bored with her job, about to throw in the towel. She was a middle manager in a development area. She was going through the motions with her work. Both Gwen and her organization were suffering. Her malaise could spread readily to others, undermining morale and commitment. Through a process of self-assessment and reflection Gwen clarified what she would find fulfilling and how to achieve it. She began to create a path forward that worked for her and for the organization. Her value contribution started to rise. She was able to create a path forward that drew on her own interests and abilities and that matched needs in the organization. Her energy and enthusiasm grew and the organization benefited.

Unfortunately, this critical step of creating a mutually satisfying path forward often does not begin within organizations; rather, it occurs with a move to another organization, because there is little in place to support internal movement. Steve had changed jobs three times in three years. Each time he began a new job with enthusiasm, mastered it, and then lost interest as it provided no learning and development at that point. He sought development by moving to another organization. When faced with the prospect of a fourth move he began to question this approach. We explored alternatives that involved remaining and developing with his current organization and this path opened to both his and the organization's benefit. When an organization creates an internal job market that is more efficient than the external one, both employees and the organization benefit.

Ahr and Ahr (2000, 32) quotes studies that build on an approach by

Table 3-1
Organization and Individual Parallels

Organization	Individual
Create value, realize purpose	Express meaning, realize dream
Structural complexity	Components of life
Evolving through life cycle	Maturing through life cycle
Interconnected in business system	Interconnected in personal system
Self-sustaining	Self-developing
Global	Universal

Meyer and Allen looking at various forms of organizational commitment. Meyer and Allen defined three forms of commitment:

- Affective commitment, where individuals want to remain with an organization because they identify with the organization and are highly involved with its activities.
- Normative commitment, where individuals feel they ought to remain with an organization because of a sense of personal obligation.
- Continuance commitment, where individuals feel they need to remain with an organization because they believe that they do not have good alternatives.

Ahr cites a number of studies that demonstrate a correlation between affective commitment and strong performance. Conversely higher continuance commitment is correlated with undesirable outcomes such as fewer commendations for work. Not surprisingly, those who stay because they want to are stronger performers. People stay when they can see options and a path for their development. Those who stay because they feel they have no other choice don't contribute as effectively to organizational value creation. In this case there is neither individual development nor effective organizational value creation.

The direct link between individual affiliation and organizational value creation is clear. Chapter 6 will explore how to quantify this link. There are strong parallels between critical factors for the organization and those for the individual. This is illustrated in Table 3-1.

Organizations exist to create value and achieve a purpose, individuals seek to express meaning in their lives and realize a dream. In both cases this may be explicit and clear or it may be implicit and uncertain. Greater clarity of purpose enhances value creation or individual fulfillment. This underlines the importance of organizations clarifying the nature of their relationship with their employee constituencies and individuals clarifying their own aspirations. Both may change over time and both need to be recalibrated over time. Even small organizations are complex with people specializing in different areas, and being of various ethnicities, ages and responsibility levels. Similarly as individuals, our lives reflect a delicate interplay of personal needs, family requirements, work expectations and social obligations. Organizations evolve through a life cycle, and a few successfully negotiate the difficult transitions needed to retain their vitality. Navigating the difficult rapids of transition requires forward-looking employees who themselves are able to express their unfolding life needs. As individuals mature through a life cycle, needs change. Organizations are interconnected in complex external systems that include competitors, customers and suppliers. As individuals, we are interconnected in complex social systems that typically involve hundreds of contacts at any time. Organizations need to be self-sustaining and individuals need to be self-developing. Both organizations and individuals need to link to their environment. Finally, many organizations today—and most in the future—operate in a global arena either as a result of competition or as a result of customer needs. As individuals, we operate in a universal environment where our colleagues represent many ideologies and cultural backgrounds. There can be a natural alignment of individual and organizational factors that strengthens the linkage of one to the other.

Community Implications

What does this mean at the community level? Up to now organizations have operated largely independently with regard to their workforce, viewing other organizations as competitors for a limited talent pool. On the other hand, business partnerships are common; typically involving sharing of business practices or complementary know-how to meet customer needs. For example, the partnering of a regional airline with an international carrier such as Atlantic Coast Airlines in the United States with United and Delta allows each organization to focus its resources on areas of greatest competence for the benefit of the consumer. However, partnerships that involve the workforce are rare. Community considerations are currently addressed by entities such as the Employment Development Department in the United States, which provide shared services that meet the community need for redeployment and the individual need for support in transition. For-profit organizations such as DBM also play an important role in supporting the transition of individuals from one organization to another. However, there are few examples

Figure 3-1
Financial Measures in 2000 by Industry Sector (Bubble Size Proportional to Sector Profit)

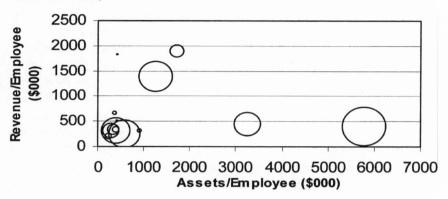

where organizations work jointly to strengthen and develop their work-forces.

In moving into a world of people scarcity, from a communal and organizational perspective it becomes increasingly important to maximize the contribution of each person. This occurs when people are working in situations well aligned with their aspirations. Such alignment is a cornerstone of a dedicated and committed workforce. In some cases this can be a difficult task for a single organization to accomplish given limitations of individual development inherent in some positions, particularly for unskilled jobs. To address this, an important area for future exploration is to develop enabling frameworks that encourage organizations to cooperate on workforce deployment, for their benefit and for the benefit of their employees. For example, an organization seeking to fill unskilled positions may support individual development to enhance productivity and affiliation, with a view to eventually helping individuals transition to more highly skilled positions in a neighboring organization. Each party, and the community, can benefit from such cooperation. This will be explored in more detail in Chapter 10.

INDUSTRY SECTOR COMPARISONS

Within a given organization the role of the workforce in creating value will vary by industry sector. Figure 3-1 shows some sector examples. These industry median financial measures for selected sectors are expressed on a per employee basis for organizations in the global Fortune

500 in the year 2000 (*Fortune*: www.fortune.com); bubble sizes are proportional to total sector profit.

The cluster of sectors in the lower left corner of the chart, with revenue per employee below $750,000 and assets per employee below $1 million, are the most people-intensive sectors. They span a broad range of industries. Included here are healthcare, chemicals, telecommunications, network and other communications equipment, food production, pharmaceuticals, entertainment, computers and other office equipment, and airlines. Companies in the global 500 in these sectors in 2000 had combined revenues of $2 trillion. The wide diversity of sectors with higher people intensity reflects the broad scope of people-intensive operations in today's global economy. The quadrant at the lower right with revenue per employee below $750,000 and assets per employee above $1 million contains the diversified financial and commercial banking sectors. These are asset-intensive businesses where the primary value creation contribution of each person is in leveraging effective utilization of these assets. The upper left quadrant with revenue per employee above $750,000 and assets per employee below $1 million contains the wholesalers healthcare sector (a single point on the chart). Here employees' contribution to revenue generation is a key to value creation. The two sectors in the upper right quadrant, with revenue per employee above $750,000 and assets per employee above $1 million, are petroleum refining and energy. Employees generate value by maximizing the leverage of assets to generate profitable revenue. Major profit generation can occur in multiple sectors as shown by the larger bubbles in multiple quadrants.

The matrix in Table 3-2 characterizes implications for the workforce of the different sectors. Employee affiliation is a key component of success regardless of the quadrant.

THE WORKFORCE AT EVOLVING ORGANIZATIONAL STAGES

The framework in Table 3-2 is based on large organizations that are part of the global Fortune 500. Do the same considerations apply at different stages of the organizational life cycle? Let us consider the evolution of an organization. Organizational growth can be characterized schematically by the well-known s-curve relationship (Foster 1986). This shows slow initial revenue growth followed by rapid acceleration as the organization's products or services are more broadly adopted with eventual slowing of growth, and the possibility of decline ultimately. Successful organizations avoid the decline phase by repeatedly adapting and

Table 3-2
Industry Quadrant Characteristics

Quadrant Descriptor	Revenue/ Employee ($000)	Assets/ Employee ($000)	Value Creation	Workforce Implications
People Intensive	<750	<1,000	Maximize effectiveness of people interactions and idea generation and implementation.	Strong emphasis on relationship building, internal and external. Support for rapid testing of new ideas. Affiliation is key in building these relationships.
Asset Intensive	<750	>1,000	Maximize asset utilization.	Workforce with deep extended knowledge of effective utilization and deployment of assets. Affiliation needed to build knowledge base.
Sales Intensive	>750	<1,000	Maximize customer interfaces to secure sales growth.	Workforce with extended, embedded customer relationships. Affiliation is key to allowing growth of strong customer relationships.
Sales and Asset Intensive	>750	>1,000	Maximize asset utilization and secure embedded customer relationships.	Workforce with deep knowledge of asset utilization and deployment, and extended customer relationships. Affiliation is key to building both internal knowledge and external links.

innovating to bridge from one s-curve to another. In this bridging step the steady progression of the first s-curve may be punctuated by a slight dip in revenue and then acceleration up a new s-curve that provides for even greater value creation potential. Various changes can enable the transition to the new curve, for example technology or a redefined business approach.

An example of an organization demonstrating this ability to sustain growth and transition is the Thomson Corporation. This organization was rooted in traditional publishing and in the late 1990s and early 2000s achieved a transformation to an organization building a business around electronic provision of information and learning. Similarly Hewlett-Packard migrated from its beginnings in the field of scientific measurement in the late 1930s to broadly diversified technology areas such as computers and related equipment. At each stage, whether it involves the successful navigation of the early growth period or the later mature phase, the leadership of the organization and the workforce drive success. The basis for value creation, organization and leadership needs and the role of the workforce shift with different phases. What are the implications for the workforce at each stage? The stages are as follows:

1. Initiation
2. Early growth
3. Accelerated growth
4. Maturity
5. Transition

In the initiation and early growth stages primary organizational needs are to test new concepts with customers, learn rapidly about evolving needs and quickly modify and adjust business concepts. This requires fleetness of foot, creativity of concept, and imagination. There are no operating rules in place as it is not clear how to best structure the approach to the operation. The best approach to engaging customers is uncertain and the distribution channels need to be developed. Questions that arise at this time are as follows:

• What are primary customer concerns and needs?
• How can solutions be tailored to address these concerns and needs that create value for the organization and the customer?
• What alternative approaches are available?
• What extensions of the basic approach are possible?

- What technology enablers need to be incorporated?
- How can credibility for solutions be established with customers?
- Who are the primary competitors and how can the new concept be distinguished?
- What resources are needed and how can they be obtained?
- Who can be most effective in helping move this forward?

These questions are focused on clarifying which tree to climb, and climbing it, rather than defining the most elegant climbing technique. One framework that describes well the characteristics of different team members needed in these stages is the innovation framework of Inscape (2002). This framework identifies five primary roles in the creation of a new business or organizational concept. Inscape provides a system that readily identifies each person's natural style. The five primary roles are as follows:

- Creator
- Advancer
- Refiner
- Executor
- Facilitator

The Creator excels at generating new ideas, fitting them into an overall concept of a path forward and handing them to an Advancer. The Advancer is able to take new ideas at an early stage and craft them in such a way that they move forward effectively and are ready for a Refiner. The Refiner hones the ideas, identifying problems and ensures that there is circling back as needed to optimize the approach. At this stage the Executor takes over to guide implementation and ensure that details and processes are installed as appropriate. Supporting all of these steps is the Facilitator, who ensures that the team members work together effectively and that the development process stays on track. Effective commercialization of a new business or development of a nonprofit organization requires that all of these roles be addressed and filled by those with requisite interests and abilities.

As a concept moves from initiation to early growth the primary driving force moves from the Creator to the Advancer, with the other three roles also becoming more prominent. In the early growth phase the most critical need is to obtain market validation for the concept and to adjust the approach according to customer needs. This stage requires insight, persistence, creativity and belief. It is not possible to know in advance which approaches will be most successful, so the willingness to explore options is critical.

The accelerated growth phase occurs when a concept takes hold, customer and market interest is substantial, and primary issues are the ability to move quickly to meet demand and pre-empt competition. While there is a continued need for innovation, particularly in areas with short life cycles, the key at this point is successful execution. It is no longer enough to have a novel concept and pique interest. Systems and processes become critical and the Executor role is essential for success.

As the concept moves into maturity, which can take many years in a traditional business such as transportation, or months in a rapidly evolving field such as software, there is a growing need to stimulate the cycle, both managing the mature components for efficiency and identifying and exploring new concepts to sustain the organization. Here the roles of the Executor and the Creator overlap as the need for new concept creation again becomes paramount. In this ongoing cycle of innovation there is a major benefit to be garnered from continuity of experience, coupled with infusion of new ideas. Such a combination provides a strong platform from which to launch new initiatives. This means creating an environment where people choose to affiliate with the organization, transferring their learning from one phase to the next.

VALUE CREATION IN THE EMERGING ECONOMY

Having examined the path an organization concept can take, a central issue is how to measure the value created. In this apparently simple question lies much of the organizational dilemma in moving into the emerging world of work. In a predictable work world, with product cycles extending over decades, measuring value based on hard assets and past returns from the assets met the tests of repeatability, validity and some predictive capability. In a world with product cycles in months, and much of organizations' assets in intangible form such as sophisticated distribution systems (Wal-Mart), protected technology (Merck) or novel applications of technology (Cisco Systems), hard assets do not adequately reflect the real value of the organization. Value is the potential for future economic performance rather than a reiteration of past performance. In the organizational world, past performance is not necessarily the best predictor of future performance. Leaders can quickly lose their pre-eminent position (Tushman 1993). This flies in the face of approaches that are built on past performance being the best predictor of the future. Past performance may, in fact, bear little or no relation to future success in emerging or declining areas. Furthermore, in this information-based world, concepts of value creation need to expand to reflect the central role of the workforce. While value can be readily calculated as the discounted sum of future cash flows, in emerging areas it is highly uncertain because the terminal value for this calculation dominates the total. Further compounding the uncertainty is the discount rate, which must reflect the uncertainties inherent in growing businesses.

With this in mind, approaches to estimating value creation need to build on the concept of the value created by each individual, magnified by networking and connecting and consolidated for the whole organization. This differs from the traditional view of the workforce as a cost to be minimized, instead viewing it as a resource to be developed and maximized. Figure 3-1 showed revenue per employee for the sectors shown varying from about $200,000 to almost $2 million. In other sectors of the economy not shown in Figure 3-1, such as professional services, the revenue per employee can be less than $100,000. Just for the sectors shown in the lower left quadrant of Figure 3-1, with the highest people intensity, total 2000 revenues are $2 trillion. To put this in perspective, this small sampling of sectors is equivalent to more than 20% of U.S. GDP in 2000. So with people-intensive businesses again a growing part of the U.S. economy, organizational value estimation needs to start with an understanding of the value contributed by each person, while also estimating the gap between this actual value and the ultimate potential contribution. Closing this gap is one of the primary responsibilities not only of leaders, but also of everyone in the workforce. HR plays a key role in this. Building on the understanding of individual value contribution, the impact of interconnections can then be incorporated.

What factors need to be in place to maximize individual potential? They include:

• Communicating an inspiring organizational purpose
• Establishing a clear organizational direction
• Providing support for individuals to clarify their own preferred path
• Providing flexibility to enable each person to align their attributes and aspirations with their work
• Aligning reward and recognition systems with desired behaviors
• Distributing decision making to those closest to each situation
• Eliminating barriers that inhibit development or effective decision making

- Encouraging diversity of viewpoints and perspectives to increase options and the likelihood of making sound choices
- Understanding and defining the preferred relationship with each employee segment to align expectations to reality.

How can this be accomplished? Unlike the traditional command and control approach, addressing these factors means enabling each person to take control of his or her own destiny within a clear organizational framework. This places a burden on managers to demonstrate effective interpersonal skills as they engage with each person individually.

Estimates of the value generated by each person can be approximated by proxy measures such as operating income per employee that reflect ongoing financial performance linked to the workforce. They can be extrapolated to project potential future contributions. Encouraging each person to assess his or her own situation and aspirations can provide a qualitative assessment of the gap between actual and potential contribution. It is a basis for supporting each person to move closer to their full potential, thereby maximizing organizational performance.

Knowing the gaps and opportunities to help people more fully realize their potential leads to interventions the organization can provide. These interventions add value through their impact on individuals who then enhance workforce effectiveness. How can this impact be described? One approach that was developed in the training field, and has been subsequently extended, provides a potential framework. The original formulation was proposed by Kirkpatrick (1998) and consists of the following four levels to describe the impact of organizational interventions:

- Level 1: Reaction and Planned Action
  - Measures participant satisfaction and planned action (sometimes known as a smile sheet)
- Level 2: Learning
  - Measures changes in knowledge skills and attitude
- Level 3: Individual Performance/Behavior
  - Measures changes in on-the-job behavior
- Level 4: Business Results
  - Measures business impact, for example increased sales or productivity

Phillips (1997) added a fifth level:

- Level 5: Return on Investment
  - Compares program benefits to costs

Elsdon and Iyer (1999) added a sixth level:

- Level 6: Prediction
  - Estimates the impact of resources committed on future performance

These levels provide a framework for assessing the value creation impact of interventions and a basis for making decisions about future resource commitments. A practical application will be illustrated later as a case study in Chapter 7.

IMPLICATIONS FOR ORGANIZATIONAL STRUCTURE

What does this mean for organizational structure? In a world where flexibility, distributed decision making and speed are prized, the traditional hierarchy begins to look shaky. Rather than distributing decision making, it concentrates the process and, in so doing, slows down decision making. It is not flexible, requiring that adjustments to structure proceed through laborious approval processes. It was more effective in stable conditions, where risk avoidance was a primary consideration—for example, for large capital investment decisions in mature businesses.

Variants of the traditional structure include the following:

- Structure by function (e.g., sales, manufacturing, research and development)
- Structure by geography (e.g., Europe, Americas, Asia)
- Structure by business unit (e.g., specialty chemicals, polymers, fabricated products)

Frequently organizations will move among these three variants according to changing business needs and management preferences, or employ a matrix structure that attempts to blend attributes of more than one variant. The functional structure excels at building strong content knowledge. Unfortunately, it can impede rapid progress in new business areas due to the many interfaces and political issues that can arise. It is also less effective in supporting cultural differences in different regions. This latter point is a strength of the geographic structure, which, however, suffers from the downside of duplication of effort and slower decision making on global opportunities. The business unit approach is strong in supporting rapid decision making, both because of a natural convergence of functional interests on business unit objectives and some distribution of decision-making authority. An example of an organization that used this approach successfully to spawn new businesses is 3M, which deliberately subdivided business units on reaching a certain size to avoid perceived dis-economies of scale. The disadvantages of this approach include duplication of resources and a tendency to form business unit silos that are barriers to individual movement and development.

These structures possess some common characteristics, namely hierarchical decision making as a means to minimize risk, and strong process and procedural components. The first two versions—functional and geographic—are most effective in relatively stable situations where the need for speed is not paramount.

It is important to evaluate these variants of the traditional structure against primary organizational needs today and in the future. They are as follows:

• Instant awareness of customers' changing expectations
• Ability to respond rapidly to change
• Flexibility
• Distributed decision making
• Ability to attract and retain key employees
• Global reach
• Ability to include a diverse workforce
• Innovation
• Efficiency

These characteristics are not easily created and sustained by the traditional organization structure variants. Indeed, some of the needs create natural tensions; for example, the need for innovation and entrepreneurial behavior implies a fluid structure, whereas efficiency implies a well-defined structure. The demands of the emerging work world may require simultaneously executing seemingly contradictory approaches in different parts of the organization. For example, it may mean simultaneously being opportunistic and planning, taking risks and being prudent with spending. It will mean reexamining the structure and systems used to build organizations. It is likely that organizations in the future will need to experiment with radically new approaches to structure. These approaches will step outside traditional boundaries, recognizing the needs of a workforce that is freed from geographical ties by communications technology, and is unwilling to accept the decision-making constraints placed on its predecessors. One example of a nontraditional approach is that of the guild. MIT's Malone (Rosenfeld 2001) pointed out the natural evolution of today's workforce toward the formation of guild-like structures where affiliation is based on functional skills much as in medieval guilds. Suggesting that organizations may evolve more to this form implies a much greater democracy of decision making than was true in the past and is true today.

What does this mean for the relationship between organizations and individuals? Here is an example. Stuart was a successful doctor struggling with the challenges of an emergency room environment when he came for career counseling. His work environment had deteriorated to the point that he was ready to leave the profession. He felt unsupported by his hospital, was at odds with his nursing colleagues, angry, and unclear that he was making a meaningful contribution. We explored his options and a path forward into new areas. It raised a question as to how a profession built upon the helping orientation of the Hippocratic oath could struggle so with the needs of its constituents. This brings us back to the Hawthorne experiments mentioned earlier that demonstrated convincingly the key role of management in understanding and responding to the needs of the workforce, while creating a sense of community. This was lacking in Stuart's case and his response to consider leaving is increasingly common. Leaders and HR must create an environment where expectations are clear and mutually agreed with employees, supporting a strong sense of community.

A challenge faced by leaders and HR is creating this strong sense of community in the face of growing role complexity for each person. For example, managers are now expected to be mentors and coaches to their employees, to maintain leading-edge functional knowledge, to stay alert to changing customer and environmental signals, while attempting to have a life outside work. There are similar expectations of others in organizations who are not in management positions. It is not surprising that stress levels are rising in the work environment along with a steady increase in hours worked in the United States (International Survey Research 2000). One means of addressing this problem is to reexamine expectations regarding internal skill capabilities in the future. Use of external specialist resources will likely be needed in some areas to meet organizational skill needs.

By framing relevant questions about workforce evolution and metrics, appropriate targets and outcomes can be established that address value creation. For example, one measure of workforce strength that directly impacts value creation is the attrition rate. Zero attrition is undesirable as it can inhibit the introduction of new ideas into the organization. Likewise an attrition rate of 100% is undesirable, bringing with it the loss of intellectual capital and high costs. So there is an attrition rate between these two extremes that optimizes value creation. This optimum will vary by industry sector, by organization and by functional group within an organization. Several factors influence this optimum as follows:

- Rapidity of changing skill needs
- Opportunities for employee development
- Replacement cost and availability of people
- Criticality of potential lost knowledge
- Impact on productivity
- Impact on institutional knowledge
- Impact on morale

The more rapidly skill needs change in a given area, the more likely it is that there will need to be some attrition to infuse new ideas. In some organizations there are natural limitations to development, for example in certain unskilled jobs. The organization may elect to support individual development recognizing that at some point individuals need to leave to fulfill their potential. The more difficult and costly it is to replace one person or a group, and the more critical their knowledge is to the organization, then the lower the optimum attrition rate. Similarly the more significantly individuals impact productivity, institutional knowledge and morale, the lower the optimum attrition rate. Establishing and regularly revisiting targets for attrition becomes essential with changing business and workforce situations. Quantitative approaches to defining this optimum and relating it to value creation will be reviewed in Chapter 6.

This exploration of value creation began with an image of a peopleless organization. It avoids all the messy ambiguities that people introduce. It also eliminates the creativity, ingenuity and flexibility that people bring into an organization. Sometimes traditional hierarchical structures have this same inhibiting effect. The emerging workplace is unconstrained by geography and by ideology. There is an opportunity to enable each person to reach his or her full potential, in interconnected, supportive and flexible systems. Such systems will need to continually restructure to meet changing business needs. They will link the individual to the work group, the division, the organization and the community.

Value is created by the individual and magnified or attenuated by the organizational environment. The challenge is to create environments that magnify. Such environments are sector specific, matched to the evolutionary stage of an organization, and based on aligning individual aspirations with organizational needs. They will require:

- New approaches to enhancing and measuring value creation that are driven by the workforce and its contribution to future potential
- Models that describe and predict the impact of resources committed on individuals and organizations
- Radically new organizational structures that democratize decision making
- Listening to the organization.

We will explore modeling and measurement later in the book. Listening to the organization is the subject of the next chapter.

— 4 —

Listening to the Organization

Organizations like crowds take on characteristics of their own. When I was a youngster in England, my father would sometimes take me to see a local football match, the kind with the round ball. This was in the days when a seat for a spectator was a luxury. We stood in a seething mass of people that moved and swayed with the ebb and flow of the game. Some weeks it was a benign crowd, other times aggressive and at other times sad. While the fortunes of the local team had much to do with the mood of the crowd later in the game, at the beginning the crowd took on a personality formed by the reaction of each person to the world around them. On one occasion at the local football stadium, I was standing in the car park with friends and about 10,000 other people waiting to begin an overnight walk to raise funds for local charities. The driver of a car made the unfortunate decision to drive through this crowd to a small exit gate. Those at the back, thinking that the walk was beginning, began to press forward and many at the front fell. It was a calamity with many people including myself trapped. I was fortunate to survive this event. Four people perished and many others were hurt. The memory of this is still with me, many years later, along with the sense that I failed to help protect those who perished. In the same night I came to see the great destructive power of a crowd, and the redemptive role of individuals who went on to struggle twenty-four miles for charitable causes. I can still recall the pain of aching limbs after this walk but a greater pain is the memory of my failure to listen to and understand the needs of those around me. This is a mistake that we cannot afford to make in our organizations.

There are several purposes to listening to our organizations:

- Build understanding
- Diagnose problems
- Prescribe solutions
- Build consensus
- Provide a basis for action

When a person knows they have been understood they are ready to act for a cause. Until then they will likely resist moving forward, often becoming active opponents to movement. In our changing world we need employees who are partners in forging a path forward. That means leaders and HR listening to the voices of the organization to build understanding of individual needs and general themes that arise from these needs. Generating this understanding provides a basis for diagnosing problems, concerns and opportunities. Such a diagnostic step is a prerequisite to designing interventions that enhance the effectiveness of the organization and strengthen affiliation with each person. It is tempting to bypass this step but a major mistake. The history of many organizations is replete with examples of missteps arising from a lack of understanding of workforce needs. For example, one organization moved its U.S. headquarters and, in the process, lost most of the workforce from the original location. There was little focus on employee needs and concerns. Problems are often evident after acquisitions when the acquirer makes assumptions about the acquired workforce, promptly losing its greatest asset. It is also true after major change events such as downsizings when the retained workforce is particularly vulnerable. In another situation an organization repeatedly increased compensation to try and stem the tide of attrition only to find that compensation was not central to employee concerns.

An effective diagnostic stage leads directly to steps that create needed outcomes. For example, if employees identify management behavior as a major concern, then prescriptive actions might include coaching or other forms of management training and support. Proposed prescriptive approaches can also be tested with the organization as part of a diagnostic phase to build consensus on a path forward. Listening helps create such consensus. Just as in individual relationships, listening is central to creating closeness, so in an organization context listening is central to building affiliation and establishing a foundation for action. Once the voices of the organization are clearly heard and understood, they form a basis for crafting and implementing a path forward.

It might seem that listening occurs naturally without effort. In fact it is a learned skill, like many interpersonal interactions. Bolton describes the nature of this skill at an individual level (Bolton 1986). The challenge is to extend such concepts from the individual to the organization. One approach to categorizing organizational listening is to consider the following dimensions:

- Process—how listening occurs
  - Informal or structured
- Emphasis—the orientation of the listening
  - Analytical or emotional
- Content—the analytical basis of the listening
  - Thematic or anecdotal
- Context—the setting in which listening occurs
  - Individual or group

Regarding the process, both informal and structured approaches make important contributions. Informal listening is an important means to identify issues at an early stage. These are issues that may not have gathered momentum at an organizational level but are beginning to surface. Informal listening is a safety valve that allows people to express concerns and introduce new opportunities. It occurs most effectively when it is spontaneous and there is a high degree of trust among participants. However, from a leadership and HR perspective it is imperative to set aside time for such listening, even though the event itself is spontaneous. Structured listening, on the other hand, occurs when a specific topic has been identified and a mechanism established to gather feedback. Examples of structured listening include employee surveys or focus groups. It is effective when the topic is well defined and known in advance. A hybrid of the two types of listening is a brainstorming session, which provides for some informality in a structured format.

The second dimension is the emphasis of the listening, whether analytical or emotional/affective. While these are not mutually exclusive, there is often a tendency in an organizational setting to focus only on the analytical at the expense of the emotional/affective component. Both are important. Individual preferences and the specific situation will determine the appropriate balance of these aspects. A structured process is more likely to address analytical aspects while an informal process can more readily surface emotional components.

The third dimension is that of content and the extent to which it is anecdotal or thematic. In other words, does it consist of stories recounting individual experiences or does it consist of general themes identified by synthesizing input from many people. Again, both have an important role to play in the listening process. Anecdotal listening gathers insights from the recounting of experiences. It usually carries a strong emotional message that represents one person's reaction to experiences and situations. Processing this type of listening is primarily about accurately understanding individual observations and feelings, as opposed to observing the entire organization accurately. As the results of anecdotal listening carry a strong emotional component they can lead readily to action, which is its strength and weakness, since an individual's perspective may not represent an overall organizational need. Organizational needs are identified through thematic listening, which is a process of gathering information from individuals so that it can be combined, allowing conclusions of general relevance to be identified. It is inherently a more analytical process. A combination of the anecdotal and thematic listening approaches is particularly powerful, as the results combine an emotional call to action with a rational determination of key issues.

On a practical level listening can occur in an individual or group context. The benefits of the former approach include confidentiality, which greatly enhances the likelihood of open disclosure, and an in-depth focus on the individual that enhances the likelihood of gathering an informed perspective. The group approach, on the other hand, is beneficial where idea building occurs from the interaction of multiple participants, such as in brainstorming. It is also possible, but more difficult, to respect confidentiality in a group setting. Again, according to context, both individual and group listening can be valuable.

This brings us to the characteristics that lead to effective organizational listening. These are the key components:

- Openness
- Confidentiality
- Respect
- Responsiveness and reinforcement
- Active engagement
- Inclusion

Open listening occurs in a nonjudgmental setting where there is a willingness to hear sometimes disquieting or unpleasant feedback. It is easy to adopt a defensive posture when receiving feedback if that feedback is critical. I have observed very different reactions in leadership groups learning about organizational issues. These reactions vary from a search for a major flaw in the data (there isn't one), to denial, to acceptance of the results and a search for solutions. The first two reactions will perpetuate the problem; the last reaction can lead to rapid, effective action. The first two reactions also inhibit additional feedback.

Confidentiality is an absolute requirement where sensitive personal issues are involved, as is often the case when seeking to understand concerns in an organization. This is particularly true when the concerns relate to management or leadership behaviors. It is difficult to create an environment where individuals know that their disclosures will be held in confidence, if the recipient of the information is internal to the organization. Use of a third party to gather information can be an effective means to guarantee confidentiality.

In one organization a primary concern raised by employees was lack of respect exhibited by management. This meant that suggestions went unheeded, that statements from top management appeared to demean segments of the workforce, and that there were few expressions of value or recognition for employees. Respect means accepting the validity of the opinions expressed, that they are given in good faith with honorable intentions. It is analogous to the unconditional positive regard of Rogers (1995) for an effective therapeutic relationship. Respect encourages further openness and expression.

Flowing directly from respect is responsiveness. This means acting on the information generated by organizational listening. It is interwoven with reinforcement, where feedback and actions in response to listening demonstrate both an understanding of the issues and a willingness to take action to address concerns or seize opportunities. Responsiveness and reinforcement lead to further open disclosure, which results in a growing cycle of actions that strengthen the organization and the affiliation of employees.

Employees in one organization kept a log of how many days it had been since their division director last visited one of their buildings. This time frame would often stretch to a month or more. The employee population viewed it as a visible reminder of their lack of importance. Active engagement by leadership and HR is crucial to maintaining open communication and allowing organizational listening to occur. This means a combination of the informal and the structured listening approaches covered earlier. It means displaying openness, respect and responsiveness and demonstrating action through feedback and reinforcement.

The final characteristic of effective organizational listening is inclusion. All employees in the organization have a contribution to make. Listening needs to occur broadly and deeply in an organization, not just in select groups or at certain levels of management. Identification of concerns needs to occur where the concerns are most strongly felt. Opportunities can be surfaced at many levels in the organization; the barrier is often that no one is listening.

These characteristics of organizational listening include aspects of both the process by which listening occurs and the environment that frames it. Process aspects are the mechanics of the listening activity such as responsiveness and reinforcement. Framing aspects include the context in which listening occurs, such as inclusion and openness. Both process and framing are largely determined by the behavior of leadership, guided and supported by HR.

Listening leads directly to action through synthesis of the information generated, development of potential solutions and feedback about the efficacy of these solutions. The process is continuous, with leadership and HR actively engaging in organizational listening, supporting development of solutions that address concerns and opportunities, and then implementation of these solutions, and soliciting feedback. Organizational listening occurs in the context of broader listening by leadership that includes listening to other core constituencies of the organization, namely customers, suppliers, shareholders and the community. The combination of such listening provides the basis for a blueprint for action.

Let us look at examples of organizational listening, first considering broad input from people in many organizations, and then considering pooled results of in-depth studies in selected organizations.

WORKFORCE PERSPECTIVE SURVEY RESULTS

To understand people's perspectives about their work and to begin examining approaches to modeling their work relationship, surveys were conducted with individuals across a wide range of organizations. These surveys were administered in conjunction with forty-five briefings at different locations in North America on the subject of employee retention. The survey instrument used is included in the Appendix. Participants completed the survey at the time they attended the briefing. It was designed to elicit basic demographic information, information on participants' work history, their organizations' attrition levels and their perceptions of their relationship to their work. Participants could identify themselves or remain anonymous at their discretion; 55% chose to identify themselves. The majority of people were in human resource functions in a broad range of positions ranging from entry-level generalists to vice presidents. The size of organizations represented ranged from one person to 350,000 people. A total of 920 surveys were completed by individuals; however, not all participants answered all questions. The two largest industry sectors represented were healthcare with sixty-four participants and manufacturing with fifty-two participants. Other sectors with twenty-five or more participants were financial services, retail, insurance and telecommunications. The remaining sectors covered a broad cross section of for-profit, nonprofit and public sector organizations. Survey participants thus represented a broad range of sectors and North American geographies.

Overall results from the surveys will be reviewed as well as findings from the two sectors with the most participants, namely healthcare and manufacturing. The sizes of respondents' organizations were as follows:

- Overall average: 9,725 people (standard deviation: 24,232)
- Healthcare average: 7,972 people (standard deviation: 15,035)
- Manufacturing average: 3,804 people (standard deviation: 5,880)

In each case the standard deviation significantly exceeds the average size, underlining the broad range of organizational sizes involved.

The need to build affiliation with employees is emphasized by these statistics that summarize voluntary attrition rates (voluntary attrition is employee initiated):

- Overall annual voluntary attrition rate: 20% (standard deviation: 18%)
- Healthcare annual voluntary attrition rate: 25% (standard deviation: 13%)
- Manufacturing annual voluntary attrition rate: 12% (standard deviation: 7%)

This underlines the challenge for the healthcare sector, which is facing a combination of increased demand for healthcare services as the population ages, and decreased supply of people as other sectors attract potential recruits and current employees. The average annual financial impact of attrition per organization based on average annual compensation of $50,000 and an attrition cost of 1.5 times annual compensation is $146 million. The annual cost of attrition for this group in total is more than $125 billion. Attrition has a major financial impact on individual organizations and it is a major cost to the community.

Given this information it is not surprising that 82% of participants rated employee retention as a critical issue (6 or 7 on a 7-point scale). The average rating overall was 6.2, with a higher rating for healthcare participants at 6.6 and a lower rating for manufacturing participants at 5.9. These differences reflect the greater degree of people scarcity felt in the healthcare sector. Healthcare can be viewed as a leading indicator for general workforce trends in the future, given demographic projections of growing employee scarcity.

Turning now to the perspective of individuals, we asked how many organizations people had been employed with on a full-time basis since completing a first degree or leaving high school. The overall average was 4 organizations with a standard deviation of 2.1. The numbers for healthcare at 4.3 (standard deviation of 1.9) and manufacturing at 4.1 (standard deviation of 2) were close to the overall statistics. Movement from one organization to another is a fact of organizational life for this population.

We also asked how long people had been with their current organization. The overall average was 6.3 years. A standard deviation of 7.2 years highlights the broad range in this area. Tenure for healthcare participants was close to that of the overall population at an average of 6.4 years (standard deviation of 7 years). Participants from manufacturing had longer tenure at 9 years (standard deviation of 9.8 years). These trends are directionally consistent with the overall attrition rates, which were lower for manufacturing, indicating longer tenure. The tenure for this predominantly HR population can be compared with the average expected tenure in the sector based on overall attrition rates (bearing in mind that the HR numbers will understate actual tenure as the individuals are still with their current organization). For the overall sample having an attrition rate of 20%, the average expected tenure is 5 years (1/0.2) vs. an observed 6.3 years for the HR-dominated sample. For the healthcare group it would be 4 years (1/0.25) vs. an observed 6.4 years for the HR-dominated sample, and for the manufacturing group it would be 8.3 years (1/0.12) vs. an observed 9 years for the HR-dominated group. In all cases the actual tenure of this largely HR group exceeds that of the overall organization in the respective sector. The smallest difference is observed in manufacturing. This greater tenure for HR has organizational benefits, as HR to a degree is the keeper of the organization's cultural history. An important question for leaders and HR professionals looking to the future is what attrition rates and tenure are appropriate for the various segments of the workforce. This subject will be explored in more depth later in the book.

Now let us look at individuals' perspectives on their relationship to their work and to their organization. We first asked about the extent to which people felt they could articulate the primary purpose of their organization. Overall, 77% of responding participants were confident in this area as shown by a response of 6 or 7 on a 7-point scale. The average response was 6 (standard deviation 1). Responses for healthcare at 6.2 (standard deviation 1.2) and manufacturing at 5.9 (standard deviation 1.3) were close to the overall responses. For this sample, individuals are clear about the purpose of their organizations.

Similarly we explored the degree of clarity people felt about their own career aspirations. Overall, 69% of those responding indicated a high degree of clarity (6 or 7 on a 7-point scale). The average overall response was 5.9 (standard deviation 1). Responses for healthcare at 5.9 (standard deviation 1.1) and manufacturing at 6 (standard deviation 1.2) were close to the overall responses. Individuals in this sample know their preferred career direction well. This is perhaps not surprising given that this is a predominantly HR population that is attuned to career options. We can conclude that we are working with a sample population that is both well informed about its own organizations' driving forces and clear about its own career aspirations.

Now let us look at the alignment of the individual with the organization. We asked how well aligned people felt their aspirations were with the purpose of their organizations. Here we see a significant change. Less than half of those responding, 46%, indicated a high degree of alignment (6 or 7 on a 7-point scale) of their aspirations with their organization's purpose. The average overall response was 5.2 (standard deviation 1.3). Again responses for healthcare, 5.1 (standard deviation 1.6), and manufacturing, 5.1 (standard deviation 1.4), were close to the overall responses. This disconnect between individuals' aspirations and organizational purpose can lead to a reduced sense of affiliation and increased attrition.

To explore this in more depth we asked questions about the extent to which people found their organization's purpose inspiring, the extent to which they felt a strong degree of affiliation with their organization, and how long they anticipated remaining with their organization. Only 49% of those responding overall found their organization's purpose highly inspiring (6 or 7 on a 7-point scale). The average overall response was 5.2 (standard deviation 1.4). Responses for healthcare, 5.6 (standard deviation 1.5), were significantly higher, reflecting the mission-driven nature of organizations in this field and that of employees. Responses for manufacturing at 4.9 (standard deviation 1.6) were lower.

This rather tenuous connection with organizational purpose is reflected in the sense of affiliation people feel with their organization. Only 53% indicated a strong sense of affiliation (6 or 7 on a 7-point scale). The average overall response was 5.3 (standard deviation 1.4). Responses for healthcare were higher, 5.5 (standard deviation 1.5), again reflecting the mission-driven nature of organizations in this field and that of employees. As with responses about organizational purpose, responses for manufacturing participants were lower at 5.2 (standard deviation 1.4).

Given these perspectives by individuals about their current situation, what does this mean in terms of future intentions? Specifically what does this mean regarding anticipated tenure with the organization and how is this related to the degree of inspiring purpose? The overall responses about how long people expected to remain with their organization were as follows:

- Less than one year: 12%
- One to two years: 19%
- Two to three years: 16%
- Three to four years: 7%
- Four to five years: 14%
- Five to ten years: 16%
- More than ten years: 16%

The three-to-four-year time horizon is a watershed. It forms a natural division of the respondents into two groups. The first group includes those people who anticipate remaining for up to three years. They represent 47% of the total. The second group includes those people who anticipate remaining for four or more years, accounting for 46% of the total. What causes an individual to be in one group or the other? We can gain insight into this by looking at the relationship between anticipated tenure with the organization and leadership's ability to create a sense of inspiring purpose. This is shown in Figure 4-1.

The three charts on the left show, in three dimensions, the relationship between anticipated tenure and inspiring purpose. The top chart is for the overall sample, the middle chart is for healthcare and the bottom chart is for manufacturing. In each chart the vertical axis shows the number of responses, the bands on the chart show these responses in bands of five for the overall group of respondents and bands of one for healthcare and manufacturing. The axis from left to right in the foreground shows the degree to which people agree with the statement that their organization's purpose is inspiring to them on a scale from 1 (strongly disagree) to 7 (strongly agree). The axis receding into the background shows anticipated tenure. The three charts on the right show this same information in the form of contour plots, for the overall group at the top, healthcare in the middle and manufacturing at the bottom. The topography from the three-dimensional plots on the left is converted into two dimensions in each of the charts on the right.

What do these unusual shapes indicate? Let us walk along the inspiring purpose axis from a low value for the overall sample shown in the top two charts. As the sense of inspiring purpose reaches about 4, we come to a plateau where the number of responses peaks. People indicate intent to stay less than three years up to this point. As we increase the sense of inspiring purpose to about 5.5 there is an abrupt change. There is a dip in response that then increases dramatically when the sense of inspiring purpose increases to 6 and 7. Respondents in this region indicate an intention to remain with the organization for a significantly longer period of time.

We can also consider this to be a proxy for a map of an individual's perspective, such that as the sense of inspiring purpose moves through this small range from 5 to 6, the anticipated tenure increases dramatically. We see a similar pattern in healthcare, the second set of two charts, although the sample is much smaller. In this case the high peak is narrower, it occurs at a higher point on the inspiring purpose scale, and the divide between the two regions is greater compared to the overall group. The pattern for the manufacturing population shown in the bottom two charts is also similar, only the responses are more broadly distributed, both peaks occur at lower values of inspiring purpose and the anticipated tenures are shorter. All of the patterns shown underline the critical importance of leaders' ability to create a sense of inspiring purpose as a key determinant of individuals' decisions to remain with the organization. A mathematical model is developed in Chapter 6 that describes the driving forces leading to this behavior.

The patterns shown in Figure 4-1 can also be considered signatures of the organization describing the relationship of individuals to it, and their likelihood of staying or leaving. As such this signature is a diagnostic tool to help identify interventions that address attrition concerns. Since the samples for healthcare and manufacturing are small we cannot draw definitive conclusions for these sectors. However, we can gain insights into the value of this approach as an analytical tool from the responses in these sectors. For example, there is a significant opportunity to increase tenure for the HR population in manufacturing by broadly

Figure 4-1
Inspiring Purpose and Tenure

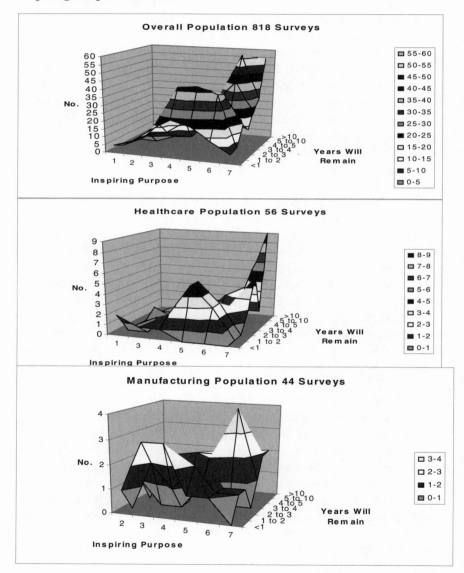

Figure 4-1 Continued

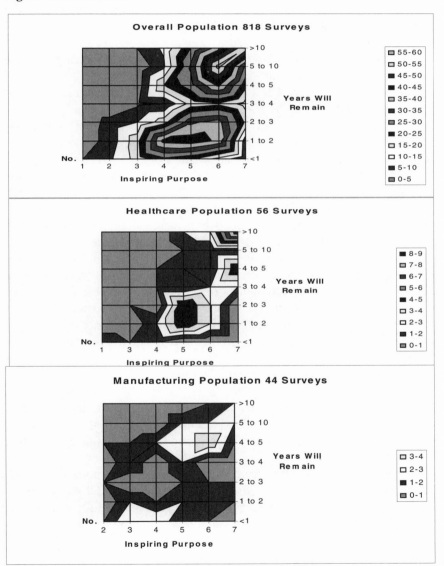

addressing the sense of inspiring purpose. This population exhibits lower scores for both inspiring purpose and tenure compared to the overall group and the responses are broadly distributed. The projected future tenure for this population is significantly lower than the historical average of 9 years for the same group, indicating future attrition problems if no action is taken. For the HR population in healthcare, the opportunity to secure long-term commitment is high given the peak at a high level of inspiring purpose and extended tenure.

Looking at the relationship between affiliation and inspiring purpose provides additional insights. This is shown in Figure 4-2.

The layout of the charts is similar to Figure 4-1. The changes are that the axis receding from the foreground for the three charts on the left now represents affiliation rather than anticipated tenure, and the bands for the overall population (the top two charts) are in groups of ten rather than five. The affiliation axis now shows the extent to which people agree with the statement that they feel a strong sense of affiliation with the organization on a scale from 1 (strongly disagree) to 7 (strongly agree). The sense of affiliation for the overall population increases steadily with an increase in inspiring purpose up to a value of 6 on each scale as shown by the top left chart. The middle and lower charts for healthcare and manufacturing respectively each have two peaks, similar to the results with anticipated tenure. In each case high levels of affiliation are associated with high levels of inspiring purpose. The responses for all populations lie on a diagonal band stretching from the lower left corner to the upper right corner of each chart. This means there are no examples of a low degree of inspiring purpose being associated with a high degree of affiliation (the top left corner of each of the two-dimensional contour charts), nor are there any examples of a high degree of inspiring purpose being associated with a low degree of affiliation (the lower right corner of each of the two-dimensional contour charts). These findings again underline the importance of leaders' ability to create a sense of inspiring purpose as a key determinant of the strength of affiliation people feel with the organization.

Let us recap the findings from these workforce perspective surveys. Based on a broad sampling of the for-profit, nonprofit and public sector areas in a wide range of geographies in North America for a predominantly HR population, we can conclude the following:

• Driven by attrition rates averaging 20%, translating to an average annual cost per organization of $146 million, and an annual community cost of more than $125 billion just for the organizations sampled, employee retention is a critical business issue. The survey participants confirm this, 82% of them rating employee retention as 6 or 7 on an importance scale of 7.

- The high level of attrition is reinforced by respondents' own proclivity to move. Respondents, on average, were employed full time with four organizations since high school or since obtaining a first degree for an average historical tenure of 6.3 years.

- Respondents understand clearly their organization's purpose and their own career aspirations.

- Analysis of the link between leadership's ability to create a sense of inspiring purpose and anticipated tenure of individuals, and the link of inspiring purpose to the degree of affiliation individuals feel, provides a signature of the workforce relationship for an organization and points to the potential for interventions.

- The analysis connecting inspiring purpose to affiliation demonstrates a strong linkage between these two elements. It underlines the necessity for leaders to focus on building and maintaining this sense of inspiring purpose. This is reinforced by strong linkage also, between the length of time people intend to stay with their organization and their sense of inspiring purpose. In this case respondents can be assigned to one of two groups with either short or long anticipated tenure. Leadership's ability to create an inspiring purpose is a key determinant of which group people occupy.

- Significant differences in the workforce relationship profiles of different industry sectors, in this case healthcare and manufacturing, underline the importance of building industry-specific information. By extension it will also be important to build organization-specific information. This is addressed in the next section.

PERSPECTIVES FROM WITHIN ORGANIZATIONS

The previous section examined the perspectives of individuals across a wide range of organizations. We took the pulse of the individual in relation to his or her worklife and from this could draw conclusions about issues to address at an organizational level. This section addresses organizational perspectives in more depth. The approach is to probe vertically within organizations for the characteristics and views of the workforce. By combining results from several organizations we can identify trends, draw conclusions of general relevance, and provide benchmark information. This analysis is based on studies conducted in 2000 and 2001 in five different U.S. organizations. The organizations span a range of industry sectors that include different elements of high technology, healthcare, financial services and manufacturing. Organization sizes ranged from just over 10,000 people to almost 200,000 people,

Figure 4-2
Inspiring Purpose and Affiliation

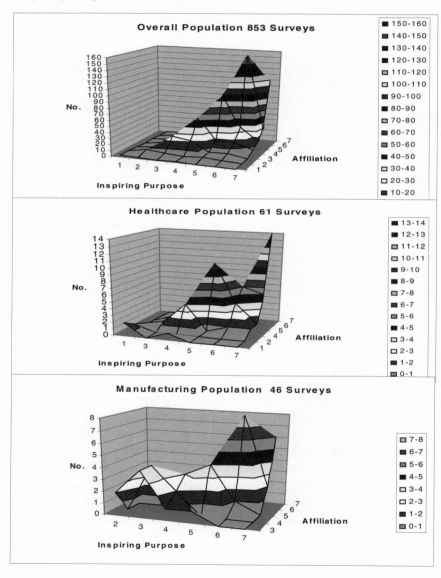

Figure 4-2 Continued

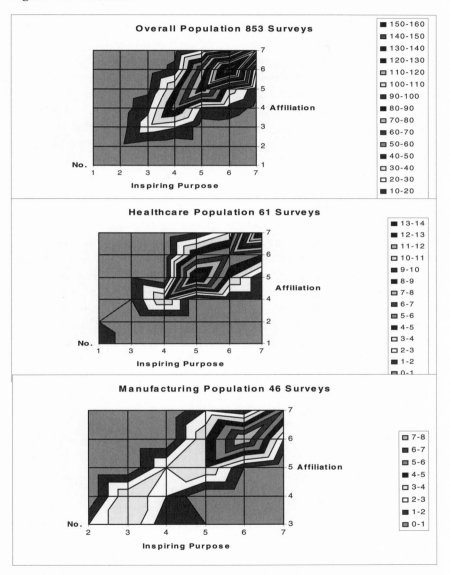

with data generated in specific business or geographic units within each organization.

The studies consisted of two diagnostic components. The first was an attrition demographic study that focused on providing quantitative understanding of workforce attrition for organizational units ranging in size from 1,300 to 12,000 people. This is the "what" of attrition. The second component consisted of interviews, primarily with people who left the organization and some who transferred internally. This is the "why" of attrition. The two components together incorporate the analytical and emotional/affective aspects and the thematic and anecdotal content described earlier. Prior to the interview each person received a letter or e-mail explaining the rationale for the interview, namely that the organization's leadership was seeking to understand how the internal environment could be improved. This communication also explained that individual responses would be held in confidence with only aggregated data being reviewed with the organizations. It was also stated that participation in the interview process was voluntary.

Consultants who were experienced in discussing sensitive information conducted the interviews. Prior to conducting these telephone interviews, which typically took twenty to forty minutes to complete, the consultants were able to review background information about each person. The consultants utilized an assessment instrument that was developed with the organization prior to the start of the study. The consultants were free to probe in depth into the assessment questions. Many of the questions were the same across the various organizations; some were tailored to individual organizational needs. Sample sizes for the interviews ranged from 53 to 498.

Let us first look at some of the findings from the demographic analysis focusing on the following four components:

- Years of service
- Age
- Ethnicity
- Gender

Knowing the variation of attrition with years of service has important implications for the effectiveness of selection, integration and development processes. It is also a key element in projecting attrition in the future. For the organizations studied we found higher attrition rates for people with up to four years of service. The attrition rate averaged 14% for those people with up to one year of service, 28% for those with one to two years, 18% for those with two to four years, then less than 10% for those with four to thirty years of service, rising again to 25% for those with more than thirty years of service as retirement became a major factor. For those with tenure between fifteen and twenty-five years the average attrition rates were in the 3–4% range.

These findings raise important questions. How effective are selection processes given the high early losses? Are integration processes adequate given the significant increase in losses in the second year? The effectiveness of development processes is also a question given the higher losses in years two through four. Regarding the population with fifteen to twenty-five years of service, having very low attrition rates, we might ask whether some degree of stagnation has set in. Regarding those with short tenure, some might take the view that there is nothing to be done about the higher attrition rates, as it is a fact of organizational life. The information generated in these studies refutes that argument as the range of attrition rates for those with 1–2 years of service varied from 7% for one organization to 78% for another. It is possible for leaders and HR to have a major impact on attrition in the early years.

Now turning to attrition by age, we see a similar profile with attrition rates for those under 25 at 24% on average, rising to 25% for those 25 to 30, and then falling to 13–16% for those 30–40, and 7–8% for those 40–55, then rising again up to 20% for those over 60 as retirement becomes a major factor. The high attrition rates for those under 30 raise particular concerns about the ability of organizations to create a sense of community for this population. Again, organizations vary greatly in their effectiveness in building affiliation with this population, as attrition rates vary from 7% to 34% for those 25–30 years old.

Now we will look at the variation of attrition by ethnicity. The highest average attrition rates were observed for the Asian and Pacific Islander population at an average of 15%, slightly greater than the Hispanic population at 14%, and the Caucasian population at 13%. Attrition rates for the African American population were 11% and they were 8% for a small sample of American Indian/Alaskan Natives. Perhaps most significant in the variation of attrition by ethnicity is the wide variation by organization: for example, the range from minimum to maximum for the Asian/Pacific Islander population was 7–30%, while for the Caucasian population it was 8–21%. Again it is possible for leaders and HR to have a major impact on the variation in attrition rates by ethnicity, as some organizations experience a much lower attrition problem with minority populations than others due to their more effective leadership and human resource practices.

When we look at the variation of attrition rates with gender an interesting trend appears to emerge, although more data will be needed for a definitive conclusion to be reached. Considering six cases (a given organization for a given year), where women were in the minority (9% to 46% of the population), in five of these cases the attrition rates for women were significantly higher than for men, and only in one case were they equal. Overall for the six cases the average attrition rates for women were 14%; for men they were 11%. Similarly for three cases where men were in the minority (7–33% of the overall population), in two of these cases the attrition rates for men were significantly higher than those for women, and in the third they were lower. The average attrition rates for these three cases for men were 10%; for women they were 8%. It appears that attrition rates for the minority gender in an organization are higher than for the majority gender, regardless of whether women or men are in the minority. This points to the importance of the organization's leaders, managers and HR staff paying particular attention to the needs of the minority gender to avoid experiencing higher losses.

Now let us look at the results from the interviews. We will look at the following characteristics:

• Motivation for leaving
• Level of active search
• Search time for those looking
• Reasons for leaving
• Attractors to the new organization
• Influencers of retention

Sometimes there is a myth in an organization that all is well internally and people are leaving just because of a plethora of good alternatives. While the availability of alternatives does have an impact on the decision to leave, it turns out that the major factor causing people to look elsewhere is dissatisfaction with their current position. For the sample studied, 71% of people left because of dissatisfaction, only 13% because of a new opportunity and 16% for a variety of other reasons, such as a spouse moving. The results were similar for men and women. Losses due to dissatisfaction are an avoidable cost since they are driven by internal factors that are controllable. This is also true for some of the other items such as leaving to reduce commute time, which may be addressed by providing telecommuting options. The range of responses is quite narrow, with the minimum % for dissatisfaction being 63% and the maximum 88%.

Of those leaving, an average of 42% were actively seeking a new position, 17% were recruited away and 41% were not actively looking but a serendipitous event linked them to a new opportunity, for example contact with a friend. There is considerable variation here; for example, for one organization, 40% of those leaving were recruited away, and for another it was only 3%. In the former case it would be appropriate to develop tactics to address the recruiter problem, such as limiting access into the organization. Ultimately though it is the organization's ability to create a positive work environment that will cause individuals to reject the recruiter's overtures. For those actively looking, productivity will suffer during the search process, much of which occurs during working hours.

Typically the search time is short, with 53% of people on average finding a new position in two months or less and more than 70% in three months or less, with some evidence that women were able to find a new position more quickly. If an employee expresses a concern it is not appropriate to defer discussion until the next performance or development review, which may be several months in the future. By that time the person will likely be gone. Certainly the search time will be influenced by the economy and the availability of other positions; however, in the work world driven by employee scarcity we are entering, it is likely that search times will remain short.

Now let us look at the reasons people leave. There are two components to this, first what prompted them to look elsewhere and second what was the "final straw" that prompted their acceptance of another position. These decision points are different. The first is the most critical decision since it is the beginning of the departure process for an individual. The top five reasons causing people to make a decision to leave (to look elsewhere) in order of priority are:

1. Lack of career development opportunities
2. Lack of recognition/appreciation
3. Negative work environment
4. Financial reasons
5. Lack of promotional opportunities

This can be contrasted with the top five "final straw" factors that caused people to accept another position as follows:

1. Financial reasons
2. Lack of career development opportunities
3. Negative work environment
4. Poor communication
5. Lack of promotional opportunities

Financial reasons are fourth in priority in terms of why people look elsewhere, but first in terms of the factors that cause a person to accept another position. This is why financial factors sometimes obscure the major causes of attrition, which lie elsewhere. Financial factors may be perceived as the main reason for attrition, when in fact other factors are much more critical in influencing a person to begin looking outside. There is a broad spread in the importance of the financial factor, with some organizations staying close to competitive compensation levels and others delinquent in this area. The impact of financial factors on the decision to look elsewhere is higher for those 34 years of age and younger (second or third in importance), compared with their older colleagues (seventh or eighth in importance). Career development heads the list of critical factors in terms of why people look elsewhere. It is often relegated to a "nice-to-have" rather than a "need-to-have" issue in the organization. These findings indicate it will be a "need to have" in the future. In the world we are entering it will be essential for organizations to provide an effective career development framework or people will leave.

Recognition and the nature of the work environment are also critical issues and are often viewed as "touchy-feely" and of secondary importance. They are not. A negative work environment can include many factors, such as lack of provision of resources or lack of consideration when personal emergencies arise. These items are central to building a sense of affiliation for individuals. Financial reasons are important to the extent that the organization must be competitive with compensation and stay abreast of changes in the labor market. Lack of promotional opportunities is an important factor. Here organizations need to set appropriate expectations on entry, and educate people about growth being primarily associated with personal skill development. This is intimately connected with career development. Providing a process that enables people to understand, in depth, who they are and where they will be most fulfilled is critical.

Another observation from the results is that there is a broad spread in the importance of the issues in moving from one organization to another. Some organizations have demonstrated an ability to address certain employee concerns so that they do not surface as prominent issues. The issues that were identified are attributable to the practices of immediate management and, in turn, to top leadership. This is consistent with the observation that dissatisfaction drives most people to look elsewhere. The top five reasons by gender that people decided to leave, for a smaller sample than the overall group, were as follows:

Women	Men
1. Negative work environment	Lack of career development opps.
2. Poor communication	Lack of meaningful work/adding value
3. Manager did not accept input	Lack of promotional opportunities
4. Lack of career development opportunities	Financial reasons
5. Lack of recognition/appreciation	Negative work environment

For women the priorities more reflect internal feelings about their work environment and relationships with others, whereas for men they more reflect external accomplishment. Again this underlines the importance of understanding the different perspectives that each person brings.

The top five attractors to the new organization were as follows:

1. Greater career development opportunities
2. Financial reasons
3. More meaningful work/adding value
4. Increased promotional opportunities
5. Greater challenge

Career development surfaces as a key issue again, identified by one in three people as critical. Financial reasons are important in the final decision to move. The last three items relate to the ability to make a difference and reflect a perception that the new organization carries a more inspiring purpose to which the person can contribute. Here again we see the importance of creating a sense of inspiring purpose, both to reduce attrition and to attract new people to the organization. The gender breakdown for attractors to the new organization, for a smaller sample than the overall group, is as follows:

Women	Men
1. Financial reasons	Greater career development opportunities
2. Greater career development opportunities	Financial reasons
3. More meaningful work/adding value	Improved promotional opportunities
4. Better teamwork	Greater challenge
5. Better family/work management	More meaningful work/adding value

These are similar reasons to those shown earlier. However, we now see the importance of family/work management and teamwork for women. Again this highlights the importance of understanding issues at an individual level.

The final area explored was a series of items that influence retention, including relationships with others, clarity of expectations, resource availability, valuing of individual ideas, recognition, development and the opportunity for a person to do his or her best work. We found significant concerns in all areas except in the area of relationships, where people were positive about the presence of a person viewed as supportive and caring (often not their manager). The item that scored lowest was the opportunity for people to do their best work. This is consistent with lack of career development opportunities and the mismatch between people and their work. This is an area of opportunity for leaders and HR.

These in-depth studies of listening to organizations show how the intricacies of attrition vary within and across organizations, and how attrition needs to be understood from a number of demographic dimensions so that interventions can be targeted to the appropriate areas and resources can be used most effectively. The studies also highlight the critical individual issues that cause people to stay at or leave an organization. These issues are about a person's ability to grow and develop, and to connect their work with a deeper purpose. The issues vary for each person and need to be understood at the individual level. Generic fixes for attrition will not work. Listening to the organization provides the basis for developing interventions that strengthen the sense of affiliation.

What does this mean for leaders and HR? We see that the motivation for movement from one organization to another is driven by factors that transcend the purely financial. These factors address the deep-seated need for each of us to find a place where we can express who we are, and in so doing make a meaningful contribution. Leaders and HR have the responsibility to create an environment where this can occur and as a result generate organizational value. This is not a minor undertaking. It is an undertaking of the heart as well as the head that will mean much for individuals, for organizations and for the community. The synthesis of organizational demographics is largely an exercise of the head drawing on analytical tools and processes. Understanding individual needs is largely an exercise of the heart. It is through understanding and respecting individual perspectives, listening to and projecting organizational needs, and creating and communicating an inspiring organizational purpose leading to individual fulfillment and organizational value that leaders build a strong sense of affiliation and a foundation for future prosperity.

— PART II —

CREATING MODELS OF THE FUTURE WORKFORCE

We are not developing . . . wealth for its own sake. Wealth is the means—and people are the ends. All our material riches will avail us little if we do not use them to expand the opportunities of our people.

> John F. Kennedy. State of the Union Address.
> The Capitol, Washington, DC, January 11, 1962

And we shall, I am confident, if we maintain the pace, in due season reap the kind of world we deserve and deserve the kind of world we will have.

> John F. Kennedy. Remarks upon receiving
> Annual Family of Man Award, New York,
> Protestant Council. New York City,
> November 8, 1963

— 5 —

Creating Models of the Future Workforce: Rationale and Linkages

There is a story about one of the colleges at a long-established university in England (DePree 1992, 227–228). A committee had been formed to discuss the renovation of one of the beautiful halls in the university. The roof of the hall was deteriorating. As the committee debated its task it became concerned about its ability to find wooden beams long enough to replace those that were in need of repair. The architect hired for the renovation project and the committee representatives understood that their predecessors had made provision for this situation. They visited a nearby wood, finding the grove of oak trees planted a century earlier from which the replacement beams could be hewn. Would that we had the foresight to support future generations in such a way. Hamel (2000, 183) quotes the French novelist Antoine de Saint-Exupéry as saying, "We do not inherit the land from our forefathers, we borrow it from our children." This is true also of our responsibilities in organizations.

PURPOSE OF MODELING

The focus now is to begin exploring approaches that help us look forward and anticipate the impact of today's decisions and situations on future outcomes, that help model the future. This is a challenge, since the social sciences lack the precision and descriptive and predictive capability of many elements of the pure and applied sciences. But the potential impact and importance are immense. Here is how Beveridge expressed it (Beveridge 1957, 212–13): "Civilization started only some 10,000 years ago. The mind staggers at what will be accomplished in the future. . . . But more urgent than finding out how to control (our physical world) . . . is the need for our social development to catch up with our achievements in the physical sciences." So we step into this arena on modeling knowing that these are baby steps, only beginning to point to some possible paths forward, but knowing this to be an important journey. Beveridge (1957, 205) reports Isaac Newton having said near the end of his life: "I know not what I may appear to the world, but to myself I appear to have been only like a boy playing on the seashore, and diverting myself in now and then finding a smoother pebble or a prettier shell than ordinary, while the great ocean of truth lay undiscovered before me." It is with this thought in mind that we begin the exploration of modeling workforce dynamics.

These are proposed characteristics of an ideal framework that could be used to describe the relationship of individuals to organizations, and guide related decisions. Such a framework would have the following attributes:

• Describes causal relationships between individual fulfillment and organizational value creation
• Predicts the impact of organizational changes on decisions individuals make about staying or leaving
• Predicts the value created by the organization under various workforce scenarios
• Provides a basis for optimizing the use of human resources.

Some existing approaches focus primarily on the individual (Brewer 1996; Jung 1976; Levinson 1978) or on financial tools that address organizational projections. There is a need for additional conceptual development that blends individual and organizational perspectives including quantitative application. At one level there is a need to project workforce demographics. For example, what will the attrition rate and hiring needs be for the organization in the coming years? At another level there is a need to incorporate the complexities linking individual choice to workforce dynamics. For example, incorporating the relationship between leaders' ability to create an inspiring purpose and a sense of fulfillment in an organization and the likelihood that people will stay. This requires a modeling framework that describes observed behavior and can predict the future impact of individual choices made today. Additional complexity is also introduced when the framework is expanded to address outcomes at the community rather than the organizational level. For example, addressing a question such as: What is the likely unemployment rate next year if the economy only grows at 1%? This requires a model linking unemployment rates to economic performance.

DEFINITION AND TYPES OF MODEL

These are examples of the types of issues that can be addressed by a model. What does the word model mean, for it is used in many contexts? For example, the word model can mean a qualitative conceptual description. The description of the evolution of a person's life developed by Levinson (Levinson 1978) is a good example. Some of the constructs earlier in the book would fit this definition. However, the intended meaning for the word model here is more focused. In the current context the word model means a mathematical description of a conceptual framework that can be validated by observation. This means being able to quantitatively describe a situation and make predictions from it.

Within this definition there are many subsets. Models can be divided into three primary categories based on intended outcomes: descriptive, predictive and prescriptive.

- Descriptive models characterize observed behavior.
- Predictive models estimate the result of a new course of action.
- Prescriptive models suggest a preferred course of action.

There are two principal model constructs that are used: statistical and deterministic. Statistical approaches describe observed relationships without attempting to explain underlying mechanisms. They are most effective in the descriptive area and they become progressively less effective in moving to predictive and prescriptive approaches. Deterministic models, on the other hand, address underlying mechanisms and are designed to address predictive and prescriptive outcomes. Econometric models are an example of the statistical category. They are based on statistical correlations of economic factors, for example the impact of the number of housing starts on demand for a given plastic. This does not explain the underlying cause-and-effect mechanisms; instead it describes historically what happened to product demand as the number of houses built changed. Whether product demand changes due to change in demand for window frames, flooring or other items is not captured. A statistical correlation, such as this, is the most basic approach and it provides primarily a descriptive capability.

Predictive models provide the ability to estimate outcomes that either fall outside the original data (extrapolate) or are within the data elements (interpolate). For example, what would happen to demand for plastics if the number of housing starts increased 20% above the previous high, or conversely fell to a level between that of the last two years? Deterministic models are the most powerful for predictive purposes. They are based on mathematical approaches that describe underlying mechanisms in accounting for observations. In doing this they address cause-and-effect relationships from which predictions of the impact of future changes are created. An example would be the projection of changes in the future population based on an understanding of birth rates, death rates and immigration rates. In some cases the statistical correlation approach is combined with a deterministic framework to create a hybrid model.

The predictive approach can lead to the next level, the ability of a model to offer insights into preferred paths forward—to be prescriptive. Such a capability is a natural attribute of a deterministic model. It can be further refined by the incorporation of mathematical techniques such as optimization that estimate inputs needed to give the most desirable outcome. For example, the level of HR spending needed to minimize costs associated with employee attrition.

APPLICATION OF MODELS

Which approach to use in a given situation depends upon the purpose of the activity and approaches that may be available. Here are some general attributes needed of models addressing workforce dynamics in the evolving work world. These attributes are as follows:

• Recognize the central importance of individual decision making regarding work choices
• Can readily address different external scenarios
• Accommodate different organizational structures and approaches
• Based on intuitively sound reasoning
• Can be validated by observation
• Provide insights that strengthen decision making
• Address significant organizational issues.

Traditional approaches to workforce planning involved constructing large, matrix models that explored supply and demand balances for people in an organization (Ward, Bechet and Tripp 1994). Initially developed in the mainframe computer world of the 1960s and 70s, these models excel at describing the flows of people through an organization, built on the premise that such movement is organizationally mandated. They are consistent with a hierarchical model of an organization operating in a relatively stable environment. The use of such models has declined because they are less effective in a turbulent outside world. Furthermore, they neglect a key aspect of today's work world—the growing ability of people to make their own work-life choices. No longer can the organization unilaterally decide about individuals' work direction based solely on organizational need. Today individual aspirations are a critical component and models need to reflect this aspect.

The need for flexibility is another major shift relative to highly structured modeling approaches in the past. Today organizational structures change frequently as dictated by external business needs, and modeling approaches need to support this. We are looking for the SWAT team model to fight the battle of workforce dynamics, not massed Roman battalions. We are also seeking models that by their structure can provide insights about directions and approaches to explore. This is more important than numerical precision.

Having defined modeling, identified different types of models and proposed criteria to characterize their effectiveness, we can explore in more depth the rationale for developing models. The three broad goals for the modeling process identified earlier are:

- Provide insights into system behaviors (descriptive)
  - For example: What is the historical relationship between economic growth and unemployment rates?
- Predict the impact of solutions and resources committed (predictive)
  - For example: What is the impact of adding further human resource staff on attrition in the organization?
- Suggest approaches to achieve given objectives (prescriptive)
  - For example: What is the optimal level of human resource expenditures in the organization?

Prescriptive approaches will necessarily include predictive and descriptive components. Let us construct an ideal situation, if there were no limitations on our modeling capability. The fictitious company is Morgan Ceramics and the year is 2025. The company's headquarters are in a traditional U.S. midwestern city, with a strong manufacturing base. The company has been around for sixty years, beginning life making ceramic rings for heavy industrial applications. In the last fifteen years the business has grown dramatically as the company leveraged an acquisition to build a business in manufacturing ceramic components that are incorporated into integrated circuits. The rapid growth in this segment greatly increased technical demands for the company's product offerings. Karen Morgan, the current CEO and the founder's daughter, is wrestling with some difficult questions about the company's workforce. The attrition rate has doubled in the last two years to 20%, and worse yet, the attrition rate for highly skilled ceramicists is almost 30%, and for employees under 30 it is 30%. In fact there is a revolving door in key technical areas and for younger employees. The organization's ability to grow is at stake, as it seems to be turning into a training ground for the competition. This, at the same time as the organization is breaking ground on a new facility in the Pacific Northwest. Karen is wondering what the future holds and what steps she could take to better understand the situation and a possible path forward. She approaches her vice president of HR, Dave Livingston, with this dilemma and asks for his recommendations on a path forward. Dave has been closely involved with the unfolding developments in modeling workforce dynamics. His approach is as follows:

- Characterize the environment regarding availability of people.
  - Use modeling to estimate unemployment rates for the next five years, and the availability of people in the current location and the new facility location.
- Confirm the organization's analysis of its workforce segmentation and update as needed using the latest perspectives on business direction.
- Analyze internal attrition demographics to describe what is happening and conduct extensive interviews to understand people's issues and concerns.
- Develop a specific set of possible solutions addressing each workforce segment and then define the resources required to implement these solutions.
- Using the latest modeling approaches, predict the impact of the proposed solutions on employee perspectives and workforce dynamics.
- Predict the financial impact of resources committed.
- Using optimization techniques combine the internal modeling results with modeling of the external environment to prescribe the optimum mix of resources to drive needed solutions.

- Implement solutions at the defined resource levels.
- Install an ongoing monitoring system.

With the analytical tools at his disposal Dave is able to complete this in two days and demonstrate a $10 million annual benefit for an expenditure of $200,000. Pie in the sky? Not at all. While much development is still needed for the modeling described here, the foundation is forming. Let us look at some of the components.

First the statistical or econometric approach. The basis of this approach is to define a mathematical relationship between a key dependent variable (for example unemployment rate) and one or more independent variables (for example gross domestic product). Tools of statistical analysis are used to create a descriptive equation that minimizes the difference between the observations and the equation. Techniques such as least squares regression are well proven in doing this. The equation can take many forms with the simplest being a linear (straight line) relationship between the variables. The most sophisticated econometric models contain many independent variables such as in studies of job embeddedness (Mitchell et al. 2001). Successful application of this approach depends on access to a consistent set of data, sufficient to support the estimation processes. The resulting equations provide a basis for prediction based on interpolation. They are not appropriate for extrapolation. One of the dangers of this technique is an implied causality where none exists. Box, Hunter and Hunter (1978) show an example where there is a strong correlation between the population in the town of Oldenburg and the number of storks observed. While few would suggest that the increase in the stork population caused the increase in the human population, we can sometimes fall into such traps with regression models. In spite of such potential pitfalls statistical regression techniques can be an effective means of characterizing observations.

Deterministic modeling, as described earlier, is potentially a more powerful tool. It has so far seen limited application in the human resource area. A simple example of this from the physical sciences is an equation linking distance traveled to speed and time. This equation is not dependent on a single set of observations, but has general applicability to any situation involving motion. It provides a basis for interpolation and extrapolation, and it is not limited to any particular object. Such an equation is powerful in its predictive capability. If this were now coupled with an equation describing fuel required to generate movement, and one describing the cost of time spent traveling, then it would be possible to find an optimum average speed that minimizes the costs involved. Fur-

Figure 5-1
Model Linkages

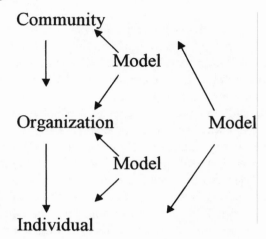

thermore, mathematical systems are available to identify this optimum using computer tools, which through a series of well-chosen guesses, converge on the optimum. If the models used in this optimization process are deterministic then the results can be extrapolated outside the domain of the initial data. If the models include statistical regression elements as part of a hybrid, then interpolation is possible. Models with these characteristics can be developed to address workforce dynamics.

Given that deterministic models are potentially so powerful, it is perhaps surprising that they are not used more broadly in the human resource field. What is the barrier? It is largely the difficulty of creating such models. They require a conceptual and analytical capability that often exceeds our current state of knowledge. This is Newton's great ocean. We are still in our infancy in terms of how to construct such systems. However, there is much potential to bring the approaches from other fields to this area.

Let us examine a structure that provides examples of opportunities to develop modeling capabilities in the field of workforce dynamics (Figure 5-1).

The three primary levels of application, or nodes, are the community, the organization and the individual. Models can be developed that address the linkages among these nodes. An example of the linkage between the community and the organization is the relationship between the number of organizations and their size. Models linking the individual to the organization address issues such as the linkage between employee fulfillment and organizational value creation, the optimum attrition rate and the impact of HR expenditures on value. At the organizational level models address issues such as workforce and attrition demographics, predictions of attrition and hiring needs, and costs of attrition. Ultimately a construct may be possible that incorporates all of these elements into a single structure. Models at the various application levels can include examples of each of the primary outcome categories we identified: descriptive, predictive and prescriptive. The focus of the next chapter is on beginning a process to create such models.

— 6 —

The Imprint of the Organization in the Past, Present and Future: Modeling Frameworks

As an organization grows it leaves an evolving imprint in its surrounding communities. Employees, who are both givers to and receivers from the organization, feel this imprint most strongly. Mathematical modeling can provide a link between decisions made by individuals about their direction, and by leaders and HR about the organization's workforce. Both relate to the imprint of the organization in the community. Exploring modeling techniques is the subject of this chapter. Some sections require an understanding of basic calculus. So that the content is accessible to all readers regardless of mathematical background conclusions from all sections are summarized at the end of the chapter. The meaning of symbols used in the equations is defined in the text and again in the Nomenclature section of the book.

"That is concerning, we have high attrition rates for people who have only been with the organization two to three years. I see also that about half of our employees have been with us less than two years. What will happen to our employee losses in the next two to three years? We are facing a major crisis." These were the comments of one HR leader recently as we reviewed the attrition profile for his organization. Here is another HR leader: "We looked at the ages of our employees. There are quite a few people who have been with us less than three years, and a large number who could retire in the next five years. What if they do retire, what will our workforce look like and how will we conduct our business? We may soon have a major problem, what can we do to understand the issues more clearly?"

These are examples of questions that are central to organizational direction, that require estimates of likely changes in the future workforce, and that can be addressed by modeling. In the first case a model is needed that builds on historical attrition and workforce demographics to create projections of future alternatives. In the second case a model is needed, based on workforce demographics, that identifies the impact of alternative choices made about retirement. In both cases the models provide frameworks for quantifying future changes in the workforce, building on information about workforce and attrition demographics. Beyond these examples we need to know what drives individual decisions to stay or leave and how to characterize the link between individual aspirations and organizational value creation.

Before beginning this exploration it is helpful to return to the three ethical questions posed in Chapter 1 (Rhodes 1999). They are:

- How do we as a community honor work that sustains and supports our lives?
- How do we support each person in expressing the unique gifts they have to offer?
- How do we integrate meeting our individual aspirations with seeking the common good?

In the struggle for organizational survival and prosperity it is easy to lose sight of these questions. It is easy to view people as a disposable commodity, whose sole purpose is to add to the bottom line of the profit and loss statement. It is easy and wrong. The goal of this chapter is to explore approaches to workforce modeling that help organizations become more effective in accomplishing their mission as well as become more fulfilling places to work. This means helping organizations craft an imprint that has personal meaning for employees, that creates value for the organization, and that strengthens communities within which the organization operates. People choose to join and stay with such organizations that support the life spark rather than extinguish it. The models need to help us ask the right questions about strengthening connections between organizations and individuals. They need to provide insights into the answers. This is a challenge given the complex issues involved, so we will content ourselves with taking a first step in framing possible approaches. The general categories addressed are as follows:

- The community as a network of individuals and organizations
- The organization as a unit
- Links between the organization and the individual
- The individual

Where appropriate the exploration of each area begins with an introduction to descriptive modeling methods. It proceeds with an examination of predictive models, in some cases from a statistical perspective, in others from a deterministic perspective. Where possible it concludes by examining prescriptive implications. The models vary from a statistical link between two variables to an exploration of connections between individuals and organizations. These models are offered as initial ideas with the hope that they will help stimulate further thinking and development.

THE COMMUNITY AS A NETWORK OF INDIVIDUALS AND ORGANIZATIONS

One area that directly impacts prosperity of the community, and each person in it, is the level of unemployment. Higher unemployment means more individuals and families struggling to meet basic needs and reduced purchasing power in the economy. Gross Domestic Product (GDP) as a primary measure of the strength of the economy can be expressed independently of the effect of inflation as Real GDP. Establishing a relationship between Real GDP and unemployment rate provides a basis for estimating changes in unemployment rate with fluctuations in the economy. To normalize Real GDP with respect to the workforce, it is calculated as Real GDP per capita, where the population used is the workforce. Figure 6-1 shows the unemployment rate and Real GDP (1996$) per capita for the U.S. workforce from 1947 to 2000, a fifty-three-year time span (Bureau of Labor Statistics: ftp://ftp.bls.gov; Bureau of Economic Analysis: www.bea.doc.gov).

Real GDP per capita grew slowly in the 1970s and then more rapidly during the mid and late 1980s and particularly in the 1990s. The unemployment rate fluctuated over the time period with oscillations every four to ten years. In exploring the linkage between the two measures, the rates of change (or first derivatives) each year provide the point of connection as shown in Figure 6-2.

Sixty-three percent (the coefficient of determination $R^2 = 0.6269$) of

Figure 6-1
U.S. Unemployment Rate (%) and Real GDP per Capita (1996$) (Based on Workforce)

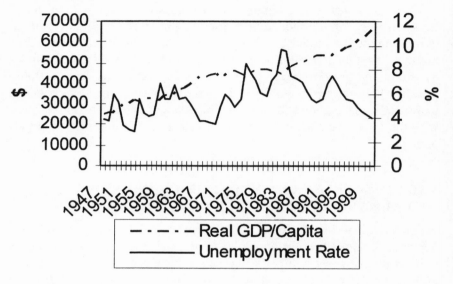

Figure 6-2
Rate of Change of U.S. Unemployment Rate and Real GDP per Capita (Based on Workforce)

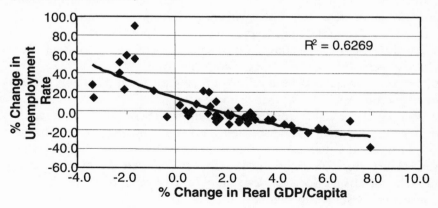

the variation of the change in unemployment rate is explained by the change in Real GDP per capita. The form of the equation is as follows:

$$\Delta UR = 0.4691 * \Delta GDPC^2 - 8.6888 * \Delta GDPC + 13.692$$

where ΔUR is the % change in unemployment rate and $\Delta GDPC$ is the % change in Real GDP per capita (where the per capita population is the workforce).

This equation implies that the unemployment rate will remain unchanged when the rate of increase in Real GDP per capita is 1.7% per year. For slower growth in the economy, the unemployment rate increases, for faster growth it decreases. This relationship provides insights into likely changes in future unemployment rates given projected changes in the economy. For example if growth in Real GDP per capita dropped to 0, then based on the equation shown, unemployment rates would be expected to increase by 13.7% of the base amount, for example from 5% to 5.7%.

This example illustrates the predictive capability of a statistical model. It works as long as the variables remain within the range of the data used to generate the correlation. The leveling of the curve at 8% Real GDP per capita growth is intuitively reasonable. It is also the upper limit of the data set and the upper limit of applicability of the equation. This model illustrates the linkage between the experience of individual unemployment and the strength of the national economy. It can be used to estimate the impact of changing economic conditions on the availability of people.

Most individuals link to their work through organizations. Are there naturally observed relationships describing the formation and size of organizations? A statistical descriptive model offers insights in this area. Figure 6-3 shows the relationship between the number of organizations in the United States on September 30, 2000 and the number of employees in these organizations. This is based on information in Dun & Bradstreet's Million Dollar Database for organizations ranging in size from 1,000 to 1,000,000 employees.

The linear relationship shown fits the data well, expressed in the form of natural logarithms. The equation shown accounts for 99.5% of the observed variation. While a slightly closer fit to the data can be obtained with a quadratic equation (it accounts for 99.9% of the variation), the linear model provides a good starting point. The linear equation provides a sound means of estimating how many organizations have at least a given number of employees. For example the estimate for the number

Figure 6-3
Size Distribution of U.S. Organizations (Logarithmic Plot of No. Organizations)

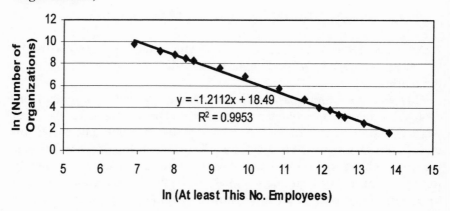

of organizations with at least 5,000 employees ($\ln(5000) = 8.5172$) is 3,547. This is within 7.2% of the actual 3820.

The equation describing the relationship shown in Figure 6-3 can be written as:

$$\ln(N) = -1.2112 * \ln(E) + 18.49$$

where N is the number of organizations with at least E employees. Why is the relationship of this form? Organizational structure provides an insight into this. Defining the span of control at any level as s (the number of people reporting to a given manager), then at the first level of management the organization has $(s + 1)$ employees. At the second level there are $(1 + s + s^2)$ employees, at the j level there are $(1 + s + s^2 + \ldots + s^j)$ employees. The sum of this geometric progression, which is the number of employees, E, in the organization, is as follows:

$$E = (s^j - 1)/(s - 1)$$

By taking natural logarithms of both sides, and simplifying, this becomes:

$$\ln E = \ln(s^j - 1) - \ln(s - 1)$$

for $s^j \gg 1$, which is true in most instances, this can be further simplified to:

$$\ln E = j \ln s - \ln(s - 1)$$ **Equation 6-1**

The relationship between the number of organizations, N, and the number of organizational levels can be expressed as follows:

$$N = d * \exp(-k_l * j)$$ **Equation 6-2**

where d and k_l are constants and j is the number of organizational levels. This equation describes the rapid decrease in the number of organizations as the number of levels increases.

By substituting for the number of levels j from Equation 6-1 into Equation 6-2 and simplifying, a relation between the number of organizations and the number of employees can be derived with the following result:

$$\ln N = \ln d - k_l * \ln E/\ln s - k_l * \ln(s - 1)/\ln s$$

The ratio of the number of organizations N_1 with employees E_1, and the number of organizations N_2 with employees E_2 then follows by subtracting this equation for case 2 from the equation for case 1 and simplifying. The result is as follows:

$$N_1/N_2 = (E_2/E_1)^{(k_l/\ln s)}$$ **Equation 6-3**

This equation describes the fundamental relationship between the number of organizations and the number of employees. It is based on deterministic modeling and can be used for predictive purposes. It can be tested with data linking the number of organizations to the number of employees. Equation 6-3 can be expressed in logarithmic terms as:

$$\ln(N_1/N_2) = (k_l/\ln s) * \ln(E_2/E_1)$$

A plot of $\ln(N_1/N_2)$ vs. $\ln(E_2/E_1)$ should be linear with slope $(k_l/\ln s)$. The actual data are shown in Figure 6-4 where the points again are based on the Dun and Bradstreet database for U.S. companies on September 30, 2000. The size ratio (E_2/E_1) is based on companies with at least this number of employees.

The data points do indeed follow a linear relationship with 99% of the variation explained by the least squares line shown. This line has a slope of 1.14, which indicates that Equation 6-3 can be written as:

Figure 6-4
Ratio Chart for the Number of Organizations of a Given Size
(Logarithmic Plot of No. Organizations Ratio and at Least No. Employees Ratio)

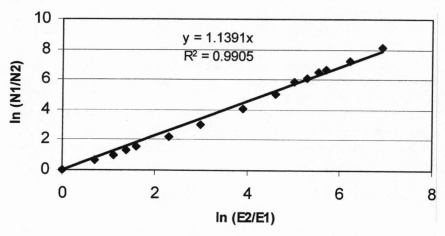

$$N_1/N_2 = (E_2/E_1)^{1.14}$$ **Equation 6-4**

This means that with each doubling of organization size there are only 45% of the number of organizations ($(1/2)^{1.14} = 0.45$). For example, in going from 10,000 to 20,000 employees the number of organizations is projected to drop from 1,927 (the actual number with at least 10,000 employees) to 867. The actual number of organizations with at least 20,000 employees is 880, close to the calculated number. For the size range of 1,000 to 100,000 employees the slope of the line in Figure 6-4 is 1.04, so that an approximate metric is that the number of organizations is cut in half each time the size doubles. In this case, to a first approximation, the number of organizations of any given size is inversely proportional to size. This can be expressed as

$$N_1/N_2 = E_2/E_1$$

Returning to Equation 6-4, since $k_1/\ln s = 1.14$, when s is equal to 4, k_1 is equal to 1.5804, and when s is equal to 3, k_1 is equal to 1.2524. When a value of k_1 in the range of 1.25 to 1.58 is substituted in Equation 6-2 it provides an intuitively reasonable profile for the variation of organization size with the number of levels. There is evidence that the span of control decreases with increasing size. By dividing the companies into two groups, those between 1,000 and 100,000 employees, and those between 100,000 and 1,000,000 employees, two separate least squares lines can be generated. The slopes of these lines are respectively 1.0369 and 1.2923. If a k_1 value of 1.5804 is used then the span of control for companies in the larger size range is 74% of the span of control for companies in the smaller size range.

If we make the assumption that the relationship of number to size reflects an optimum that is determined by the operation of an efficient market, then the equations are naturally occurring relationships linking frequency and size of organizations under efficient market conditions. It suggests that the equations describe an optimum configuration to seek either in a community or potentially, by extension, in a large organization with multiple business units.

THE ORGANIZATION AS A UNIT

Descriptive Approaches Using Demographic Analysis and Interviewing

Chapter 4 showed, by example, the value of probing in depth into attrition and affiliation issues across a number of organizations. Now let us consider a single organization and explore how to use demographic analysis and interviews to better understand the dynamics of the workforce. Demographic analysis means quantifying selected characteristics of the workforce and its segments. Understanding demographic characteristics and listening to the workforce provide a basis for:

• Identifying where critical issues, such as attrition, are most severe
• Building a framework that captures the needs of each workforce segment
• Designing interventions to achieve targeted objectives
• Predicting likely future changes in the size and nature of the workforce and the impact of proposed interventions.

Viewed from the perspective of the modeling taxonomy defined in Chapter 5, workforce demographic and attrition analyses begin with a descriptive component that includes some or all of the following variables:

• Gender
• Ethnicity

- Years of service
- Age
- Geographic location
- Function
- Position
- Grade level
- Performance rating

The analyses address both the overall workforce and those leaving or moving internally, ideally over the past two fiscal years. This provides a signature of the organization at one or more points in time. Inclusion of a variable such as performance rating provides an indication of the effectiveness of performance management systems. Even organizations with sophisticated performance management systems can show significant gaps in their implementation.

Attrition demographic analysis needs to address the movement and separation of people both in terms of absolute numbers and rates. For example, the number of people with less than two years of service who are leaving, and their rate of departure relative to this segment of the population. Moves can be both external and internal. Attrition demographic analysis generates a prioritized list of concerns in terms of both absolute and relative importance. For example, large numbers leaving from a key sales area or high rates of departure for those new to the organization. Knowing this focuses resources on the areas of greatest need in the organization. Attrition demographic analysis also provides the basis for deterministic modeling to predict future workforce trends.

Attrition demographic analysis does not address the reasons why people move or the nature of individual concerns. As reviewed in Chapter 4, there are various organizational listening approaches to gather this information. One important approach is that of interviewing. Exit interviews, interviews with people moving internally, and interviews with other selected, existing employees, conducted confidentially with a sound, consistent methodology, provide this information. They can elucidate underlying themes and root causes of concerns, and they can be focused on key employee populations with a major business impact. This information, coupled with the prioritized areas from the attrition demographic analysis, provides a strong framework for identifying specific, actionable, prescriptive steps to enhance affiliation. This approach avoids the knee-jerk response to anecdotes from one or two vocal individuals that may bear limited relation to overall themes of importance.

Here is a description of a combined attrition demographic analysis and interview study for a single organization. In the high-tech industry few organizations have survived and thrived as successfully as Applied Materials, Inc. Founded in 1967, Applied Materials—with $7.3 billion in annual sales in fiscal year 2001 and about 20,000 employees worldwide—is the world's largest supplier of equipment and services to the global semiconductor industry. In 2001 it was rated by *Fortune* magazine as one of the 100 best companies to work for in America (*Fortune* 2001: www.fortune.com). And in an industry notorious for defections to competing companies or new opportunities, Applied Materials' turnover rate has been among the lowest in the industry.

So why are the corporation's executives worried about attrition? "We're a knowledge organization, and when you lose top talent you lose your corporate memory," explains Debra Scates, Applied Materials' senior director of Talent Strategies. "We came to believe that no matter how low turnover may be, *any* turnover can have a significant impact on performance." That realization came to the fore after the 1998 economic downturn in the high-tech sector. At that time, retention issues were handled by the company's Employment Group, a highly decentralized department that was achieving mixed results. The company's vice president of HR at the time, Sam Ishi, decided it was time for a more strategic approach. The Employment Group was reorganized into a new team called "Workforce Management." Under the initial direction of Vice President Susan Kaminski, the mandate was to develop more effective assimilation and retention strategies. Debra, who had been head of the company's training and development and college recruiting, joined the team.

"The assimilation of employees during their first year with us and the retention of our more experienced workers were especially important, as we were heading into a tight labor market at two of our key locations: Austin, Texas and Santa Clara, California. In both places, unemployment rates were reaching extremely low levels—as low as 2%. With that kind of competition for talent, we knew we had to look for new ways to keep our 'best and brightest.' "

Debra says that one of the team's first tasks in holding on to talent was to figure out who was leaving the organization—and why. To do that, Susan Kaminski retained DBM to conduct exit interviews with employees who were voluntarily leaving the company. The exit interviews were conducted in two phases. The first round of interviews, which began in May 2000, focused on the people who had left Applied Materials during the previous six to nine months. After that, the company began feeding DBM the names of employees to interview every other week. Eventually, DBM interviewed these same employees six months after the initial interviews to elicit additional perspective on their decisions to leave. "We suspected that the reasons people gave our Human Resources department for leaving were not the *real* reasons," Debra reports. "Having an objective third-party . . . conduct the exit interviews confirmed our suspicions."

Debra says that while the information gained was "eye opening," she and her team were looking for even more information to shape any retention strategies they might develop. They wanted a profile of the type of person most at risk of resigning. "We had a general number that indicated how many people were leaving the organization," Debra says, "which, by any industry or competitive standard, was low. But we had never really studied the data behind the number. We wanted to 'slice and dice' the data to find out exactly who was leaving." Here again, Applied Materials looked to DBM for assistance. To create an attrition demographic profile for Applied Materials, DBM analyzed information on all employees who had voluntarily left the organization over the previous two years. They also studied what Debra calls "internal churn," employees who moved to different opportunities within the organization. "We wondered if people were moving within the organization for the same reasons they were leaving the organization," she says. "For example, were both groups frustrated by lack of opportunity in their current positions? Was it easier to find a new position internally or externally? We felt that by examining these issues as objectively as possible we'd be better able to create effective assimilation and retention strategies." Debra says that she and her team have gained valuable insights that will help them formulate effective retention strategies. "For example, turnover percentages in certain segments of the employee population are higher than we are comfortable with. Knowing this makes it possible for us to identify specific, actionable strategies for addressing the problem. We wouldn't be able to do this if we hadn't parsed the attrition data more finely." Debra reports that DBM also provided them with models that forecast the impact turnover will have on the organization in the future if key issues aren't addressed. "We can attach a dollar figure to the impact of retention now and in the future."

Projecting Future Workforce Needs

How do we leverage the attrition demographic information to make predictions about future workforce dynamics? Here is an example of a modeling approach to do that. The example is an organization of 15,000 people that has existed for fifteen years. Exploring the implications of different workforce and attrition profiles provides insights into the possible future evolution of this organization's workforce. The modeling simulation looks at three variables, tenure of the workforce, historical attrition by length of service and the desired future growth of the workforce. There are many possible combinations of these variables. The cases selected include combinations from the following pairs of alternatives:

- Even distribution by tenure or a greater number of more recent hires
- Constant attrition over time or higher attrition in the early years with the organization
- Constant workforce size in the future or 10% annual growth in the future workforce

The example simulation demonstrates the application of a modeling approach to project attrition and hiring needs five years into the future for each of the alternatives. It also demonstrates the estimation of financial impact. Five cases were examined to illustrate the modeling methodology. These five cases are as follows:

- Case 1: Each cohort group, identified by years of service, going back fifteen years contains 1,000 people. The annual attrition rate is 10% for each of these cohort groups. The workforce remains at 15,000 people for the next five years.
- Case 2: Each cohort group going back fifteen years contains 1,000 people. The annual attrition rate is higher for those with shorter tenure. It is 20% for those with up to one year of service, 30% for those with one to two years of service, 30% for those with two to three years of service, 20% for those with three to four years of service, 10% for those with four to five years of service and 5% for those with more than five years of service. With this profile the average attrition rate is 9.25%. The workforce remains at 15,000 people for the next five years.
- Case 3: In this case more people have shorter tenure. 3,000 people have up to one year, one to two years and two to three years of service, while 500 people have years of service from four to fifteen. The attrition rates for those with shorter tenure are higher as in Case 2. The workforce remains at 15,000 people for the next five years.
- Case 4: Each cohort group going back fifteen years contains 1,000 people. The annual attrition rate is 10% for each of these cohort groups. The workforce grows 10% each year for five years into the future.

Figure 6-5
Workforce Profiles for Case 5

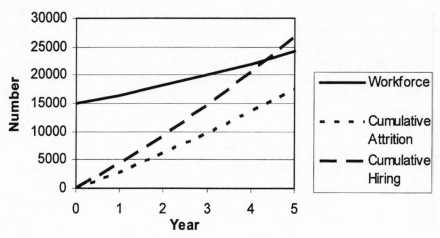

- Case 5. More people have shorter tenure, and there is higher attrition for those with shorter tenure as in Case 3. The workforce grows 10% each year for five years into the future.

The modeling software used for these calculations was Mathcad 2000. The modeling logic used an iterative approach to calculate attrition and then hiring needs each year to match predetermined population targets. Future attrition was calculated based on the historical attrition and workforce profiles by tenure. The model advanced the calculation one year at a time up to the fifth year using the prior year as a starting point each time. An example of the projected population, cumulative attrition and cumulative hiring is shown in Figure 6-5 for Case 5.

A total of 17,584 people are projected to leave over the five years in this case. Attrition averages 3,517 people each year. Hiring needs are 26,742 over this time period to support the 10% annual average population growth. The workforce increases from 15,000 people to 24,158 after five years. If a recruiter could find and hire two people each week, thirty-five full-time recruiters would be needed just to offset losses due to attrition. The relatively high total attrition is driven by a combination of high attrition rates in the early years and a population with relatively few years of service. Both of these conditions are common in today's workforce. The stress it places on the organization is evident from these numbers.

Examining the population after five years and the total attrition and

Figure 6-6
Workforce Projections

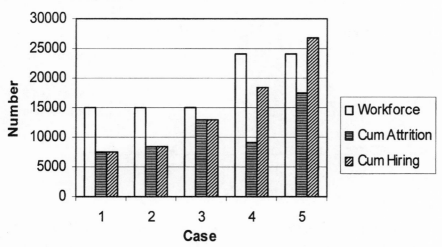

hiring over the five-year period provides a basis for comparing the five cases. This summary information is shown in Figure 6-6.

The first three cases are based on a constant workforce of 15,000 people. Cumulative attrition and hiring both total 7,500 people over the five years for Case 1. When the attrition rate is higher for those with shorter tenure as in Case 2, the cumulative attrition and hiring increase to 8,350 even though the average attrition rate over the fifteen years is less than in Case 1. There is a dramatic increase in attrition and hiring when the workforce profile has a higher proportion of shorter tenured employees as shown in Case 3. Cases 4 and 5 show the impact of growth in the workforce. The historical tenure profiles for Case 4 match those of Case 1 and for Case 5 they match the tenure profiles for Case 3.

Implications for Organizational Value

An estimate of the financial impact of these cases is built from two factors. The first factor is the cost of attrition and the second factor is the opportunity cost due to lost potential revenue and income. An average cost of attrition of 1.5 times annual salary is used combined with an average annual salary of $50,000. For the simulation the multiple of 1.5 is used as a representative average. It includes direct costs such as hiring and training, productivity losses, termination costs, lost revenue, productivity impact on others in the organization, and the costs of strategic missteps.

Figure 6-7
Attrition Cost by Performance and Level

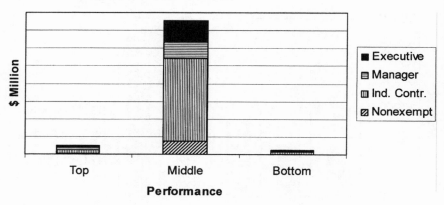

Additional detail about attrition costs by performance and level is not used in the simulation since it is intended to demonstrate the overall impact of future attrition and hiring. However, it is instructive to look at the information such detail can provide. We will digress briefly to examine this then return to the simulation. The cost of attrition varies by level, function and performance. A detailed analysis shows the attrition cost as a multiple of annual salary for nonexempt staff to be about 0.95, for individual contributors about 1.55, for managers about 2 and for executives about 3.4. An example of the variation by function is the sales area, where a case can be made that for a salesperson the multiple should be linked to annual quota rather than annual salary. While there is uncertainty about the specific cost impact of losing people with different levels of performance, some prior work suggests that a reasonable initial approximation is to use a salary multiple of about 3 for top performers, 1 for mid-range performers and 0.5 for low performers (Bliss & Associates 2000). With these detailed cost metrics it is possible to estimate the cost impact of attrition by performance and level in an organization. Figure 6-7 shows an example of this.

This is a representative example of a high-tech organization. It shows the dominating cost impact of losses from the middle-performing group, in particular individual contributors. They represent the engine of the organization and the area of greatest vulnerability. Identifying the financial consequences of attrition in this way helps ensure that resources are focused on the areas of greatest need.

Returning now to the simulation and the financial impact of the five cases, the second factor to consider is the opportunity cost of lost income

Figure 6-8
Costs for Modeling Cases

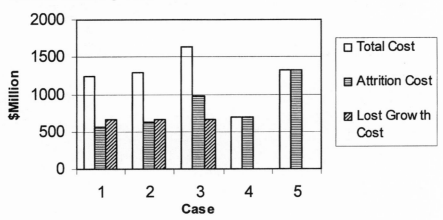

because there are insufficient people to secure potential growth. For the purposes of the current analysis an average income per employee (net income/number of employees) of $26,000 is used. This is calculated from the average of the industry sectors shown in Figure 3-1. As with attrition costs, the income per employee should be calculated for each organization, as it is specific to a given organization. The cost implications for each of the five cases are shown in Figure 6-8.

Figure 6-8 shows the total cost, attrition cost and opportunity cost of lost potential income for the five-year period in millions of dollars. The opportunity cost calculated relative to the higher growth case results in a growth penalty of $669 million for the first three cases. The cost of attrition, on the other hand, is directly proportional to the number of people leaving the organization, so that Cases 3 and 5 show the highest attrition costs. With the assumptions shown, Case 3 shows the greatest cost penalty. This would apply to an organization with a relatively short tenured workforce, having higher attrition for those with shorter tenure, and constrained by lack of people while operating in a growth market. This is a common situation for many organizations. The cost penalty over five years in this case is $1.6 billion. The lowest cost case has a cost penalty of $0.7 billion. These are huge financial impacts that address the fundamental wealth creation capability of the organization. For the case of the organization of 15,000 people in Case 3, using an average income per employee of $26,000 and valuation of 10x earnings, the value of the organization five years into the future is about $3.9 billion. For Case 3 the cost penalty over five years is 41% of the total value of the

Table 6-1
Impact on Organization Value over Five Years ($ Million)

	Constant Workforce (Case 3)	10% Annual Workforce Growth (Case 5)
Attrition Cost	968	1,319
Opportunity Cost of Lost Income Relative to Growth Case	669	0
Total Cost	1,637	1,319
Company Value After 5 Years (based on 10x Earnings)	3,900	6,281
Costs as a % of Company Value	42%	21%

organization. Each year these costs average 8.4% of the value of the company. For Case 5 the company value is $6.3 billion at the end of the five-year period and attrition costs are 21% of the total. Even the proverbial Sisyphus would have trouble pushing this stone up the hill. These costs are often either underestimated or not estimated at all by organizations. On the other hand, some organizations, being aware of the significance of attrition costs, are beginning to note these costs in internal profit and loss statements. In the future it will be critical to include economic estimates of the cost of attrition in the basis for decisions about resource allocation. The results for Cases 3 and 5 are summarized in Table 6-1.

There is hope however. Cutting the attrition rate in half for only the first five years reduces total attrition costs by about half for both cases. The incentive to reduce attrition in the early years is substantial. Coupling this information with feedback from interviews provides a basis for moving from the descriptive and predictive to the prescriptive. This includes estimating the economic impact of resources committed to enhance affiliation.

Defining the impact of attrition on company value establishes a direct link to the primary financial goal of a for-profit organization, namely maximizing the net present value of future cash flows. This can be generalized by a deterministic approach as follows, considering only attrition costs and not opportunity costs. Defining the value, V, of a for-profit organization as the net present value of future earnings (as a proxy for cash flow), the income per employee as i (= Revenue per employee*Return on revenue), the total number of employees as E and the discount rate as $r\%$, then using continuous compounding (Uhl and Hawkins 1971, 59):

$$\int_0^V dV = \int_0^t i * E * e^{-r*t/100} dt$$

so that:

$$V = (i * E * 100/r) * (1 - e^{-r*t/100})$$

and for $t = \infty$

$$V = i * E * 100/r \qquad \textbf{Equation 6-5}$$

The annual cost of attrition (C_a) is given by the following expression:

$$C_a = 1.5 * s_a * a * E/100 \qquad \textbf{Equation 6-6}$$

where s_a is the average salary, and a is the attrition rate expressed as a %.

Dividing Equation 6-6 by Equation 6-5, multiplying by 100 to convert to %, and simplifying gives the following, where A_v is the annual cost of attrition as a % of company value:

$$A_v = 0.015 * r * a * s_a / i \qquad \textbf{Equation 6-7}$$

For $r = 10\%$

$$A_v = 0.15 * a * s_a / i \qquad \textbf{Equation 6-8}$$

The cost of attrition as a percentage of company value is directly proportional to the ratio of salary to income contribution per employee (s_a/i). For a salary to income contribution ratio of 2, and an annual attrition rate of 20%, the annual subtraction of value due to attrition at a discount rate of 10% is 6% of total organizational value. Over five years 30% of the organization's value is lost. This does not take into account opportunity costs due to lost growth that can substantially add to this total. This major financial impact is one reason why attrition should receive attention at the highest levels in the organization.

If attrition continues indefinitely at a rate of $a\%$ then

$$\int_0^{C_{aT}} dC_a = \int_0^t (1.5 * s_a * a * E/100) * e^{-r*t/100} dt$$

for $t = \infty$

$$C_{aT} = 1.5 * s_a * a * E/r$$

where C_{aT} is the total cost of attrition in perpetuity.

Dividing by Equation 6-5 and multiplying by 100 to convert to % yields

$$A_{vT} = 1.5 * a * s_a/i \qquad \text{Equation 6-9}$$

Where A_{vT} is the cost of attrition as a % of company value in perpetuity.

In this case, for an annual attrition rate of 20% and a salary to income ratio (s_a/i) of 2, the total subtraction of value over time is 60% of the value of the organization. By allowing the losses to continue indefinitely the value of the organization is severely curtailed. Fiduciary responsibility demands that this area receive attention.

The *Fortune* assessment of the 100 best companies to work for in the United States (*Fortune* 2001: www.fortune.com) provides data that illustrates the application of this approach. This data includes the average starting salary for people joining the organization. The average starting salary can, as a first approximation, be converted to average overall salary by adding 50% to the starting salary. This is based on independent information for one organization. The *Fortune* data also includes average attrition rates, worldwide company earnings and the total number of employees. Applying Equation 6-8 to data for 2000 yields the following estimates for the reduction in value due to attrition in 2000 for some example organizations:

• Men's Wearhouse: 36% reduction, based on a 44% voluntary attrition rate
• Four Seasons Hotels: 49% reduction, based on a 22% voluntary attrition rate
• American Express: 3.6% reduction, based on a 20% voluntary attrition rate

- Sun Microsystems: 3.4% reduction, based on a 6% voluntary attrition rate
- Applied Materials: 0.9% reduction, based on a 9% voluntary attrition rate
- Microsoft: 0.5% reduction, based on a 10% voluntary attrition rate
- Eli Lilly: 0.3% reduction, based on a 3% voluntary attrition rate

The challenges facing the retail (Men's Wearhouse) and hospitality (Four Seasons Hotels) sectors are evident from these figures. While American Express and Sun show a much lower impact, the impact is still substantial, translating to a 36% and 34% subtraction in value respectively should attrition occur at the levels shown in perpetuity. Applied Materials, buoyed by high earnings in 2000, shows a lower impact of attrition on value aided by a voluntary attrition rate below 10%. Microsoft benefits from a disproportionately large earnings stream that mitigates the impact of attrition. The benefit of very low voluntary attrition is evident from Eli Lilly, where attrition only subtracted 0.3% of value in 2000.

Does this mean that zero attrition is an ideal? Not at all. Organizations need a continuous infusion of new ideas, which means movement of people into and out of the organization. Furthermore, as individuals our priorities and preferences change over time. As Carl Jung expressed it so clearly (Jung, 1976), "We cannot live the afternoon of our life according to the program of life's morning—what was great in the morning will be little at evening, and what in the morning was true will at evening have become a lie." Today there can be many mornings, afternoons and evenings in our evolving lives.

Would 100% attrition be desirable? For the organization, 100% attrition is a problem for many reasons, including the high cost it involves. For individuals, excessive movement exacts a penalty in terms of increased stress as well as limiting the ability to grow and contribute. By definition there is an optimum attrition rate for the organization that lies between 0 and 100% and there is likely an optimum movement rate for each individual.

LINKS BETWEEN THE ORGANIZATION AND THE INDIVIDUAL

Optimizing Attrition Rates

Deterministic modeling offers insights into the optimum attrition rate for the organization. The starting concept is that the economic value of the organization is equal to the sum of the value created by each individual, minus the costs of employee losses, plus the synergies resulting from people working together. The individual's contribution to economic value (v) can be expressed as a multiple of individual expertise (e), commitment, strategic focus and impact, minus the investment in the individual by the organization (x). Ultimately each of these elements can be characterized and measured. In this work we are simply seeking to demonstrate the presence of, and rationale for, an optimum. The conceptual statement can be expressed as follows:

$$v = k * e - k_d * x \qquad\qquad \textbf{Equation 6-10}$$

where k and k_d are constants, and k is a multiple of commitment, strategic focus and impact.

Expressing an individual's expertise (e) as a function of knowledge (n), capability (p) and obsolescence (o), building with time during which the individual is with the organization (t_t) leads to the following equation:

$$e = (n * p - o) * t_t \qquad\qquad \textbf{Equation 6-11}$$

where n and o are expressed per year.

If the attrition rate for the organization is a % per year, and the total number of employees is E, then by definition:

$$t_t = 100 * E/a * E$$

which can be simplified to:

$$t_t = 100/a \qquad\qquad \textbf{Equation 6-12}$$

Substituting for t_t from Equation 6-12 in Equation 6-11 yields:

$$e = (n * p - o) * (100/a) \qquad\qquad \textbf{Equation 6-13}$$

Substituting for e from Equation 6-13 into Equation 6-10 yields:

$$v = (n * p - o) * (100/a) * k - k_d * x \qquad\qquad \textbf{Equation 6-14}$$

For simplification we assume that average values of the components over time can be used. Incorporating functional time relationships and integrating over both time and the population could introduce time dependency of the components. For the organization in total, economic value (V) at a point in time is equal to the summation of the value created by each individual, minus the cost of employee losses, plus the value created from the synergy of individuals working together. This can be expressed as:

$$V = \int_0^E v \, dw - \int_0^E (a * k_3/100) * A_E \, dw + \int_0^E k_s \, dw \qquad \textbf{Equation 6-15}$$

where A_E is the cost of attrition per person, w is the number of people in the organization, k_3 is a constant to account for varying population over time and k_s is a constant. Substituting for v from Equation 6-14 into Equation 6-15, integrating and dividing by E yields:

$$v = (n * p - o) * (100/a) * k - (a * k_3/100) * A_E \qquad \textbf{Equation 6-16}$$
$$- k_d * x + k_s$$

This can be simplified by defining:

$$k_0 = n * p * k * 100$$

$$k_1 = o * k * 100$$

$$k_2 = A_E * k_3/100$$

to give:

$$v = ((k_0 - k_1)/a) - k_2 * a - k_d * x + k_s \qquad \textbf{Equation 6-17}$$

This equation yields an optimum in the relationship between individual economic value (v) and attrition rate (a). Now we can compare the prediction from this equation with observations. Figure 6-9 shows the actual data for five profit centers in a high-tech organization. Operating income per employee is a proxy for value creation per employee. The solid line is a best fit developed for the top four data points with the linfit function in Mathcad.

The equation representing the solid line in Figure 6-9 is as follows:

$$v = -9836/a - 95.1 * a + 2063 \qquad \textbf{Equation 6-18}$$

Figure 6-9
Observed and Modeled Organization Value

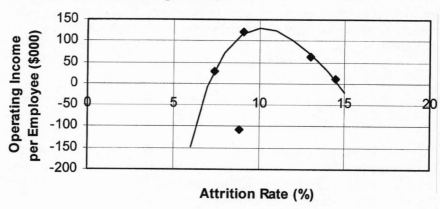

Attrition Rate (%)

where $k_0 - k_1 = -9836$, $k_2 = 95.1$, $k_s - k_d * x = 2063$. Figure 6-9 shows that this equation form represents the optimum well. An analytical expression for the optimum can be derived as follows:

Differentiating Equation 6-17 with respect to a yields:

$$dv \, / \, da = -(k_0 - k_1)/a^2 - k_2$$

$dv/da = 0$ at the optimum, hence

$$-(k_0 - k_1)/a^2 = k_2$$

Therefore

$$a = \overset{+}{\underset{-}{}} \sqrt{-(k_0 - k_1)/k_2}$$

Since the positive root is the only relevant root

$$a = \sqrt{(k_1 - k_0)/k_2}$$

Equation 6-19

This means that the optimum attrition level decreases as knowledge, capability, commitment, strategic focus and impact, k_0, increase; as obsolescence, k_1, decreases; and as the attrition cost per person (proportional to k_2) increases. Using the values of 9836 for (k_1-k_0) and 95.1 for k_2 results in an optimum attrition level of 10.2%.

Figure 6-10
Relationship Between Attrition Rate and HR Spending (Attrition Rate vs. HR per Employee High-Tech Organization)

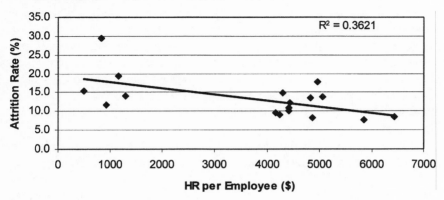

If $(k_1 - k_0)$ and k_3 are constant then the ratio of optimum attrition levels (a) for two different costs of attrition (A_E) for particular positions is given by the following expression:

$$a_1 / a_2 = \sqrt{A_{E2}/A_{E1}}$$

Equation 6-20

This means that each time the cost per person of attrition quadruples the optimum attrition rate is halved. We can compare the optimum attrition rate for a nonexempt position with annual compensation of $30,000 using a cost of attrition salary multiple of 0.95, with the optimum attrition rate for a manager compensated at $100,000 per year and an attrition cost salary multiple of 2. In this case the optimum attrition rate for the nonexempt position is 2.65 times that of the manager position (square root of (200,000/28,500)).

The analysis of the optimum attrition rate can be combined with a relationship between attrition rate and HR spending to model the optimum level of HR spending, focusing only on the contribution of HR to reducing attrition. Here we introduce a statistical component into the modeling process so this becomes a hybrid approach.

First we need to identify the relationship between HR spending and attrition. An example showing one approach to estimating this relationship is given in Figure 6-10, which covers three fiscal years and six business units for one organization.

The linear relationship shown has the following form:

$$a = -0.0017 * h + 19418 \qquad \text{Equation 6-21}$$

where h refers to HR expenditures per employee. The coefficient of determination shows that 36% of the variation is defined by the linear relationship underlining the approximate nature of this relationship. The investments in HR per employee are small compared with revenue per employee of about \$400,000 and operating income per employee of about \$50,000. The slope of the line, -0.0017, means that for this data, each \$1,000 invested in HR per employee yields a 1.7% reduction in attrition. This relationship can be used to estimate the optimum level of HR expenditures as follows.

Using b to represent the slope of the line relating a and h, and d_h to represent the constant in the relationship, the observed relationship is:

$$a = -b * h + d_h \qquad \text{Equation 6-22}$$

If the annual cost of attrition, with no investment in HR, is C_0, the total employee population is E, and the cost to the organization per employee lost is A_E, then the annual benefit (B) from reduced attrition by investing in HR is:

$$B = C_0 - (a/100) * E * A_E \qquad \text{Equation 6-23}$$

Furthermore the cost addition (F) due to the investment in HR is:

$$F = h * E \qquad \text{Equation 6-24}$$

When $h = 0$, $a = d_h$ from Equation 6-22, and $B = 0$ by definition. Therefore inserting $a = d_h$ into Equation 6-23 when $B = 0$ yields:

$$C_0 = d_h * E * A_E/100 \qquad \text{Equation 6-25}$$

Substituting for C_0 from Equation 6-25 and a from Equation 6-22, into Equation 6-23 and simplifying yields:

$$B = (b * h/100) * E * A_E \qquad \text{Equation 6-26}$$

The net value (V_a) from the investment in HR is equal to the benefit minus the cost, that is Equation 6-26 minus Equation 6-24, which after simplification is as follows:

Figure 6-11
Benefits from Investing in HR (Benefit from H.R. Expenditures at Three
Levels of Attrition Cost/Employee [$])

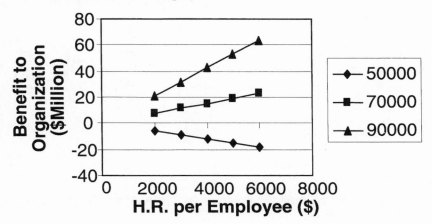

$$V_a = h * E * ((b * A_E/100) - 1)$$ **Equation 6-27**

The benefit equals the cost when $V_a = 0$ in Equation 6-27 and $A_E = 100/b$. For the data analyzed in Figure 6-10, $b = 0.0017$, which means that the benefit of investing in HR equals the cost when the attrition cost per employee (A_E) is $58,823. For this company the average annual compensation of employees was about $70,000. Using a salary multiple of 1.5 for the cost of attrition leads to an estimated attrition cost per employee of $105,000.

Figure 6-11 shows the annual benefit to the organization in millions of dollars, from Equation 6-27, using the line slope from Figure 6-10, assuming an employee population of 12,000 people, at three different levels of attrition cost per employee, $50,000, $70,000 and $90,000. As shown in Figure 6-11, for an attrition cost of $50,000 per employee, HR expenditures decrease overall value since this is below the break-even level of $58,823 identified earlier. However, at an attrition cost of $70,000 per employee, each $1,000 of investment in HR adds about $2 million annually to the organization; at a $90,000 attrition cost per employee the annual addition is about $6 million. While this analysis is based on a limited data set, it does illustrate the potentially substantial benefit of investing in HR, and it underlines why optimizing resources in this area can be a significant source of competitive advantage.

We can now return to the calculation of the optimum level of spending

Figure 6-12
Optimum HR Spending

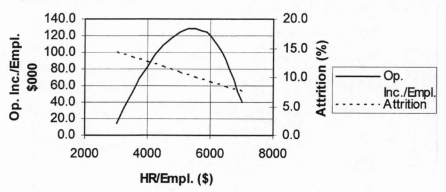

on HR. Substituting the retention rate a from Equation 6-22 into Equation 6-17 yields the following:

$$v = (k_0 - k_1)/(-b * h + d_h) - k_2 * (-b * h + d_h) \qquad \text{Equation 6-28}$$
$$- k_d * x + k_s$$

Using the constants shown in Equations 6-18 and 6-21 results in the attrition and value profiles shown in Figure 6-12.

Again, it is possible to develop an analytical expression for the optimum as follows. Differentiating Equation 6-28 with respect to h, using the rule for differentiating a quotient, and setting the result equal to 0 for the optimum yields:

$$b * (k_0 - k_1)/(-b * h + d_h)^2 = -k_2 * b$$

This can be simplified to give the value for h at the maximum, since only the negative root is relevant, as follows:

$$h = (1/b) * (d_h - \sqrt{(k_1 - k_0)/k_2}) = (1/b) * (d_h - a) \qquad \text{Equation 6-29}$$

(Substituting the optimum attrition expression from Equation 6-19 into Equation 6-22 also results in this equation.)

In this case, as the impact of HR spending on attrition increases (as b increases), the optimum level of HR spending decreases. Also, as the attrition cost per person (and k_2) increases, so does the optimum HR spending level. This provides a prescriptive basis for estimating the optimal spending on HR.

Organizational Growth

Now we will examine another area, namely organizational growth. The basic model of organizational growth so far considers steady and uniform growth over time, for example in projecting 10% per year growth in the earlier simulation. While this is a good overall approximation, in practice as the workforce in a growing organization builds, this steady growth is often punctuated by periodic contractions. Is there a model that describes such behavior? Here is one approach, which begins with two assumptions. The first is that the rate of growth of the employee population is directly proportional to the value addition of each person. When adding a person adds disproportionately greater value than the existing workforce, then rational decision making at the organizational level will lead to more rapid addition of people.

This can be described by the following equation:

$$dE/dt = c_1 * v + c_2 \qquad \qquad \text{Equation 6-30}$$

where E is the size of the employee population, t is time, v is value creation per employee and c_1 and c_2 are constants.

The second assumption is that the rate of increase in value addition per employee is, as a first approximation, linearly related to the size of the workforce due to the benefits of networking, minus the cost of supporting each person. The cost of supporting each person decreases over time due to productivity improvements. These productivity improvements can be expressed by a variant of the well-known experience curve. It shows a logarithmic decline in unit costs with an increase in the logarithm of production volume. In this case we substitute productivity for unit costs and time for volume. These assumptions are represented by the following equation:

$$dv/dt = c_3 * E - c_4 * t^{c_5} \qquad \qquad \text{Equation 6-31}$$

where c_3, c_4 and c_5 are constants.

Differentiating Equation 6-30 with respect to t, substituting for dv/dt from this into Equation 6-31 and rearranging leads to the following expression:

$$d^2E/dt^2 - j_k * E + q * t^{c_5} = 0 \qquad \qquad \text{Equation 6-32}$$

where j_k $(= c_3*c_1)$ and q $(= c_4*c_1)$ are constants. This second-order, linear, nonhomogeneous, ordinary differential equation describes the growth of an organization's population over time. It can be solved given either an initial value for E and the initial slope of E with time, or an initial and a later value for E. We will use the former approach, setting the initial condition of $E = 1,000$ and $dE/dt = 4,000$ per year for illustrative purposes. Using parameter values of 0.7 for c_5 (which is a typical value for an experience curve relationship), -1 for j_k and 2,500 for q we generate the prediction for growth in the organization's workforce shown in Figure 6-13 using the numerical odesolve capability in Mathcad. The vertical axis shows the number of people in the workforce and the horizontal axis shows time in years.

The population grows steadily over a thirty-year period from 1,000 to 25,000 people. However, this growth is punctuated by contractions every six years. This behavior conceptually mirrors that observed in practice in many growing organizations. The parameters of the equation define the overall growth rate and the periodicity and magnitude of the contractions. Equation 6-32 can be used as one basis for predicting growth of the workforce for an organization. This approach is readily extended to include a rate of increase in value addition per employee that varies as a power of the size of the workforce, for example varying with the square of the workforce size.

THE INDIVIDUAL

The focus up to now in the area of organization/individual connection has been on the organization. The other critical component is the perspective of the individual, particularly regarding his or her future relationship with the organization. This is intimately connected to the degree of fulfillment that a person experiences in his or her work. In constructing a model that links individual fulfillment to organizational value creation, it is necessary to create equations that address each of these two aspects separately, the organization and the individual perspective, and then identify a bridging mechanism to link them together. The bridge used in this model is affiliation. This can be expressed in measurable form as the length of time a person intends to stay with an organization, their anticipated tenure. The two anchor points for the bridge are first a description of individual fulfillment, and second an extension of the description of organizational value defined earlier.

The deterministic modeling so far has used continuous functions to predict continuous behavior. Catastrophe theory (Varian 1979) is a modeling approach in which continuous functions predict discontinuities in behavior such as the decision to leave an organization. Sheridan, using

Figure 6-13
Workforce Growth with Periodicity

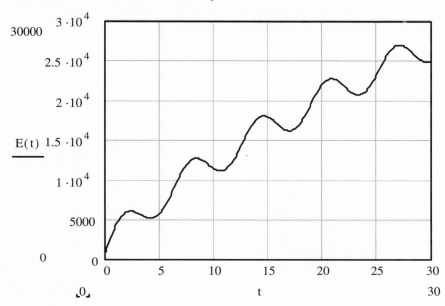

a different approach to that developed here, also examined the application of catastrophe theory to attrition (Sheridan and Abelson 1983; Sheridan 1985).

The proposed approach consists of the following components:

- Constructing an equation that relates individual fulfillment to time with the organization
- Converting individual fulfillment to perceived economic value using a utility function
- Constructing an equation that relates organizational value created by an individual to time with the organization
- Defining regions of stability by equating individual utility to organizational value created by an individual.

The first step is defining the relationship between individual fulfillment (f) and anticipated tenure (t_t). The starting postulate is that the rate of change of individual fulfillment with anticipated tenure is directly proportional to current fulfillment and the gap between individual aspirations (calling or meaning) (A_i) and actual fulfillment. This can be expressed mathematically as follows:

— 137 —

$$df/dt_t = k_i * f * (A_i - f)$$ **Equation 6-33**

where k_i is a constant linked to the ability of leadership to create a sense of inspiring purpose and fulfillment for individuals.

The solution to this equation is as follows:

$$-(1/A_i) * \ln((A_i - f)/f) = k_i * t_i + k_b$$

where k_b is a constant.

Simplifying and normalizing yields the following:

$$f/A_i = 1/(1 + B_i * \exp(- A_i * k_i * t_t))$$ **Equation 6-34**

where $B_i = \exp(-A_i * k_b)$

The individual contribution to organizational value was derived previously as Equation 6-17. Transforming the equation from attrition rate to time by setting $a = 100/t_t$ and simplifying by grouping constants together leads to the following expression:

$$v = - D_i * t_t - E_i/t_t + C_i$$ **Equation 6-35**

where $D_i = - (k_0 - k_1)/100$, $E_i = k_2/100$ and $C_i = k_s - k_d * x$

From Equation 6-35:

$$dv / dt_t = -D_i + E_i / t_t^2$$

At the optimum, $dv/dt_t = 0$, so that:

$$t_{tm} = \sqrt{E_i/D_i}$$

where t_{tm} is the anticipated tenure at the optimum.

Value created per person at the optimum, v_m, can be determined by substituting for t_{tm} in Equation 6-35. Equation 6-35 can be normalized by dividing v by v_m, which results in the following equation:

$$v/v_m = -D_i * t_t/v_m - E_i/(t_t * v_m) + C_i/v_m$$ **Equation 6-36**

The individual and organizational perspectives can be linked by introducing the concept of individual utility, which is the translation of fulfillment into an economic equivalent. Defining utility $(u) = k_u * f$, where k_u is a constant, and equating this to individual value creation v, then from Equation 6-34 multiplied by k_u and Equation 6-36:

$$k_u/(1 + B_i * \exp(-A_i * k_i * t_t)) = - D_i * t_t/v_m$$
$$- E_i/(t_t * v_m) + C_i/v_m \qquad \textbf{Equation 6-37}$$

This can be further simplified to:

$$1/(1 + B_i * \exp(-A_i * k_i * t_t)) = -G_i * t_t - H_i/t_t + L_i \qquad \textbf{Equation 6-38}$$

where G_i, H_i and L_i are constants.

This equation describes the equilibrium relationship between individual utility and the individual contribution to organizational value creation. What does this mean?

Figure 6-14 shows the equation describing individual utility (ind(t_t) in the figure), the left-hand side of Equation 6-38, and the equation describing individual contribution to organizational value (org(t_t) in the figure), the right-hand side of Equation 6-38, both plotted against anticipated tenure (t_t) in years.

For this chart B_i = 403(A_i = 1, k_b = −6), k_i = 1.3, G_i = 0.027, H_i = 4.9 and L_i = 1.8. The equation describing individual utility (ind(t_t)) is an s shape as the rate of change first accelerates and then decelerates. The equation for individual contribution to organizational value (org(t_t)) shows a continuous increase over the range shown, although outside this range it has an optimum. For the parameter values shown, the curves cross as three points, which represent potential points of equilibrium. The variable A_i*k_i through k_i is directly related to the ability of leadership to create a sense of inspiring purpose and fulfillment for an individual; t_t is tenure with the organization. Examining the three-dimensional surface that is generated by varying k_i and t_t in Equation 6-38 (expressed as the value of L_i) shows the form this equilibrium takes. The equilibrium surface is shown in Figure 6-15.

The value of the expression (L_i) is shown on the vertical axis, k_i is varied from 1 to 2 on the axis in the foreground, and t_t is varied from 2.5 to 10 on the axis in the background. This is a complex surface with a fold discontinuity. This can be seen more clearly in Figure 6-16, which is a two-dimensional cross-section of Figure 6-15.

The contours are the equilibrium values of L_i. The horizontal axis is k_i and the vertical axis is t_t. k_i in the language of catastrophe theory is known as a slow variable. This means that a small change in the value of this variable can cause a major shift in the value of the fast variable t_t, intended tenure with the organization. The slow variable, k_i, is directly proportional to the ability of leadership to create a sense of inspiring purpose and fulfillment for an individual. Examining the contour with a

Figure 6-14
Utility and Value Curves (Variation of Individual Utility and Organization Value with Tenure)

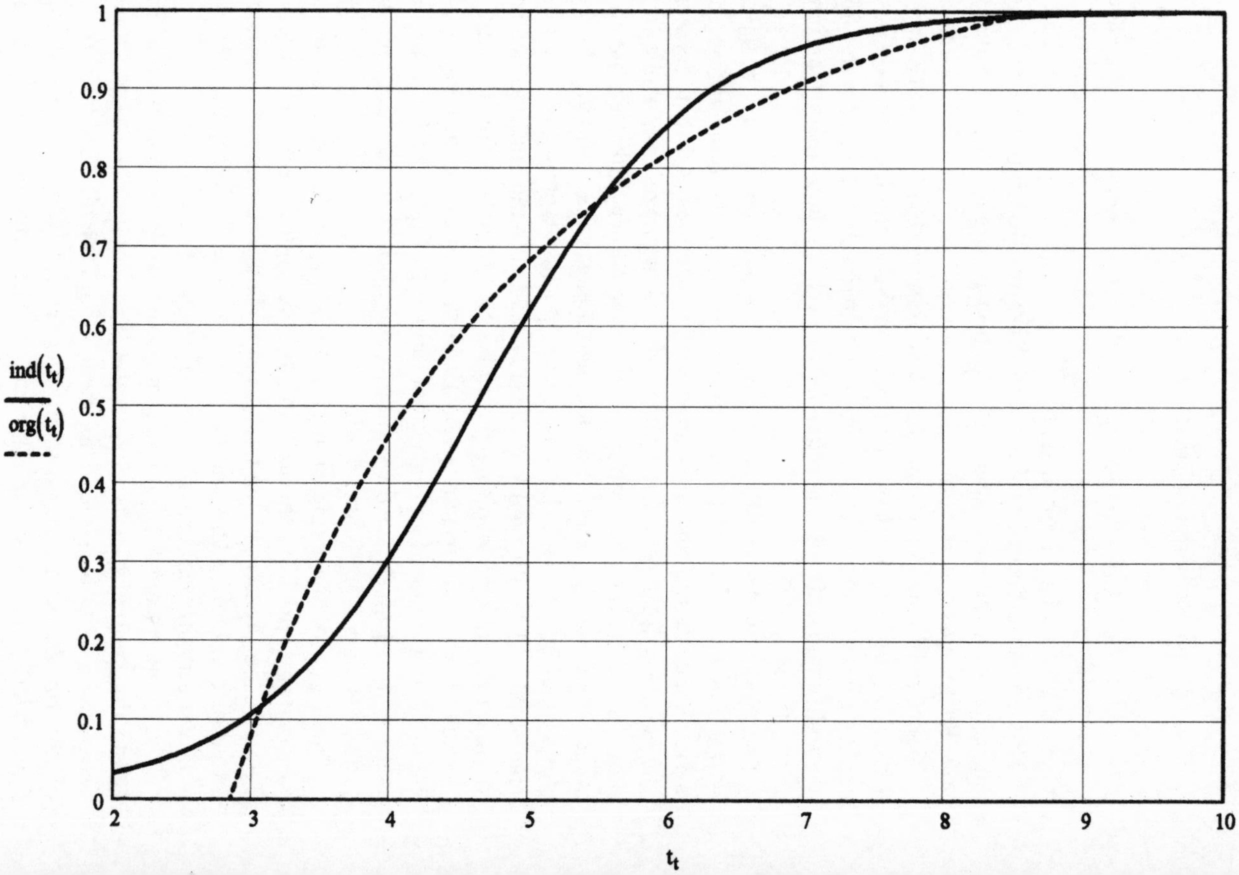

Figure 6-15
Equilibrium Surface Linking Inspiring Purpose/Fulfillment and Tenure

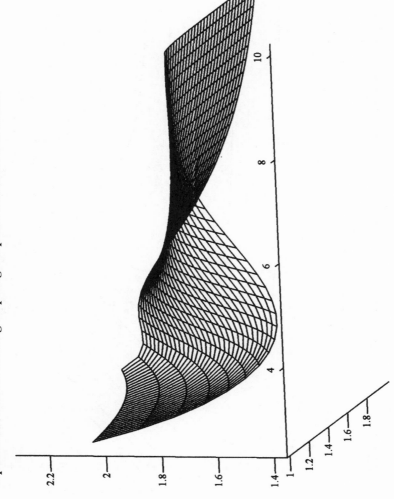

Figure 6-16
Contour Lines Linking Inspiring Purpose/Fulfillment and Tenure

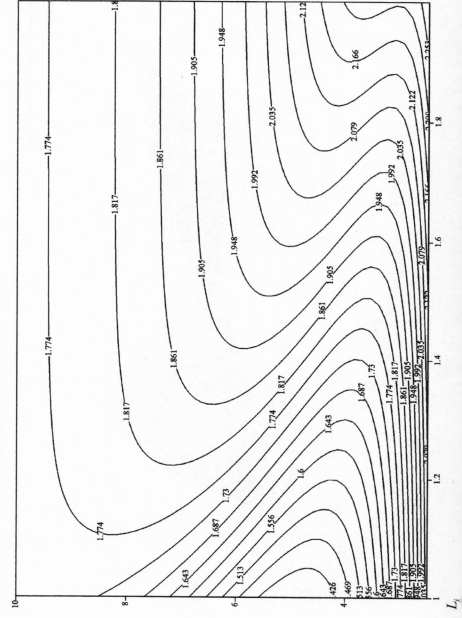

value of 1.817 illustrates the predicted behavior. As k_i increases from 1 to about 1.5, t_t suddenly jumps from 3.6 to about 8.2. This means that as leadership creates a greater sense of inspiring purpose and fulfillment the individual feels a dramatically increased sense of commitment, as shown by a substantially longer intended tenure. Conversely when k_i declines from a value above 1.5 to about 1.2, t_t drops suddenly from about 7.2 to about 3 on the 1.817 contour line. This means that as the sense of inspiring purpose and fulfillment declines there is a sudden major decrease in commitment and an increased likelihood of leaving.

We can compare the predicted behavior for individuals with observations from a broad range of people in many organizations described in Chapter 4. Figure 4-1 shows the relationship between anticipated tenure with an organization and leadership's ability to create a sense of inspiring purpose and fulfillment for the overall sample and for the healthcare and manufacturing sectors. The observed pattern is one of regions of stability. In each case there are two regions of stability. One shows high anticipated tenure and a strong sense of inspiring purpose and fulfillment, the other shows a low anticipated tenure and a lower sense of inspiring purpose and fulfillment. A small change in the degree of inspiring purpose and fulfillment can result in sudden movement from one region of stability to the other. This is exactly the behavior predicted by Equation 6-38 and shown in Figures 6-15 and 6-16. Leadership plays a key role in determining the region of stability that people will occupy. On an individual level as a person's sense of inspiring purpose and fulfillment increases there is a sudden, dramatic increase in anticipated tenure with the organization and the reverse is also true. This sense of purpose can be directly influenced by leadership. If conditions in the workforce provide ready alternatives and people lack a sense of inspiring purpose and fulfillment in a given organization, they will likely leave quickly. This short time to departure is observed in practice as described in Chapter 4. A future opportunity is to develop specific parameter values for the model for individual organizations that lead to prescriptive approaches. Initial work using the observations in Chapter 4 and optimization techniques to fit theory to data has demonstrated the feasibility of such an approach.

The regions of stability predicted by this model and observed in practice are analogous to the patterns that might reflect other major life decisions. Indeed, an analogy that could represent this behavior is that of a traveler on a boat traveling through an island chain. He or she chooses to alight on an island for a time and then abruptly departs for another venue. The length of stay directly depends on the island community, and how it captivates and embraces the traveler, just as with an individual in an organization. Organizations today are such islands, and the strength and extent of purpose, fulfillment and community are largely leadership issues. These issues directly determine the sense of affiliation and length of anticipated stay of individuals with organizations.

SUMMARY

The approaches to modeling began at the community level, then extended to the organization, the link between the individual and the organization and finally focused on the individual. The key points that were identified are as follows.

- A relationship between the change in unemployment rate and changing economic conditions was identified. It provides one means of estimating future employee scarcity based on changing economic conditions. The equation linking the % change in unemployment rate (ΔUR) to the % change in real GDP per capita based on the workforce ($\Delta GDPC$) is as follows:

$$\Delta UR = 0.4691 * \Delta GDPC^2 - 8.6888 * \Delta GDPC + 13.692$$

This means that the unemployment rate remains unchanged when real GDP per capita increases at 1.7% per year; for slower GDP increase the unemployment rate will increase and vice versa for faster GDP increase.

- A relationship linking the number of organizations to size was identified. This likely represents the operation of an efficient market and therefore is a potential target for communities and by extension large, individual organizations with multiple units. The equation linking the number of organizations (N) to size, having at least E employees, is as follows:

$$\ln(N) = -1.2112 * \ln(E) + 18.49$$

The ratio of the number of organizations N_1 with employees E_1 to the number of organization N_2 with employees E_2 is as follows:

$$N_1 / N_2 = (E_2 / E_1)^{(k_t/\ln s)}$$

where k_t is a constant and s is the span of control. Estimating the exponent from observations leads to:

$$N_1/N_2 = (E_2/E_1)^{1.14}$$

which in many cases can be simplified to:

$$N_1/N_2 = (E_2/E_1)$$

This final equation means that the number of organizations of a given size is inversely proportional to that size.

- The percentage reduction in organizational value due to attrition is directly proportional to the ratio of salary to net income contribution per employee.

The annual cost of attrition as a % of company value (A_v) is given by the following expression where r is the discount rate, a is the attrition rate, s_a is the average annual salary and i is the organization income per employee.

$$A_v = 0.015 * r * a * s_a/i$$

If attrition continues at the same rate in perpetuity then the total cost of attrition as a % of company value (A_{vT}) is given by the following expression:

$$A_{vT} = 1.5 * a * s_a/i$$

- An equation was developed that predicts the optimum attrition level for an organization based on value creation. The relation between value creation per employee (v) and attrition rate (a) is given by the following expression (the remaining terms in the equation are constants):

$$v = ((k_0 - k_1)/a) - k_2 * a - k_d * x + k_s$$

This predicts the optimum attrition rate decreasing as knowledge, capability, commitment, strategic focus and impact, k_0, increase, as obsolescence, k_1, decreases, and as the attrition cost per person (proportional to k_2) increases.

- A relationship was developed between the optimum attrition rate and the per person costs of attrition. It is given by the following expression, which indicates that as the cost of attrition per person is quadrupled, then the optimum attrition rate is halved:

$$a_1/a_2 = \sqrt{A_{E2}/A_{E1}}$$

- By defining the link between HR spending and attrition and connecting it to optimum individual value creation, an expression for the optimum level of HR investment was developed. It is given by the following expression:

$$h = (1/b) * (d_h - \sqrt{(k_t - k_0)/k_2}) = (1/b) * (d_h - a)$$

As the attrition cost per person (and k_2) increases, so does the optimum HR spending level.

- A model was developed describing the evolution of organizations in which steady growth is punctuated by periodic contractions. The differential equation describing this behavior, where E is the size of the organization's workforce, takes the following form:

$$d^2E/dt^2 - j_k * E + q * t^{c_5} = 0$$

where j_k, q and c_5 are constants.

- A model was developed linking individual fulfillment to organizational value creation with affiliation, expressed in the form of anticipated tenure with the organization, as the bridge. The model predicts discontinuities in individual behavior where departure can be triggered by a reduction in inspiring purpose and sense of fulfillment. The model also predicts regions of stability for people in an organization where individual utility (fulfillment expressed in economic terms) matches individual creation of organization value. One region shows high anticipated tenure and a strong sense of inspiring purpose and fulfillment, the other shows a low sense of inspiring purpose and fulfillment and short anticipated tenure. Predictions from the model match observed behavior. The regions of stability can be described in terms of anticipated tenure (t_t) with the organization by the following equation:

$$1/(1 + B_i * \exp(- A_i * k_i * t_t)) = - G_i * t_t - H_i/t_t + L_i$$

where k_i incorporates leadership's ability to create a sense of inspiring purpose and fulfillment, A_i is a measure of individual aspirations and the other terms are constants. This equation describes the critical impact of leadership's ability to create a sense of inspiring purpose and fulfillment on individual decisions to stay or leave.

— 7 —

Case Study: Creating Value and Enhancing Affiliation through Employee Development

It is accepted, almost as an article of faith, by many in the fields of career and human development that enhancing individual fulfillment in work will increase organizational value. This is largely due to anecdotal support of such a proposition. Furthermore, the modeling approach examined in Chapter 6 in connection with the individual showed strong links between employee fulfillment and organizational value creation. However, those charged with making pragmatic business decisions must allocate scarce resources where they can be most effective. Allocating such resources for individual development means understanding the potential economic impact. There is little data in this area, because it is complex and difficult to quantify the cause-and-effect relationships between individual development and organizational value creation. This chapter describes one case study that quantifies the economic benefit to an organization of investing in individual career development. It is a case study of Career Services at Sun Microsystems that illustrates an approach to measuring the impact of individual development on organizational value. This provides a perspective on a question posed by organizations: "Why should we invest in employee career development, won't employees just leave our organization?" In fact, as we will see, when the organization provides options and choices people self-select into the organization rather than out. This case study also provides a perspective on a question posed by many employees: "Why should I stay with your organization?" Answering this question is not easy, for we are asking employees to stay connected while the wheel of organizations turns faster. It is not surprising that sometimes employees spin out like tiny satellites from a furiously rotating sun. This chapter describes one approach to strengthening the connection between employees and an organization and how to quantify the benefits.

The case study begins with background on human resource work at Sun, and then describes the evolution of Career Services. The results of the case study are presented in terms of measurements that address activity levels of Career Services, reach into the employee population, and describe outcomes of the work. The study concludes with a brief outline of some related research and summarizes lessons learned.

BACKGROUND

"Kick butt and have fun" is Sun CEO Scott McNealy's message to employees. Sun's culture is about having fun while employees work hard at innovation and creating the future. Sun Microsystems, Inc. operates in many countries with global headquarters in Palo Alto, California. Founded in 1982, Sun is a global leader in enterprise network computing with more than $18 billion in revenue in fiscal year 2001. While Sun's name is synonymous with Java, its products range from workstations and servers to software services.

In the 1980s, Sun copyrighted its slogan "The Network is the Computer," a vision that is now ubiquitous. Sun provides enterprise-wide solutions to businesses, enabling them to leverage information resources in a stable operating system environment. This is an area where competition for employee talent is fierce.

Supporting Sun's operating divisions are core human resources (HR), finance, legal and IT services provided by a Corporate Resources group. The role of HR is constantly refined to add greater value to the organization and to keep up with the fast pace of change. In the late 1990s HR at Sun had promised to deliver a competitive workforce (W), competitive organization (O) and a competitive workplace (W), commonly referred to as the WOW strategy within the company. HR provided an extensive range of services, from the conventional compensation and benefits to fitness programs, and innovative programs like Career Services, as profiled here. Measurement of the outcomes of services and their refinement are important elements of the Sun HR culture.

In the late 1990s, Sun had begun to strongly emphasize the importance of measurement in tracking performance in all aspects of the business.

Examples of measurements that were tracked include external customer satisfaction, on-time delivery of products and internal employee perceptions. This comprehensive approach to measurement is also reflected in the current study of the impact of Career Services on the organization.

In the late 1990s, while the high-tech industry is believed to have experienced annual employee turnover of 15% and higher, Sun maintained single-digit voluntary turnover, in spite of the workforce growing by 20% worldwide each year. Sun invested in understanding what attracts employees to an organization and what will retain them. Among the top contributors to attraction and retention were work challenge, career development, financial opportunity, work variety, and organizational commitment to people. At Sun, the importance of career development was reinforced by a number of satisfaction surveys and by comments from employees. In an environment of rapid change and little hand holding, it is a major challenge to provide a middle ground between defined career paths and "figure it out for yourself" development. Working with a third party, the Career Action Center, a nonprofit organization, Sun developed an approach to support employees in taking control of their careers and identified measurable benefits to the organization.

HOW CAREER SERVICES AT SUN MICROSYSTEMS DEVELOPED

A strength of Sun's approach to employee development is long-term commitment to continuous evolution and improvement in the process. Within Sun, Career Services is a primary support mechanism for employees. Counselors from a third party provided career counseling as a benefit to employees. This approach evolved from a career center opened in 1991 that initially focused on the manufacturing area and the challenge of helping employees deal proactively with redeployment. The center provided career counseling for employees built around the concept of employees taking "primary ownership" of their career direction, with support by the organization.

This led naturally to the next evolution. Within eighteen months the focus of the center and its counseling moved to ongoing career management provided as a benefit to all employees. At this point internal reporting responsibility for the center moved to the Human Resources department. The third party continued to be responsible for delivering the services and guiding content direction. The reach of the counselors was broadened with services being offered at multiple Sun locations around Silicon Valley. Primary activities shifted from items such as resume creation to supporting individuals explore their career aspirations. This included expressing these aspirations in development plans aided by assessment instruments and workshops. The evolution of Career Services continued with an expansion in the number of counseling sessions available as a benefit to employees from two to four; inclusion of telephone counseling to reach a distributed population; dispersion of counselors to separate locations at different Silicon Valley facilities and one on the East Coast; and increased emphasis on tracking both the ability of the services to reach the Sun population and on measuring outcomes. By the late 1990s Career Services evolved to help employees make well-informed career choices and match their aspirations to opportunities within Sun. The primary delivery approach was individual career counseling coupled with supportive resources and events such as one- to two-hour group presentations tailored to employee needs.

Employees were informed about Career Services through a variety of channels. These included: Sun's website, career talks, e-mail, new hire orientation, presence at employee events, locating the counselors' offices close to high-traffic areas, and by the counselors linking closely with the local Human Resources representative.

OUTCOMES AND MEASUREMENT

In examining the value of the services to the organization, key questions that arise are their ability to address all segments of the employee population and their impact on organizational success. Much anecdotal information was gathered previously from individual employees strongly supporting the value of the services in addressing individual needs. However, there was little quantitative information available about the impact on the organization, since there is a complex chain linking work in this area to business performance. This study explored this linkage, looking primarily at the impact of Career Services.

The overall purpose was to look at connections between employee alignment with fulfilling work, employee satisfaction, retention and business performance. The components of the study included analyzing data characterizing business unit financial performance; workforce demographics, resources committed and transfers and promotions; Career Services activity; employee satisfaction; terminations and retention; and links among these elements. Over the primary thirteen-month period studied, 91% of the one-on-one counseling provided by Career Services occurred in a face-to-face setting and 9% was by telephone. The analysis addressed six separate units in Sun, which at the time of data collection accounted for about 90% of Sun's workforce, which averaged 18,000 people worldwide and 12,000 people in the United States.

The six operating units in Sun covered a broad range of types of business, from service to state-of-the-art semiconductor design, from hardware development to leading-edge software products. The units contain examples of a full range of functional capabilities including research and development, sales, marketing, production and support functions. As such they are representative of leading-edge, high-technology organizations. The results of the analysis are as follows.

Activity Level

During the thirteen-month period studied in detail, 1,033 people used Career Services. There were 2,138 appointments, of which 1,033 were initial appointments and 1,105 were follow-up. This continued use of the service beyond the first appointment indicated the value individuals placed in the service. Ninety-three percent of the appointments were made by employees seeking career counseling for development purposes, with only 3% for employees on a termination path. The remaining 4% were interns. Use by interns underlines the appeal to the population about to enter the workforce. In the six units studied, usage varied from 6% to 11% of employees in each unit, a high usage compared to benefits such as employee assistance programs. Employees who were transferred made greater use of the service than the general population. A number of these employees would likely have left Sun in the absence of support to aid them in finding suitable transfer and development opportunities. Employees who were promoted used the service less than the general population, as promotions tend to be driven more by the organization than the individual.

Reaching the Employee Population

A critical question in exploring the value of an approach such as Career Services is how effective it is in reaching the employee population. There are many dimensions to employee demographics as we saw in Chapter 6. They include ethnicity, gender, years of service, age, position, location, level, performance and function. With this in mind, the population using Career Services was compared with the overall population and in some cases with those people leaving. There was a higher usage of Career Services by non-Caucasian ethnic groups at 38% of the total, compared with their constituting only 33% of Sun's workforce. Career

Figure 7-1
Attrition and Years of Service (Attrition as % Employee Population by
Years of Service [U.S.] as of Jan. 1, 1997)

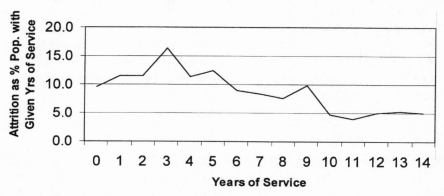

Services is seen as a valued resource by, and is used by, ethnic minorities. This is particularly important for Sun given the growing diversity of its workforce. This also underlines the ability of the career counseling process to reach ethnic minorities, even though the counselor population was exclusively Caucasian. In terms of usage by gender, female clients accounted for 59% of all appointments, significantly higher than their representation in the overall population, which was about 40% female. This underlines the effectiveness of Career Services in supporting the female population.

There was a close match between the age distribution of the population using Career Services and the age distribution of the overall population, again confirming the ability to reach into the employee population representatively. Particularly encouraging was slightly higher use of the service by employees who are younger than 35, as this group is one of the most vulnerable from an attrition perspective. The service was also used representatively by those with varying years of service.

Voluntary attrition accounted for more than 90% of all those leaving during the time studied. The overall population and the profile of those leaving showed a high proportion of employees with up to three years of service, underlining the importance of addressing the needs of this group for affiliation purposes. Attrition by years of service is summarized in Figure 7-1.

The attrition rate was highest in the first five years of service, peaking at about three years of service. This is a particularly vulnerable time in building relationships with employees for this organization and it un-

Figure 7-2
Distribution by Grade Level

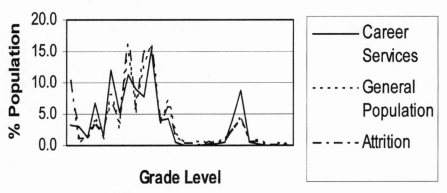

derlines the importance of Career Services support. In examining the activity level by years of service it was apparent that Career Services was able to support employees at all stages in their careers with particular strength in the early years. Broad reach was also a characteristic of Career Services when looking from the perspective of grade level, as shown in Figure 7-2.

People at many levels in the organization used Career Services. This included use by nonexempt personnel, the segment at the right-hand side, usage by the general exempt employee population, the segment at the left-hand side, and usage by senior-level employees and managers, the segment close to the middle. Grade level increases from left to right for the exempt and the nonexempt employees. Career Services reached broadly into the workforce and addressed employee groups that the organization considered critical for future success. The population using Career Services matched the overall population well, which also closely tracks attrition demographics.

OUTCOMES AND BENEFITS

Having established the ability of Career Services to reach the employee population, the question of impact now surfaces. Strong positive impact on employees is confirmed by anecdotal and qualitative comments collected after counseling sessions. How does this translate into organizational performance? One directly measurable element is attrition level. This is expected to reflect employee alignment with fulfilling work, satisfaction and ultimately business performance.

The relationship between Career Services activity and attrition in each

Figure 7-3
Voluntary Attrition vs. Career Services Use

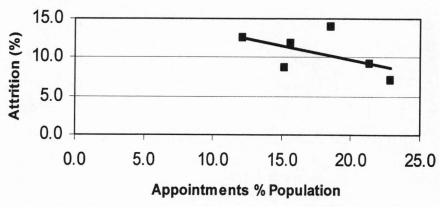

of the six operating units pointed to the benefits of the investment in career development support. Because 10% of the employee population used the service over the time studied, it would have been understandable if there were no significant relationship at the operating unit level. In fact, surprisingly there was a noticeable reduction in the attrition rate at the operating unit level, as the number of appointments with Career Services increased. This is shown in Figure 7-3 where the voluntary attrition rate in each of the six units is plotted against the number of Career Services appointments, expressed as a percentage of the employee population.

This is illustrated more directly when the attrition rate for the population using Career Services is compared with that for the overall population. Over the period studied, 1,130 people left the organization voluntarily in the six units examined in detail. For those who did not use Career Services, the attrition rate was 10%. On the other hand, for those proactively using Career Services over the same time, the attrition rate was reduced to 9%, lower by 1% than the reference group. This is true in the operating units studied where Career Services support can be leveraged into transfer opportunities for individuals. The impact is likely less in support functions with fewer alternatives for employees.

The reduction in attrition translates to significant savings for the organization, using an estimated cost of losing one person as 1.5 times their annual salary. The average salary at Sun during the study period was $70,000 per year, which means the cost of attrition per person was about $100,000. Taking the reduced attrition of 1%, and applying it to the population using Career Services of about 1,000 people per year, results in an annual cost saving due to reduced attrition of about $1 million. Furthermore for those employees in transition, use of Career Services is a cost-effective means of support. This is estimated to contribute about another $100,000 per year relative to the use of outplacement services. Since the fully loaded cost of Career Services was estimated at $600,000 per year, the return on investment is ($1,100,000/$600,000)*100, which is equal to 183%. Here we see a clear, measurable organizational benefit to complement the many qualitative benefits that are observed. Indeed, it is only necessary for Career Services to reduce attrition by one employee every other month to fully recover the cost.

CONNECTION WITH THE EXPERIENCE OF OTHERS

There is limited quantitative information available on the organizational impact of career development work. Also few fundamental models describe cause-and-effect relationships and therefore predict the impact of given interventions. The complexity of linkages between human resource practices and business performance is reflected in the eclectic range of reference sources summarized by Elsdon and Warner (1998). References vary from an academic to a practitioner focus, from an organizational to an individual, psychological perspective. Regardless of their foundation, there is a common theme, that this subject is important because of the scale of HR commitments and the significant implications of human resource decisions on the organization and the individual. The importance of HR commitments is borne out by analysis of the percentage of sales devoted to people-intensive resources: research and development, sales, general and administrative expenses in eight high-tech organizations including Sun, based in Silicon Valley (Elsdon and Warner 1998). This shows investment in these people-intensive resources to be one third of a total revenue base of $120 billion. Maintaining a fulfilled and productive workforce is critical to maximizing the value of this investment.

As pointed out in the Preface there is some support for approaches that identify best practices in HR that can be applied broadly (Delery and Doty 1996). However there is also the need to relate practices to the culture of an individual organization. Indeed Niehaus and Swiercz (1996) reinforce grouping HR practices into three broad categories: (1) those in which a best practice can be identified and applied to other organizations, (2) those which are specific to a given organization and (3) those where the link among multiple practices in a given organization is key. It is likely that much of the learning from the Sun study has general applicability. However, this should be treated with caution as approaches in other organizations need to recognize the complexities of each organization, the culture and HR and leadership practices.

We can also revisit the framework described in Chapter 3 for describing the organizational impact of development resources. The six levels are as follows:

Level 1: Reaction and Planned Action

• Measures participant satisfaction and planned action

Level 2: Learning

• Measures changes in knowledge, skills and attitude

Level 3: Individual Performance/Behavior

• Measures changes in on-the-job behavior

Level 4: Business Results

• Measures business impact

Level 5: Return on Investment

• Compares program benefits to costs

Level 6: Prediction

• Estimates the impact of resources committed on future performance

The work in this case study focuses on levels 4 and 5 and begins to explore level 6 (as outlined in Chapter 6). Increased emphasis on level 6 in the future can provide a basis for establishing sustainable competitive advantage. For it is here that proprietary approaches are possible, building on the uniqueness of a particular organization. As Wright, McMahan and McWilliams (1994) propose, an organization's workforce offers sustainable advantage if it creates value, is unique or rare among competitors, is difficult to replicate and is not readily imitated or substituted. The approach explored at Sun and the use of predictive tools provide means to create value by strengthening the links to individual employees, and tailoring an approach to the individual organization and its workforce. As evident from high attrition rates at many organizations, there is a need to strengthen connections with individual employees. For many organizations, the key to competitive survival is building the unique strengths of the workforce. This includes, for example, the need for enhanced productivity in a more stable environment and rapid response to change in a dynamic environment.

This case study points to the following conclusions and lessons learned:

Case Study

1. Enabling employees to seek greater fulfillment in their work through person-to-person career counseling creates significant value for the organization through reduced voluntary attrition. In the example studied, return on investment was well over 100%.

2. Person-to-person career counseling creates greater workforce flexibility by enabling employees to respond rapidly to a changing environment and customer needs. In so doing, this helps retain employees who might otherwise have been lost.

3. Person-to-person career counseling provides an effective means to broadly address the needs of different segments of the employee population. For example, addressing the needs of minority groups, which are of increasing importance with growing workforce diversity.

4. In supporting employees with their career development, it is important to address the different segments of the employee population and track them with appropriate metrics. Segments include those based on ethnicity, gender, years of service, age, position, location, level, performance and function. Such analysis can help establish needs of particular groups and permit the development of appropriate support approaches. Additional metrics to track include outcomes such as transfers, promotions and attrition, employee satisfaction and qualitative measures of the impact of services on an individual.

5. Particular emphasis is required to support the affiliation needs of employees with five or fewer years of service, as this is a vulnerable group. This may include, for example, provision of orientation and development support and internal networking opportunities.

6. Building on the material covered in Chapter 6, the development of predictive tools to estimate, in advance, the impact of HR on business performance is an approach that offers the potential for creating competitive advantage. This includes, for example, identifying an optimum level of HR investment, and an optimum level of attrition.

This study underlines the critical importance of people as a key source of competitive advantage for the organization. This means a shift in mindset to a focus on employees as the key source of competitive strength rather than hard assets. This study emphasizes how employee support through person-to-person career counseling helps strengthen the connection between the individual and the organization and in so doing helps build organizational value. It is in analyzing this impact, in understanding workforce demographics and in tailoring support accordingly that unique and sustainable organizational strength can be uncovered and expressed.

Having framed the environment and examined modeling approaches and case studies, we will now explore the path forward.

— PART III —

DEVELOPING A PATH FORWARD

The test of our progress is not whether we add more to the
abundance of those who have much; it is whether we provide
enough for those who have too little.
Franklin Delano Roosevelt

— 8 —

A Conversation with Leaders and HR about Affiliation

Photographs on the walls spoke to values of the organization. One was of a little girl, gazing intently at a tray of bright red, candied apples. Such a delicious sight fully engaged and entranced her. She was unlikely to leave. Sitting in a nearby room were the leaders of this organization, a publishing company, wondering how to best engage and entrance their employees. This was made all the more difficult by a recent layoff. We started discussing changing demographics of the workforce and what this would mean for organizations in the future. We talked about the growing scarcity of people and its effect on the relationship with employees. We discussed the daily focus on cost cutting and deadlines. Then we began to talk about the purpose of this organization. We heard passionate expressions about integrity in news reporting, about depth of content. We heard passion about this organization's contribution to preserving a democratic society. And interestingly, though these leaders believed intensely in these statements of purpose, they were not the primary component of the formal language describing the organization. So a new commitment was born in this leadership team to crystallize their purpose and make it real for others. Caple (1991, 13) in talking about the job interview process, observes: "All of us have glorious gifts. The challenge is to unwrap them." This is also true of organizations. This chapter will explore how leaders and HR can help unwrap the gifts of their organizations so that people choose to engage.

It begins with an examination of key processes linked to the workforce that leaders and HR must address. The focus then shifts to the various roles leaders and HR need to fulfill, the barriers they may encounter and the behaviors they need to exhibit. The chapter concludes by linking these thoughts to the stages of connection between individuals and organizations.

PROCESSES

Six key processes for leaders and HR linked to the workforce are as follows:

- Creation of a transcending purpose
- Communication
- Building a supportive environment
- Understanding of workforce dynamics and analysis
- Measurement of workforce contributions
- Prediction of evolving needs

Creation of a transcending purpose. What is meant by creation of a transcending purpose? It is not a bland statement of fiscal goodness that could be directly substituted for similar statements in many other organizations. Transcending purpose for an organization is a statement of the unique contribution it strives to make. Some tests for transcending purpose are:

- Is it unique to the organization?
- Does it speak to fundamental values that are immutable?
- Does it address the intended organizational legacy?
- Does it speak to the heart as well as the head?
- Does it guide behaviors?

Why is this critical? Chapter 4 showed the strong link between a sense of inspiring purpose and affiliation. They are intimately intertwined. A clear statement provides a touchstone for each person in the organization validating why they are there. When it is lived out on a daily basis it enables each person to step over the frustrations and minutiae of daily work. It ennobles each person and elevates work to a vocation in the terminology of Brewer (1996).

How is such a statement of purpose created? The first step is both a heartfelt and a pragmatic examination of the reason for the organization's existence. One organization assembled the entire employee population in a room for a day to work in teams to describe the essence of the purpose. For others a founder or core leadership team creates the statement of purpose. Asking questions similar to those posed above, only in open-ended form, for example, how is our organization unique, is an effective way to refine the statement. It can then be translated into a simple and clear form, for example for DBM: "We help improve people's lives." It is then ready for testing with employees and with customers for impact and depth, and modification as necessary. The final step is a conversation among the leadership team about translating this statement into behaviors, and then living those behaviors. This may sound simple or even trivial. In fact it is neither, since it is reaching depths of understanding that are neither easy to access nor easy to express.

What benefits result from such an endeavor? They include:

- Greater energy and enthusiasm in the organization
- Enhanced ability to make complex strategic decisions
- Greater commitment
- Higher productivity
- More effective selection of new employees
- Stronger affiliation with each person in the workforce
- A stimulus for more rapid growth of the organization

Communication. Having crafted a clear statement of purpose the next step is communicating it. This means constantly reinforcing messages about the direction, purpose and values of the organization. It means telling stories about the organization's values as practiced. One example that illustrates this relates to integrity. This was a business unit facing a difficult decision about supplying customers. The unit was highly successful in that customer demand exceeded the unit's ability to supply. It was faced with a question about how to allocate limited available product. One large customer demanded a disproportionate share that would drastically curtail the supply to others, including small customers who could have been put out of business by such actions. In spite of the pressure from the large customer the unit decided to continue with an equitable allocation to all, large and small. While this proved unpopular with the large customer, it did not lead to termination of the relationship. In fact it was a clear statement of the integrity of the organization both internally and externally. It signaled to customers that they could expect equitable treatment. Similar approaches to pricing questions reinforced for customers and employees the integrity of the organization and strengthened long-term relationships. Benefits from such communication of behaviors that match values and purpose accrue both internally and externally.

Communication also helps answer the question for each person about why they should affiliate with the organization. Communication is a two-way process with listening at least as important as reinforcement of the message, as was reviewed in Chapter 4. This means hearing employee issues and concerns, and integrating them with perspectives from customers, suppliers and shareholders. It is the glue that links together the community of individuals we call an organization. It is the current that flows as a result of the potential for connection. It provides the web of connection that links and sustains the sense of organizational community. There are many forms this communication can take, such as:

- Informal group discussions
- Informal individual discussions
- Focus groups
- Newsletters
- E-mail
- Individual interviews
- Surveys

Communication needs to be frequent, two-way and consistent so that messages sent by the organization are reinforced, and messages sent by individuals are consolidated into general themes as well as being received individually. Monitoring the impact of communications, and the various channels used, provides a basis for refining the approach. The benefit that accrues from attention to this process is the ability to maintain alignment of the organization's actions with both business needs and the needs of the employee population. Communication is important because it creates a framework within which the relationship between the organization and the individual can flourish. It creates a framework of mutual connection and exchange. It helps ensure that expectations are consistent and it lays the foundation for a climate of mutual trust. It lays a foundation for the next process, building a supportive environment.

Building a supportive environment. A supportive environment exists when individuals believe that leadership recognizes and supports their particular needs. In one case this may mean sponsoring a person in continuing education, in another case it may mean providing the freedom to adjust work hours or location to meet family commitments. Aspects of a supportive environment include the following four components:

- Recognition
- Flexibility
- Policies
- Compensation

People, on leaving an organization, will sometimes say that all the recognition they needed was a simple thank you, yet it was missing. Recognition needs to be genuine, frequent, immediate and personal. It is often infrequent, late and impersonal. Flexibility means stepping outside the one-size-fits-all mold. It may mean flexibility in time, in location or in appearance. Rounding out the key aspects of a supportive environment are policies that enhance rather than limit options for individuals, and compensation that is competitive. All of these elements are a direct result of leadership behaviors that recognize the need for both short- and long-term investments in people. Short term is compensation for services rendered; long term is investment for future value creation. The former is driven more by getting and the latter more by giving. Giving promises much greater and deeper impact, but it requires a higher level of trust and likely suspension of immediate gratification. At its core this means creating an environment that supports alignment of individual aspirations with organizational needs. The case study in Chapter 7 shows how increasing this alignment provides tangible financial benefits to the organization. An important aspect of this alignment is developing organizational clarity about workforce dynamics through analysis. This is the next key process.

Understanding of workforce dynamics and analysis. Workforce dynamics means the structure and composition of the workforce as it evolves over time. For example, changes in the composition of the workforce with regard to diversity, employment status (permanent or contract), or needed skills. In exploring workforce dynamics it is necessary to look back in time to establish a historical frame of reference, and forward in time to build predictive and prescriptive views. This is an area where leadership and HR can craft a clear view of the future and in so doing create a sound basis for trust. While some elements that affect workforce dynamics are outside the control of leadership, such as changing demographics of the population and changing generational perspectives, most are within leadership's control. For example, choices made about the composition and segmentation of the workforce, about policies and practices that either encourage or inhibit diverse views, and about resources committed to understanding and creating a chosen workforce trajectory.

Elements that are part of an analysis of workforce dynamics include the following:

- Workforce characterization (Chapter 2) to achieve organizational objectives
- Future size of the workforce to meet business objectives
- Attrition and hiring rates
- Promotion and transfer rates
- Measures of diversity
- Changing tenure profile of the organization
- Evolving age profile
- Evolving competency needs in the organization
- Changing skill sets of the employee population
- Changing requirements due to partnerships, mergers or acquisitions
- Changing geographic needs

Analysis of workforce dynamics requires a combination of qualitative and quantitative approaches, of descriptive, predictive and prescriptive tools. Such tools provide structure and processes to drive decisions and resource commitments. Competitive strength and long-term survival will be supported by the capability to model and explore the likely consequences of decisions that affect the organization's primary asset, its workforce. The modeling tools described in Chapter 6 can contribute to this analysis. Analysis of workforce dynamics needs to address both the overall workforce and segments within it.

The benefits of the analysis of workforce dynamics are as follows:

- Builds clarity about future workforce needs
- Strengthens capability to drive to organizational goals
- Enhances ability to quickly anticipate needed changes, likely before competitors
- Provides a basis to optimize resource commitments.

This is a fledgling area still needing methods and systems. The frequency and depth of analysis depend on the characteristics of the sector within which each organization operates. For example, in a rapidly evolving high-technology sector, quarterly updates, punctuated by additional analysis when signals suggest major shifts, may be appropriate. In an area such as professional services, where the entire business process for value creation is driven by the people component, frequent, comprehensive and deep analyses are likely appropriate. In a more established sector, with high capital rather than people intensity, the frequency of analysis may be reduced and the depth of analysis more circumspect. Most important is the recognition that analyzing the trajectory of the workforce is an important endeavor that contributes to the fundamental success of the organization.

Measurement of workforce contributions. Going hand in hand with analysis of workforce dynamics is the measurement of workforce contributions. Such measurement provides the core information needed to strengthen performance over time. Key to effective measurement is defining elements that link progress toward organizational objectives to measures of effectiveness and efficiency of the workforce. In the past, measures important to the organization's leaders and those in the HR community have sometimes differed. Leaders are concerned with financial performance; HR professionals have sometimes focused on activity levels. In moving forward it will be important to close this gap. For example, when speaking with HR groups, I frequently find that only about 10–30% of HR teams determine the in-depth financial impact of attrition. Yet CEOs are asking HR for a financial rationale for investing resources in workforce development. It will be important for HR to speak the same financial language as organizational leaders when engaging in conversations about workforce development.

There are many potential metrics related to workforce processes as described by Becker, Huselid and Ulrich (2001). They use a Balanced Scorecard method to establish overall objectives that lead to a menu from which metrics can be selected. An overarching challenge is that of adopting measures that link the effectiveness of the workforce to financial impact. Traditional financial measures are based on arbitrary time periods (usually a fiscal or calendar year), address past performance, and are focused on tangible assets, for example, return on investment. The value contribution of the workforce on the other hand is not bounded in time, and it is an intangible asset that will deliver its primary value in the future. This is a dilemma when trying to use conventional financial measures. One approach is to use a simple cascading measurement system. Here is an example showing key value adders and subtractors:

	Example Value Adders	Example Value Subtractors
Overall organization performance	Net present value of future revenues	Net present value of future costs
Workforce effectiveness and efficiency	Revenue per employee Income per employee	Value subtraction due to attrition Absentee costs per employee
Workforce processes	New hire tenure Interview acceptance rate	Number of grievances Employee losses in first year
Workforce resource investment	HR investment per employee Development per employee Integration/orientation per employee	Severance payments per employee Litigation costs per employee

The measurement flow begins with the overall organization, moves to the contribution of the workforce, continues with those workforce processes that enable this contribution and finishes with the effectiveness of resources invested to drive these processes. The benefits of introducing a measurement system that incorporates the workforce as a central element are as follows:

• Tightly links organizational drivers and workforce direction
• Aligns HR goals with organizational leadership goals
• Recognizes the key role of the workforce in creating value
• Provides a basis for resource allocation
• Provides an early warning of potential problems
• Provides a basis for predictive approaches that optimize long-term performance.

Prediction of evolving needs. The last point leads to the sixth and final process, namely prediction of evolving needs. In the ever-changing organizational world prediction of a most likely external future is fraught with uncertainty. However, it is possible to examine the implications of alternative futures. This paves the way for contingency planning and provides a sound basis for resource decisions. It also encourages a search for leading indicators that can help identify early, major shifts that signal the need for course changes. Prediction of possible alternative futures includes both quantitative and qualitative aspects. An example of the quantitative aspect is the modeling of future hiring needs summarized in Chapter 6. An example of the qualitative aspect is a description of the impact of adopting various workforce segmentation policies. HR can play a pivotal role in this process by identifying key workforce-related elements to incorporate in predictions, and sponsoring analyses that provide organizational leaders with scenarios that illustrate a range of future alternatives and their consequences.

ROLES

Having examined processes that impact the workforce, the next focus is on the roles of leaders and HR as they influence affiliation. Traditional management approaches have emphasized variants on the "plan, execute, monitor and control" theme. While elements of these themes remain relevant, the emphasis on hierarchy and structure does not meet the needs of the organization of the future. Just as a monarchy lost its relevance in the political arena for an educated and vibrant populace, so the command-and-control model is losing relevance for the workforce of the post-information society. Instead a different set of leadership and HR roles draws on concepts of servant leadership (for example DePree 1992). These roles are as follows:

- Guide
- Mentor
- Coach
- Conductor
- Artist
- Visionary
- Entrepreneur
- Innovator
- General
- Change Agent
- Connector

As an organization evolves the relative importance of these roles will shift. For example the Innovator is crucial in the early stages of an organization's life cycle, the General is important in more mature stages, and the Visionary is important at all stages. Indeed it is unlikely that any one individual will be equally effective in all areas. However, an effective leadership team will include a broad range of these skills and harness them to the needs of the organization at each point in time. This is an area where effective coaching can develop dormant skills. Let us examine each role in more depth.

Guide. Whole Foods Market Inc. has taken a concept of providing nourishing, healthy food and built a successful and growing business. This was done while respecting the value of the workforce. Whole Foods Market is one of the *Fortune* Top 100 best companies to work for in the United States. Whole Foods Market has an internal policy that the compensation of any officer in the organization is limited to fourteen times the average full-time salary of all team members (employees); amounts in excess can be deferred. No mega-salary for the CEO here, simply a level of compensation linked to others in the organization. This is a powerful values statement that shows the regard the leadership of this organization feels for its employees. It is an example of the organization's leaders and HR providing strong guidance about the kind of organization they are creating and the behaviors they encourage within the organization. Business bestseller lists have been replete with stories of CEOs who have enhanced their own egos and lined their own pocketbooks. Whole Foods Market is a telling testament to the principles of servant leadership. Their leaders act as guides not only for their own organization but also for all of us.

Mentor. I remember beginning my first position responsible for a new business area. This was in a competitive industry sector where the fledgling business was significantly smaller than its competition. On my first day in the new position my boss sat me down in front of his desk and pointed to a small rock on the corner of the desk. On that rock was an inscription along the lines of: "The customer is always right." There were many occasions over the next three years, as the business grew and flourished, when we grappled with the challenges of meeting customer needs. While there were many customer compliments, there were other times when customers were frustrated or angry and they weren't reticent. I never forgot the words on that stone. Due to the skills and commitment of others the business flourished, and it did so while respecting customers and employees. My boss had provided a simple and important example of being a mentor to a rookie. It was an invaluable lesson.

Scott Adams, the creator of "Dilbert," tells a story of his early days seeking a publisher for his work (Dilbert Zone: www.unitedmedia.com).

At that time he sent a sample of his work to Jack Cassady, the cartoonist host of a PBS television program called *Funny Business*, to ask advice about how to enter the profession. He received a complimentary letter back with details about how to proceed, encouragement to seek a publisher and advice not to be discouraged by the rejection he might receive. Buoyed by this, Adams recounts how he submitted his best cartoons to *Playboy* and *The New Yorker* only to receive cold rejections. He put away his materials at this point and decided to forget about cartooning. About a year and a half later, a letter appeared from Jack Cassady unexpectedly. In it Cassady inquired about Adams' progress and again encouraged him to press forward. Scott Adams recounts how this kind word touched him, since he hadn't even replied to the first letter. He pulled his materials out of storage and prepared samples of what would later become "Dilbert" and submitted his work again. It was accepted and "Dilbert" was born, now to be read by millions. Jack Cassady's actions were selfless here. He had nothing to gain from Adams' support, was a busy man, and yet found time to support a struggling new artist. He demonstrated the selfless act of mentoring at its best, and as a result helped bring a new talent to the world. This one act of kindness has created a ripple effect from which many benefit today. All benefit from the mentoring relationship. Imagine the power that could be harnessed in an environment where mentoring is as natural as breathing, for mentoring is born in us and somehow our organizational structures can cause it to be lost or hidden.

Coach. Closely aligned with the role of mentor is that of coach. The distinction is in the frequency and focus of the relationship. While a mentor is focused on being a resource as needed, a coach is an active supporter who is consulted regularly. As coaches, leaders and HR are there to encourage, exhort and help employees set goals that cause them to reach new levels of performance. I recall an incident from my teenage years. I had been volunteered as a member of a swimming team for an intramural event in the English equivalent of an American high school. Swimming was not my forte; in fact I was hopeless at it but had to participate. The event took place on a Saturday night in a pool with quite a few cheering (and jeering) spectators. It came to my event. Four of us were competing. It involved four laps of the pool and predictably by the end I was in last place, a full half-length behind the third-placed participant. I finally arrived at the finish point, too exhausted to even pull myself out of the pool. I was expecting a searing criticism, for that was common in that school. Then something unusual happened. The team coach, an older boy, helped pull me out of the water. He looked at me and said: "Well done, we really appreciate your efforts. Thank you." I was too shocked by these few words of kindness to say anything, but they have remained with me for more than thirty-five years. I have forgotten the many small slights and put-downs, those acts that diminish rather than elevate. But I have not forgotten the brave words of that coach.

A coaching relationship can involve elements of counseling, performance development and business consulting, with the mix shifting according to the needs of the moment. Coaching flourishes in an environment that supports individual development and decision making. For example, the apocryphal statements in the Nordstrom employee handbook: Rule No. 1: Use your best judgment in all situations. There will be no additional rules (Tushman 1993). These statements encourage the expression of individual initiative. Implicit in the role of the coach is a concern for the development of the individual, occurring in the context of organizational needs. So the coach is a source of wisdom and insight, a listener and most of all a developer of human potential. The oil that helps the gears connect smoothly. It is a role that can be adopted at any level in the organization and it is an ennobling experience for both coach and coachee.

Conductor. The conductor of an orchestra might seem like an unlikely analogy for the organizational leader or HR. After all an orchestra is tightly scripted, following a predetermined path. However, there are many similarities. The role requires the execution of complex skills that include deep functional knowledge of the creative process needed to bring music to life. The conductor must couple this functional knowledge with the ability to bring consensus to a group of creative and independent individuals. The conductor must know how to follow the script or plan he or she has been given, and how to create unique expressions from this script. The conductor has a discriminating audience that expects technical virtuosity and delivery that meet predetermined commitments. The conductor is a public figure who is an active proponent of the works of the orchestra, and who must create in such a way that the orchestra generates income to support itself. All of these aspects have parallels in the organizational world and the world of the workforce. Workforce conducting is just as creative and complex, with outcomes that can enhance organizations and communities just as the music from the orchestra enriches. An example from the corporate world is that of Microsoft and Bill Gates, where the introduction of succeeding generations of software is a series of carefully orchestrated scripts that reach millions.

Artist. Closely related to the Conductor is the Artist. The Artist is steeped in the creative process, using a given medium to generate a new vision and, in so doing, offer insights and perspectives on beauty that were previously hidden. The work of the Artist is bounded only by his or her imagination and proficiency. It comes to life in the response evoked in those receiving the gift of the Artist's creation. Likewise leadership and HR in an organization create a work of art from the medium of the workforce, with much beauty in the complexity and dynamics this represents. A business example that, both in a physical and in a metaphorical sense, demonstrates this is Apple Computer. Even the design of its products transcends a purely functional physical form, to delight customers with innovation in style. Functional performance has also reflected constant striving for new, creative approaches that expand the boundaries of prior experience and require the development of novel software and hardware. Here we see the convergence of business form and function in an artistic expression that generates an emotional response both from customers and from employees. Such artistic expression is an important part of the early creative stages of a new organization, and an established organization that views innovation and flare as core business processes.

Visionary. Tushman (1993) observed that "In real time visionaries and lunatics look the same." The visionary's novel perspective may offer only a fleeting, or worse, a nonexistent path forward. But he or she may also offer entirely new, revolutionary, fruitful landscapes. A visionary stance, that transcends the daily strife and toil, is essential to leadership and HR to engage and energize the workforce. An example is Southwest Airlines. Southwest repeatedly takes a distinctive and different position. This is evident in its operational activities, where an emphasis on efficiency and providing basics well results in rapid aircraft turnaround, low fares and lively flights. However, this approach extends beyond the operational to the organization's relationship with employees. In the aftermath of the September 11, 2001 terrorist incidents in New York, when the airline industry was reeling, many airlines were making deep cuts in the employee ranks. Not Southwest; here the emphasis was on strengthening the relationship with employees, ensuring continuity of employment, recognizing the possibility of penalizing short-term earnings, knowing the benefit of engendering longer-term employee commitment. Many would cite the visionary stance taken by Southwest's management in their business and operational practices. And they do represent impressive accomplishments. However, I suggest that the stance taken with their workforce is equally visionary, requiring organizational courage and commitment.

Entrepreneur. It might seem that the hallways of a large oil company are an unlikely place to find an example of entrepreneurial leadership. However, this example demonstrates that entrepreneurial leadership is by no means limited to the high-tech arena. Most of us come into contact with polyester daily. It could be through the fibers in clothing or in furnishings; it could be soft-drink bottles. Polyester is part of daily life, helping clothe people, insulate houses, and package food and supplies. In the mid-1950s polyester was made from a raw material that was produced by a complex, multi-step chemical process. At that time, enterprising scientists working for an organization known as the Scientific Design Company discovered a new, simpler and more cost-effective process to make a different raw material and significantly lower the cost of making polyester. At that same time, Amoco Corporation was in the process of founding a chemical company, and was able to produce from its refineries a chemical that could form the starting point for the new synthesis route to polyester.

By serendipity a chemist from Amoco met a scientist from the Scientific Design Company at a social event and together they understood the potential for the new Scientific Design discovery. Amoco's leadership, upon learning of this opportunity, immediately recognized its commercial value and purchased the rights to the technology. At this point there were still many technical hurdles to be overcome, related to the intricacies of full-scale, commercial production and securing needed purity. Nevertheless, Amoco's leadership made the investment in the technology purchase, followed by major investments in research, and in commercial facilities. At each stage there was significant technical risk of failure. Today this is a multibillion-dollar business for the organization (it is now part of British Petroleum by acquisition). The organization is now the world leader in the production of the key intermediate for making polyester. There are manufacturing plants at many locations around the world based on this technology. The entrepreneurial leadership of those pioneers led to the foundation of a company, and ripples from it benefit many of us in our daily lives today. The entrepreneurial role of the leader and HR is vital to the continued reinvention of organizations as environments and opportunities change.

Innovator. Closely related to the role of Entrepreneur is the role of Innovator. The Innovator's role is to "see what everybody else has seen, and to think what nobody else has thought" (Szent-Gyorgyi in Peter 1979) and then convert it to organizational reality. The Innovator works at the edge of the envelope, exploring new boundaries and new approaches. One company has made an art of innovation. That company is 3M, where the abilities to spot new opportunities and to harness technology to realize those opportunities are core to the company's values. In relation to the workforce this means encouraging innovation in individual businesses by keeping small units, dividing operations as needed to maintain focus. 3M views the innovative effectiveness of small tightly knit teams as outweighing the diseconomies of innovation that can arise with large scale.

An example of the Innovator role in the development and application of technology is the commercialization of xerography. The ubiquitous copy machine began as a brainchild of Chester Carlson, who recognized how to harness the natural forces of static electricity into a practical application. The leaders in the field of conventional photography rejected the idea as impractical. That rejection led to the formation of a new company, the Haloid Company, which later became the Xerox Corporation and founded a multibillion-dollar industry. As the wheel turns full circle, leaders of the Xerox Corporation now struggle to maintain the innovative spark that characterized its foundation. The role of Innovator is vital to sustaining the life spark and growth of organizations.

General. These innovative, entrepreneurial roles require structure and process to be effective. This is the role of the General. Here the focus is on organizational efficiency, on establishing those processes and systems that allow the different parts of the organization to function effectively together. An example of this is General Electric, a behemoth in organizational terms that has continued to grow and prosper. It operates under strong central guidelines, requiring individual units to be first- or second-ranked competitors in their sectors. Strict financial controls and sophisticated planning and control methodologies guide performance.

Change Agent. In a stable world the General can reign supreme seeking ever-greater efficiencies. However, the world is one of surprises. They can take the form of technology advances that can rapidly make an existing product obsolete, such as the compact disc replacing the record. They can take the form of major social change, such as the entry of women into the workforce from the 1950s through the 1980s in the United States. Changes can take the form of shifts in the economy such as the changes in GDP growth rates as we saw in Chapter 6, or shifts in political perspective such as the U.S. government's changed position in the Microsoft antitrust case. In this shifting environment the role of leaders and HR as organizational change agents is critical. An example is Sun Microsystems, where the ability to navigate the rapidly changing worlds of networking and the Internet enabled the organization to remain a leader. Cisco Systems, for many years an icon of such success, is experiencing the challenges of navigating through the rapids of change, and what this means for the workforce.

Connector. I came across an interesting example recently of an organization that ran a number of call centers. In call centers, employee attrition is typically high, to the point that it is easy to assume such attrition is inevitable. In this organization high attrition was indeed the norm. However, one of the call centers had a different profile with attrition at a much lower level. Leadership wondered why this was so and talked to the supervisor of this one call center. On being asked about what she did, her response was that she tried to find something about each new employee on a personal level she could connect with. With one person it might be their children, with another a favorite hobby. It didn't matter, just that she could connect with that employee on a personal level. Then she made a point of talking with that person regularly and asking about their personal area of interest. This single investment of her time and interest led to a dramatic reduction in attrition. This behavior was almost certainly coupled with other equally supportive practices. It clearly demonstrates the important role of connecting for organizational leaders and HR.

It might seem that fulfilling these roles well is an overwhelming challenge. Indeed it is a lot to ask of any one individual. However, it is a practical objective for a leadership team. A first step is to define the key leadership and HR roles needed to support each segment of the workforce. This can begin with the workforce segmentation approach identified in Chapter 2. Based on such an analysis, the most critical leadership and HR roles can be identified and prioritized. The capabilities of the leadership and HR teams can then be harnessed to address these roles. This involves understanding the strengths and aspirations of each person on the leadership teams, and then providing each person with development support for the roles that are a natural fit. This support may take the form of coaching, it may take the form of educational experiences or it may take the form of on-the-job experiences. Regardless, it means recognizing the importance of developing individuals who can effectively execute the needed leadership roles. It also means developing a description of expert execution in each role and a means for measuring progress against such an ideal. Here HR plays a pivotal role in creating definitions of such role behavior and the tools to continually refine the level of execution. In doing this, HR balances the needs of the organization and the needs of the individuals within it.

BARRIERS AND BEHAVIORS

Why is it difficult to excel in these roles? What are some of the barriers that prevent successful development and performance? They can be grouped into three categories:

- Social and environmental barriers
  - Changing economic circumstances that limit options
  - Changing market conditions that constrain organizational strategy
  - Unexpected major events
  - Social pressures to conform to different value systems
  - Short-term expectations of the financial community or other major owners/stakeholders
- Organizational system barriers
  - Policies and practices that limit flexibility
  - Political agendas that derail honorable intentions
  - Lack of support for individual development
  - Inappropriate organizational strategies
  - Lack of leader support
- Individual barriers
  - Lack of knowledge about role behaviors
  - Fear of change or unwillingness to change
  - Lack of motivated skills
  - Lack of self-knowledge
  - Overconfidence or lack of confidence

At first this may appear to be a daunting list with much beyond individual control. However, there are approaches that can help overcome these barriers. While it is true that external events may instantly redefine the operating environment, they do not define each person's response to it. That response is individually determined. For example, a reason often cited for corporate behavior is that investors expect continuing short-term gains with a result that investment in more risky, new endeavors is constrained. Those seeking funding for such ventures have the option to redefine their environment by seeking alternative sources of funding. The venture capital market developed to accommodate nontraditional risk/return profiles and it offers funding for high-risk/high-return opportunities.

In the organizational area there can be cultural and political considerations that constrain behavior in the roles described earlier. For example, if an organization does not support individual development it may seem like a Herculean task to adopt progressive development practices that enable leaders to excel in their role behaviors. Faced with this situation individual leaders have the choice to move the system from within, or to leave for a better organizational fit. Perhaps the most difficult area is that of individual, internal barriers because they may not be easy to identify and therefore to address. Here the perspective of a coach or mentor is invaluable to help overcome such barriers.

Understanding role requirements and barriers that may need to be overcome leads to identification of needed behaviors. Here are examples of behaviors that will be needed by leaders and HR professionals in the future. They are as follows:

- Self-understanding
- Vulnerability
- Listening
- Communicating
- Synthesizing
- Connecting

Self-understanding. This is a rare and precious gift for through the lens of self-understanding we can see ourselves clearly and be present for others. Isabel Briggs Myers, the daughter of the originator of the Myers-Briggs Type Indicator, an instrument that illuminates personality preferences, sometimes observed with pleasure the response from a client on receiving feedback about their personality preferences: "What a relief to find out that it is all right to be me!" (Myers and Myers 1995, xiv). And yet it is hard to give that affirmation to ourselves. Building knowledge of who we are is necessary to fulfill our potential and help others fulfill theirs. Here is Martha Graham (Great Quotations: www.cyber -nation.com), founder of the well-known dance company:

There is a vitality, a life force, an energy, a quickening that is translated through you into action. And because there is only one of you in all of time, this expression is unique. And if you block it, it will never exist through any other medium, and be lost. The world will not have it. It is not your business to determine how good it is, nor how it compares with other expressions. It is your business to keep it yours clearly and directly, to keep the channel open.

Self-knowledge is evident in the writing of DePree (1992), who is at the same time humble and confident, establishing values based on a clear sense of self-knowledge that also encourages others. Creating such an anchor in terms of self-knowledge is especially important in a changing organizational world, such as the high-tech arena. The promise of wealth and new frontiers drew many people. It proved to be a hollow promise for many, as in the early California Gold Rush days. Strong self-knowledge is needed to navigate such turbulent times and to repeatedly make decisions about individual life choices and organizational direction that were not available a generation ago.

Vulnerability. This might seem like an odd characteristic to include in a list of leadership behaviors. After all, isn't the leader's role to be the font of all wisdom with a clear, unquestioning view of the future? I well remember one person who was in an area I was responsible for, coming to me one day several years ago with some words of wisdom. We were struggling with difficult decisions and the path ahead was far from clear. His words were: "It's okay, we know that you don't have all the answers, we are in this together." It allowed us to talk in depth about our perspectives and uncover possibilities that otherwise would have been lost. Shying away from showing vulnerability, I had closed doors that needed to remain open. It is partly through the expression of vulnerability that our humanity shines through. It is in this expression that trust can be built. Such trust opens the door to the learning that builds effectiveness in the leadership and HR roles we examined earlier.

Listening. It is frequently clear in exit interviews that conversations took place between concerned employees and their managers but no listening occurred. Listening means understanding the entire message that is being transmitted, the verbal and nonverbal, the words, the intonations and the subtleties underneath the words. It is a skill that can be developed (Bolton 1986) just like functional skills. Techniques such as summarizing and paraphrasing are part of this skill. Listening is not easy to put into practice so there are few examples of effective listening. There are many potential inhibitors, for example anxiety or fear. At its high point listening enables the listener to put herself or himself in the shoes of the other person and walk with them, understanding their concerns and issues from their perspective. This rare and beautiful gift is one of the greatest we can give to those around us.

There is a simple, searing description of an event that illustrates the value of listening. In this narrative, Dobson (1994) describes an experience when, as a young man, he was riding a train in Tokyo. He was trained in aikido and itching to use this training, when suddenly a drunk boarded the train. The drunk began accosting and insulting passengers and Dobson readied himself to kick the drunk off the train, baiting him and eagerly anticipating a fight. Dobson describes how, unexpectedly in a small, joyous and insistent voice, an elderly fellow passenger said to the drunk: "Hey. C'mere and talk with me." He describes how the drunk turned eyeing a potential new victim, ready to attack. At this point the elderly passenger told the drunk of his liking of sake and he asked the drunk about his life. Slowly the drunk began to tell the elderly passenger his sad life story. How he had no wife, no home, no clothes and no money and he began to cry. Terry Dobson, watching this unfold, experienced a deep and profound realization of the humanity and compassion in the elderly passenger. He realized how the power of listening and compassion can eclipse the power of aggression.

Communicating. This is a two-way process that begins with listening and continues with providing information. Given the importance of defining and reinforcing overall direction, communicating becomes a critical leadership and HR trait. People need to know where the course is set and why. They need to know when changes are initiated and why, and when change is a response to outside events, what the response will be and why. Communication can occur through many media but whatever form it takes it must be respectful of the listener. It must recognize diverse perspectives and be timely, concise, accurate and personal. This is not easy given the time demands placed on leaders and HR. Again there are specific learned components of this skill that leaders and HR can acquire.

It might seem that analysis, or the ability to break down a situation into constituent parts is a critical leadership behavior, and indeed it is an important skill for a leader. However, there is another behavior, *Synthesizing*, that is the ability to connect and see patterns, that is even more critical. In the evolving world it confers the ability to extract useful information from overwhelming data. A major challenge is not to create yet more discrete bits of information; rather it is to make sense of the current avalanche of bits. With the growing ability to access vast arrays of information electronically, the challenge becomes one of sifting through this maelstrom for meaningful signals. It is here that the skill of Synthesizing is critically important, so that the signals representing sustained change can be separated from those that represent short-term perturbations. From this knowledge appropriate action is born. Synthesizing is a leadership and HR trait that helps build the bridge from organizational needs to workforce needs. It provides clarity about overall and workforce direction.

Going hand in hand with the role of Connector is the behavior of *Connecting*. This is one component of an area that has come to be known as social capital (Adler and Kwon 2002; Humax: www.humaxnetworks .com). Social capital refers to the interconnections and networks that exist for individuals, and that exist in organizations and communities. It is created through connecting processes that are vital to the health and prosperity of communities, whether at the organizational, local or national level. Effective Connecting enables the flow of information and the Synthesizing that follows from it. Connecting enriches communications and strengthens the sense of community that builds in an organization. It is an important leadership and HR skill.

STAGES IN EMPLOYEE ENGAGEMENT

We have examined processes, roles and behaviors that are important for leaders and HR to build strength and connection with the workforce. There is a complementary perspective, namely the engagement cycle for a person joining an organization, integrating, contributing and then leaving. This will now be the focus, exploring the responsibilities of leadership and HR in four stages. The four stages are:

- Selection
- Integration
- Development
- Transition

The sense of affiliation, of connection, begins at the selection process. It establishes the nature and tone of the relationship. Leaders and HR are responsible for establishing a process that provides clarity about organizational needs to potential candidates and ensures open communication with individuals. With this in place leaders, HR and the individual can each assess the likelihood of establishing a mutually beneficial relationship. With greater employee scarcity in the future, increasingly the determining factor in the hiring process will be the individual's decision to join an organization or not. The financial consequences of poor hiring decisions are substantial. One HR manager described a recent situation where a high-level position was filled. The new person was recruited and relocated. Within three months the organization determined this was not a good fit and let the person go. At this point the organization had incurred moving costs of more than $50,000, obligations to compensate the person for the loss of their prior job and an obligation to pay return moving costs. Productivity suffered throughout the process. Moreover, the individual's life and family were greatly disrupted. This is the worst case, namely filling a position with the wrong person. The components of an effective selection process are as follows:

- Characterize the needed relationship
- Define needed success factors
- Conduct the interview process
- Build connection
- Communicate organizational value
- Use an effective decision-making process
- Define the future relationship.

The process begins with a clear definition of the type of relationship sought. Is it extended or transactional? Is the organization seeking to tailor the opportunity to the individual or is it a take-it-or-leave-it proposition? Once the nature of the relationship is defined, it can be communicated to potential candidates so there is alignment of expectations.

The second step is defining key success factors for the position, taking into account the culture and needs of the position. For example, individual characteristics needed to succeed in the same software developer position would likely look quite different in a consensus-based (Hewlett-Packard) vs. a more confrontational culture (Oracle). Once success factors are defined then the interview process can begin building on the concept of hiring for fit and training for skill. Much has been written on the concepts of behavioral interviewing (for example Janz, Hellervik and Gilmore 1986). This is built on the precept that past behavior is the best predictor of future performance. This technique provides a solid foundation for gathering information. The interviewing team's ability to create a sense of connection throughout establishes the candidate's impression of the organization, as this is based on the conduct of the interview. Regardless of the outcome, it is important to create a positive experience and communicate the value of the organization to the individual. There are many components to this, ranging from compensation and benefits, support for individual development, community support, and features that are unique to a given organization. Each potential recruit is an ambassador and possible future hire if they don't join on this occasion. If the individual joins the organization then the next major stage is that of integration.

This is a crucial step in building connection. There are frequently missteps in this area. In one case, in the division of one of the world's major high-tech organizations, people completed a complex, rigorous interview process, only to arrive on their first day unannounced and unexpected. In another organization new hires were sometimes turned away on their first day.

A senior HR manager at a leading healthcare organization recounts the converse of this. Nurses were leaving at an alarming rate and the HR team identified inadequate integration/orientation as an important reason. Over the objections of management due to the costs involved, HR extended the orientation/integration process from one week to six weeks for two pilot groups. The attrition rate for the two pilot groups was one half the attrition rate for the general population. The financial benefits of this far outweighed the costs of the additional orientation/integration time. For many people coming straight out of college there is a major loss of community. It is important to recreate this sense of community quickly for new college hires. Other problems may exist at higher levels in the organization where attrition of new entrants is often high. Support is needed to connect people into the organization. An effective integration process includes the following perspectives and components:

- Begins as soon as the hiring decision is made
- Provides integration support for the first year of employment
- Includes a mentoring system connecting those with experience with new hires
- Coaches hiring managers in important interpersonal skills such as listening and provides incentives for the practice of these skills
- Creates a structured integration process for the first month for each position; for example, at DBM this is known as "thrive in twenty-five" (days)
- Provides paced training in essential skill areas
- Ensures that practical resources such as a computer, space, and a telephone are available on the first day
- Provides an opportunity for new hires to meet with upper management in the first three months
- Creates social gatherings that support building a sense of community.

Perhaps most critical is simply recognizing the importance of this stage including leadership spending time with people new to the organization. HR plays a key role in building integration processes and in educating existing employees about their roles.

After integration comes development. Chapter 4 highlighted employees' concerns in the area of career development. Employee development is an Achilles' heel for many organizations. Leadership plays a vital role in providing the resources that are required for effective development systems. There are wonderful tools available today that include virtual elements, workshops, and individual career counseling. These tools need to be woven into the organizational fabric for they help to secure the ongoing affiliation of employees. HR has a key role in structuring development processes and identifying resources to provide needed support. Providing this support also eases the pain of transition, the final of the four stages.

Transitions out of the organization will occur in the fluid environment of the future. They are less traumatic for individuals and less disruptive for organizations when people have marketable skills and are in control of their destiny. The organization's role is to provide a framework within which ongoing development can occur and to provide support in transition. Indeed there is considerable merit in building transition support into the initial employment agreement so that people know the support they will receive if business conditions necessitate their departure. Leadership is responsible for defining policies for transition support with HR accessing the resources in a timely manner to ensure effective delivery of this support.

By addressing the processes outlined in this chapter, adopting the roles and behaviors described, and applying these to the steps of employee engagement, leaders and HR will make a major contribution to securing the commitment and continuity of their workforce.

— 9 —

Bridging from the Organization of Today to the Organization of the Future

Elting Morison, who was a historian of technology at M.I.T., tells some fascinating stories about the challenge of change in his book *Men, Machines and Modern Times* (Morison, 1966). They are directly relevant to the organizational challenges we face in adapting to the future environment and the needs of the emerging workforce. Workforce change, addressing as it does core values in the relationship between individuals and organizations, is closer to the revolutionary end of Tushman's (1993) change scale that begins with evolutionary processes. This chapter explores the meaning of workforce change in bridging from the organization of today to the organization of the future. It begins with examples of the difficulty of implementing organizational change in general and then addresses barriers, in the form of myths, to changing employee affiliation. A story about the organization of the future follows this. It provides a foundation for examining the implications for leaders and HR of the emerging work world and the implications regarding processes, roles and stages of employee engagement. The chapter concludes with a discussion of practical steps for moving forward and the potential benefits.

THE CHALLENGE OF ORGANIZATIONAL CHANGE

Let us examine the ease of responding to, or creating change within an organization using two of Morison's cases as examples.

The first example concerns the use of armaments in the Second World War. In the early part of the war, when armaments were in short supply, the British were using a particular piece of field artillery towed behind trucks. This field gun was handed down from the Boer War many years earlier. There was a consensus at the beginning of the Second World War that the speed of fire could be increased, so a time and motion expert was called in. He filmed the firing sequence. On reviewing the film he was puzzled by a three-second segment when two members of the gun crew stopped all activity and stood to attention. Baffled by this he asked an experienced colonel of artillery about the reason for this behavior. The colonel looked at the film, and after a few moments' reflection said: "Ah. I have it. They are holding the horses." Here we see the difficulty of letting go of institutionalized habits that are no longer relevant. A translation to today might be policies that limit internal movement in an organization.

Now let us look at Morison's second example that relates to adoption of innovation. This is another military example, in this case from the end of the nineteenth century. It concerns the adoption of a technique known as continuous-aim firing. At the end of the nineteenth century firing from a ship was a haphazard process. The ship moved with the motion of the sea so the gun aimer had to guess when to fire during the ship's roll. Telescopic sights on guns were rare and ineffective. They were fixed to the barrel and would recoil into the gunner's eye should he choose to look through it before firing. The rapidity of fire was controlled by the time of the ship's roll and the accuracy limited by the gunner's ability to estimate the optimum firing point.

A solution to this problem was first identified by an English officer, Sir Percy Scott, when captain of the HMS *Scylla* in 1898. Scott had been pondering the challenge of improving gunnery for several years. One rough day he was walking the decks of his ship as it was engaged in target practice. He noticed that one gunner was much more accurate than the rest. The gunner did this by working the gun's elevating gear to partially accommodate the ship's roll. Scott recognized the significance of this and immediately made three changes to the guns on his ship. First he changed the gear ratio on the guns so it was easy for gunners to follow the target with the roll of the ship. Second he put the sight on a sleeve around the barrel so it did not recoil into the gunner's eye. Third he equipped the guns with a rifle and simulated target so the gunners could practice with the new techniques. The result was a dramatic improvement in accuracy. Later studies showed a 3,000% improvement in accuracy. For example, five ships firing for five minutes each using the then-conventional techniques managed, at a typical range of 1,600 yards, two hits on the sails of a target vessel. Using the new technique, one gunner made fifteen hits in one minute at the same range on a much smaller target, half of them in a bull's eye fifty inches square. This is a revolutionary improvement that addresses the fundamental capability of this organization; in this case its ability to hit an enemy target.

Scott was a colorful person, somewhat of a renegade, often railing against the "inelastic intelligence of all constituted authority, especially the British Admiralty." His prior reflections on the subject of gunnery and the serendipitous events on his ship enabled Scott to weave together the threads of existing technology and create a massive leap forward. So we come to the question of how this learning was transferred to the American navy. Scott had been transferred to the China station and there met with an American junior officer, William Sims. Sims, like Scott, was a renegade who rebelled against what he considered the bureaucratic inefficiency of his own navy. Sims learned all there was to know about continuous-aim firing from Scott and demonstrated precisely the same success with his ship's gunnery capabilities.

Sure of his success Sims now set about educating his navy. He prepared and submitted thirteen reports over two years with extensive factual data that summarized the benefits of the new approach and the techniques needed to implement it. The response came in three stages. In the first stage the reports were ignored. They were simply filed away as not credible. The second stage began with Sims adopting a more strident tone in his communications and distributing his reports more broadly. This led to the navy hierarchy meeting Sims' proposals with logical, rational rebuttal. Indeed the Bureau of Ordnance mounted experiments at Washington Naval Yard that proved to their satisfaction that Sims' proposals were impossible. This is because the tests were on dry land and did not have the ship's motion to aid the gunner. This led rapidly to the third stage, that of name-calling. Increasingly acrimonious exchanges followed. Sims, a lieutenant, then took the extraordinary step of writing to the president of the United States, Theodore Roosevelt, to inform him of these remarkable new techniques that were being ignored by the navy. Roosevelt brought Sims back from China in 1902 and installed him as Inspector of Target Practice. He stayed in this post for the remaining six years of the administration, after which he was universally acknowledged as "the man who taught us how to shoot."

This example raises the question as to why there was such resistance to a demonstrably major improvement that addressed the fundamental purpose of the organization. Morison identifies reasons. First are those more on the surface: an obscure junior officer proposed the idea; it challenged the approaches developed earlier by those in command; and improvements weren't needed. The Spanish-American War was recently won without these new techniques, even if only 121 out of 9,500 shots from other than close range found their mark. Morison goes on to explore a more fundamental issue. He proposes that the resistance resulted from the challenge these new approaches posed to the social structure of the navy, for example they immediately elevated the importance of the gunnery officer. He also identifies a central factor in this resistance. Namely the identification of those people opposing change, and to a lesser extent those people for change, with a limited purpose that is only a subset of the overall organization's goal. For example this limited identification may be to an existing narrow social structure; to a technology product (the sight) without regard for its application; or to the act of rebellion. It raises a question, posed by Morison, whether an organization should undertake reform itself, or whether it must seek guidance from the outside. Morison goes on to suggest that two possible means to offset these limiting behaviors are first to enlarge the sphere of identification from a part to the whole, and second to consider identification with the processes of adaptation and change rather than the product of this change. This means embracing the opportunities that unfold from new perspectives and their impact on our systems.

What is the relevance of experiences in military organizations 50 to more than 100 years ago to the situation in organizations today? Both of these examples are about social systems, and that is precisely the arena of today's organizational world. While the details of the changing world today are different, the barriers to change are just as real as in the examples. In the Scott/Sims case the innovation survived due to the dogged persistence of Sims. We might ask how many equally daring ideas surface in organizations only to disappear from view, suppressed within organizations that inoculate themselves against change. By identifying with the part rather than the whole we compromise the growth and success of our organizations. Some examples of this related to the workforce are:

- Parochial behavior that restricts development of employees by limiting internal movement
- Unwillingness to invest in employee development
- Limiting the decision-making capability of employees
- Failing to identify and capitalize on workforce partnership options

- Unwillingness to embrace technology tools to aid in workforce development
- Leadership insisting on rigid command-and-control hierarchies.

BARRIERS AND MYTHS

The challenge and opportunity is first to recognize those areas where the partial view limits organizational capability. Then it is possible to expand horizons and mobilize resources to address the barriers. One example of barriers to change relates to myths that surround employee affiliation. Let us look at six of these.

- It's all about money.
- What's the big deal, we'll just hire some people to replace those who leave.
- In this world of constant job hopping we can't impact people losses.
- It's somebody else's problem.
- Once they're gone, they're gone.
- With our name people will just come and stay.

It's all about money. As we saw in Chapter 4, in-depth studies of the reasons people consider leaving show compensation fourth on the list. Compensation is not irrelevant. However, it is a necessary but not sufficient condition for strong affiliation. The price that it takes to play the game is being competitive with compensation. Once competitive, compensation is no longer a primary retention instrument. Unfortunately, all too often, it becomes the primary instrument because it is easy to implement and does not require any behavior change on the part of leaders. To dispel this myth it is necessary to gather factual data from departing employees about their reasons for leaving.

What's the big deal, we'll just hire some people to replace those who leave. Long-term demographic trends highlighted in the Introduction point to future challenges in recruiting. While these challenges are less when the economy slows, they remain formidable. Indeed people with specialized skill sets are routinely in high demand. I hear many stories of the difficulties faced in this area, whether it is specialized engineering talent, creative talent or healthcare talent. Putting this myth on the table helps limit the tendency to rewrite history when someone leaves. In some organizations a person's perceived performance suddenly plummets after they leave. Such a change does not usually reflect reality. Ignoring the issues that led to the departure compromises the relationship that might be possible with this person after departure, and it interferes with steps the organization could take to address system-wide concerns.

In this world of constant job-hopping we can't impact people losses. This is a particularly dangerous myth. One study (*Business Wire* 1998) explored the links between employee dissatisfaction and the amount of training provided. The percentage of the employee population who were dissatisfied or very dissatisfied fell from 23% to 8% as the amount of training provided by organizations increased from zero to six or more days each year. Here is a direct link between an organizational intervention, training, and employee dissatisfaction. Employee dissatisfaction in turn is linked to attrition.

Another study (Watson Wyatt 2000) contrasted employee and employer perspectives about why top-performing employees resign. The top two items from the employee perspective were inadequate opportunities for promotion and dissatisfaction with company management. Third was dissatisfaction with pay and a close fourth, with a high rating, was not enough flexibility to handle personal responsibilities. In contrast, the top item from the employer perspective was pay. Employers rated flexibility as relatively unimportant and well below the employee rating. It is essential to take steps that stop this disconnect opening up with the employee population. For it is in this disconnect that many of the seeds of dissatisfaction are sown. Without knowing the reasons for employee concerns it is not surprising some organizations think there is nothing that can be done. Understanding these reasons is a key step in the path to action.

It's somebody else's problem. The top three reasons that caused people to look elsewhere in the study summarized in Chapter 4 were: (1) Lack of career development opportunities; (2) lack of recognition/appreciation; and (3) negative work environment. This raises the question, who can influence these items? While leadership and HR play a major role, everyone in the organization has an influence on the work environment. So the responsibility for building affiliation is a broadly held responsibility. Recognizing this, some organizations are now incorporating measures of overall employee attrition into the reward structure for everyone in the organization, not just leaders. This is an area where leaders' rewards need to be structured to encourage employee development and mobility within the organization. When leaders' rewards are focused only on the financial performance of local operating units, parochial behavior will result. This can lead to a perspective that employees are owned by the local fiefdom, a good example of Morison's limited identification discussed earlier.

Once they're gone, they're gone. Sometimes there is an organizational view that departure signals disloyalty and should be punished. For example at one time some organizations in the textile industry had policies prohibiting the rehire of anyone who left the organization. It may be more subtle today; for example one of my clients was uncomfortable raising the possibility of leaving a position as a vice president at a non-profit organization, for fear that even mentioning this thought would result in ostracism from the core leadership team.

The message for the future is to think of those people who leave the organization as alumni. They are ambassadors for the organization, and they can be good or bad ambassadors. They are also potential re-recruits who can be readily integrated into the organization. They are potential sources of referrals for additional new hires. One organization gives a boomerang to each person who returns, and they are not Australian. Another recently held a returning party for a whole group of ex-employees who decided to return. Such behaviors signal openness and welcoming, important elements of ready integration. They also signal support for individual development even when it entails a move outside the organization. SelectMinds is an organization that has built a business model providing a virtual platform for organizations to stay connected with their alumni.

With our name people will just come and stay. Sometimes an organization's greatest strength can become its greatest weakness. Take the example of an organization that has risen to prominence in its local or national community. This may have occurred at a time when jobs were scarce, causing top leadership to struggle up through the ranks. We have heard much about employee entitlement, the perception by people that they have a right to a job. There is another form of entitlement, namely organizational entitlement. This arises when leadership believes that people will join the organization and stay just because of its name. There are few organizations today, if any, that people will join and stay, simply because of the name of the organization.

THE FUTURE ORGANIZATION

Recognizing and overcoming these and other myths will help pave the way for organizations to build the workforces needed for the future. Here is one view of this future to help frame a review of the issues for leaders and HR in bridging to the emerging work world. It describes a fictitious morning in the life of an employee in the future (Elsdon 2002).

Jane realized this was a good day to visit Life Central. After working for ten months as an information synthesist for her local bank she was feeling anxious and bored. While tired of the incessant calls trying to entice her to a new position she recognized this restlessness may signal another move. She looked at her communicator, 7:12 A.M., January 10, 2025. Her goals for the day, clearly shown in blue and green in the latest aqua display, included a personal worklife check-up. She looked forward to this check-up. All those late-night sessions with Alvin were starting to make sense.

After a quick shower and a low chol breakfast she flipped on her communicator's audio news feed. Those depressing economic statistics, the unemployment rate had risen to a whopping 1.5%, some grumbling that Social Security benefits would have to be cut back for those workers over 75. She thought how much her father's life had changed now that he reached that golden age of 75 and could cut his workweek back to thirty hours. Oh no, another one of those intrusive ads had sneaked around her security system. This company offered ten hours of classes each week toward an MA in IS. Not a bad offer, but the place was known as a sweatshop that sent people packing with a slight dip in earnings. Her friends were still talking about those layoffs three years ago and how the CSO had so publicly missed the organization's growth targets. It was rumored that the company was now in decel, that it could not find enough people to continue operations. It's a tough world out there, survival of the company fittest, thought Jane.

She quickly checked the latest job opportunities for synthesists locally, fourteen companies hiring, all offering three-month induction training and all offering bonuses for every three months worked. Jane ran out to catch the cart to Life Central. Good to see her friends over there, Jan's and Carl's schedules matched hers. They had all started at Calway on the same day. It would be good to see Alvin again also. He was a bit of a taskmaster but good fun all the same.

Calway was a big contributor to Life Central. Many local organizations had created Life Central five years ago when they couldn't find and keep people. Funny really, thought Jane, a bank working with a supermarket, a research lab, a chocolate factory, their local university and of course the communicator company. But it really worked; it opened up opportunities days before she picked them up on her system. Some of her friends had moved easily from one organization to another.

Reaching Life Central she ran in, a bit late again. Good job she remembered her securicard, the doors opened and the umbrella system picked up her latest data. Alvin would know that she had completed the latest DRJK tests. She rushed upstairs just in time for her appointment with Alvin. She liked the way he spent a few minutes chatting with her about other parts of her life. It calmed her down and helped her focus. Today Alvin seemed relaxed. After their usual banter he began to review the results. How interesting to see the changes from three months ago. Her growing restlessness was showing. There were telling indicators, no wonder she had received such an urgent message from her Supporter. Her leaving index had jumped 20% over the past three months. She could see the economics for Calway mapped out on Alvin's report. What was going on? There were clear signals about her changing interests and growing concerns.

Jane talked with Alvin at length about her wishes. She talked about her belief in Calway, about how it was helping strengthen her community. Jane particularly liked it when Alvin came up with creative new ways for her to explore her changing hopes and dreams. She also liked how Alvin could help her connect with opportunities in the other organizations in Life Central and how they might be a good fit for her. This time they found three possibilities that might work well and, for each, two people to connect with. She realized how much she was committed to the groups in Life Central and their purpose. It's a good job; she could find some other options in the group. And then all too soon her session was over. Smiling she stood up, turned off Alvin, and walked out of the room.

IMPLICATIONS FOR LEADERS AND HR

This scenario extrapolates a number of workforce trends that are emerging today to one possible outcome. While this exact future is highly unlikely, some close variant is possible. What does it mean for organizational leadership and for HR? First, don't take employee loyalty for granted. With advances in technology and communications the job market is becoming increasingly efficient. It won't be many years before it rivals the efficiency of the stock market. Just as organizations need to attract investors today, they will need to attract employees in the future. This means more than the window dressing of branding. The decision a person makes about joining an organization is a values-laden decision that is not equivalent to buying a container of soap powder. It is about practices and behaviors in the organization. It is about the respect with which people are treated, their participation in decisions and the openness of communications. It is about the substance of the organization, not how it appears. One of the benefits of the burgeoning access to information is the ease with which employees can communicate their satisfaction or dissatisfaction with organizations (Levine et al. 2000). The employee of the future will know the reality of life in an organization from the outside.

The growing efficiency of the job market will also likely lead to continued increases in employee volatility. One of the results of limited access to information about opportunities in the past was inertia regarding movement. As information about opportunities becomes pervasive this natural inertia is reduced. Also built into the scenario is the notion that organizations can partner on workforce development to address the problem of employee scarcity. By opening more possibilities for people, organizations strengthen the connection with them. Technology becomes an enabler for this partnering and for the assessment steps that help people continually clarify their unfolding aspirations. Leaders and HR are central to ensuring that these processes occur.

Another primary implication for leaders and HR is the importance of continuing to question assumptions about the relationship between the organization and each segment of the workforce. This includes questioning the prevailing philosophy in dealing with people and introducing the concept of employees as customers as well as volunteers, for they surely are. It means supporting leaders throughout the organization in learning about their responsibilities in the new relationship and the behaviors they will need to exhibit. These behaviors are needed to function in a world that was described in Chapter 2 as moving from:

- Stability to change
- Constant skills to constant learning
- Lifelong commitment to engagement for mutual benefit
- Paternalism to self-reliance
- Local to global
- Hierarchy to fluidity
- Abundance to scarcity of skilled people
- Internal to external.

This means supporting all leaders in broadening their horizons so that they embrace change. It means providing leaders with forums for exploring the direction and path of such change and encouraging the sharing of learning across the organization. HR's role becomes that of change enabler regarding the relationship with employees. It means leaders and HR constantly probing for opportunities to introduce learning into the workplace, whether through formal courses or through direct work experiences. The concept of the corporate university has waxed and waned with business cycles, in some cases evolving to a virtual experience. Providing, as it does, core curriculum that centers the organization on key learning experiences from hard skills through interpersonal skills, it is one example of a demonstrated commitment to employee development. It is one example of a differentiator for organizations in the future that goes well beyond window dressing. Such an emphasis on learning may also force choices about committing valuable organizational resources to foster internal learning. One organization took its most skilled equipment operators and routinely seconded them to training operations for several months to transfer internal learning. This benefited the students through their new learning, the experts by allowing them to experience the richness of supporting others, and the rest of the organization by opening up development opportunities for others.

Another implication for leaders and HR is the importance of supporting people in taking charge of their own careers. Lew Platt, when he was CEO of Hewlett-Packard, described his awakening in this area in a panel discussion that was used by the Career Action Center to illustrate to organizations the importance of this subject. Platt describes the sadness of his encounter with an administrative assistant he had known for many years as an employee of the organization. She was losing her job. Platt expected a tirade about the insensitivity of the organization but instead heard a lament that this person had not stayed current in her job skills. It is a credit to Platt's leadership abilities and insight that he recognized this as a general need for the organization and acted on it. He committed the organization to providing support for employees so that their skills would not atrophy. He instituted processes to support employees in understanding how they could maintain currency with their skills and navigate the path of their careers.

As the demographics of the workforce shift and global communication enables remote working arrangements, an important implication for leaders and HR is to support the growing globalization of the workforce. A recent example I observed was the purchase and integration of a German high-tech organization into a Silicon Valley company to take advantage of the extensive, highly trained workforce in Germany. In other sectors this may mean supporting the movement of people from one region to another where opportunities abound, for example in nursing. An increasingly common trend is the movement of work to the labor force such as software creation to India or manufacturing to China. Again this requires flexibility in leaders and HR, as well as openness to different cultural norms.

These changes speak to movement from an internal to an external organizational focus. They speak to the need to institute processes that continuously capture signals, whether from the employee population, from the marketplace, from investors or from customers, and synthesize these signals into a coherent whole. This provides a firm foundation for decisions that are not driven by anecdote or whim, but by factual information fed into a passionate vision of the future.

What do the processes, roles and stages of engagement introduced in Chapter 8 mean for leaders and HR in bridging to the future connection with the workforce? The processes are as follows:

- Creation of transcending purpose
- Communication
- Building a supportive environment
- Understanding of workforce dynamics and analysis
- Measurement of workforce contributions
- Prediction of evolving needs

Critical to overcoming the problems of limited identification that Morison highlighted is creation of a transcending purpose. It is the cornerstone that enables each person to step outside his or her limited domain. When the Walt Disney Company talks about being the world's premier family entertainment company, Michael Eisner, the chairman and CEO, reinforces this by referring to employees as cast members, to customers as guests. There is no doubt about the transcending purpose of this organization. It is clearly communicated in the language used to describe each person who connects with the organization. Bridging to the work world of the future means being clear about direction and letting the organization know what this means. This includes recognizing the need to change course as opportunities and circumstances dictate. It is during times of change that people in organizations most need support—support in exploring new directions and their own aspirations. Support is needed one person at a time and then it cascades throughout the organization. Measurement and prediction of possible future paths, the final two processes, provide a link from the individual to the organization and they are central to crossing the bridge to the future workforce.

Moving forward in a sometimes calm and sometimes choppy sea, with an eye to both the horizon and the waves close at hand means leaders and HR adopting varied roles that are sometimes unfamiliar. These roles as defined in Chapter 8 are:

Bridging from the Organization of Today

- Guide
- Mentor
- Coach
- Conductor
- Artist
- Visionary
- Entrepreneur
- Innovator
- General
- Change Agent
- Connector

Just as our individual lives no longer follow a predictable, linear path, nor do the roles of leaders and HR. As organizational needs change from the entrepreneurial in the early stages of formation, to the more structured in the later stages, so the roles of leaders and HR shift in moving to new places in the relationship with employees. Steve Jobs at Apple Computer faced a very different workforce challenge when he returned to the company after being away several years than when he founded it. He faced a workforce with different expectations, sobered by challenges but still ready to be enthused by new opportunities. The role needed to galvanize the workforce on his return was that of visionary. This is a different role from the mentoring and guiding that characterized the end of his first period with Apple.

Strengthening affiliation and connection in the future work world means redefining the processes of engagement with employees that were identified in Chapter 8 as:

- Selection
- Integration
- Development
- Transition

In the future selection will need to begin with the premise that individuals are a scarce resource, continue with the recognition of technology as an enabler of a highly efficient labor market, and conclude with a process that clarifies attributes needed by the organization and recognizes individual aspirations.

The integration process has often been relegated to insignificance or to a purely transactional activity focused on the mechanics of joining the organization. Johnson (2001) cites examples of organizations that adopt a much more comprehensive approach. The Container Store, top of *Fortune*'s "100 Best Companies to Work For" list for two years, has developed a Foundation Week for integration. This includes time for new hires with the store manager to understand the organization's philosophy, visual information about the product flow in the system, exploration of sales techniques, and explanation of the role of each store person and back room operations. At the end of the week there is a ceremony recognizing completion, a rite of passage. The Container Store's attrition rates are less than half the average for competitive retail stores.

At Whole Foods Market Inc. the integration process includes an assigned buddy, hands-on experience in the store and practical support with skills and knowledge development. New hires learn about the company values and history and engage in team-building activities. At Intel the process includes both virtual and in-person activities. Integration events occur at specific points in time over a nine-month period, emphasizing that this is a process, not an event. At KDA Software most of the integration occurs through the use of online tools, recognizing the distributed nature of the workforce. Johnson (2001) underlines the importance of gathering manager input into the structure of the integration process so that it meets organizational needs, and stresses the importance of defining metrics for the process. Integration needs to focus both on enhancing productivity and reinforcing, for new hires, their fit with the organization. It will be increasingly important in the future for leaders to be active contributors to the integration of new employees. Complementing this is HR's contribution to creating a process that has strong content and builds an emotional connection with new hires.

Lack of perceived career development opportunities and lack of opportunity for a person to do their best work were pre-eminent employee concerns in the studies described in Chapter 4. This is in spite of the fact that many people were part of sophisticated organizations with a broad range of positions available. The conventional organizational model stressed business performance while relegating individual development to a secondary position. Leaders and HR are central to rebalancing this situation so that individual development is elevated in importance. This will lead to higher productivity. An example of the tangible financial benefits from career development support was described in Chapter 7. Leaders and HR must continue to challenge the organization to institute practices that demonstrate support for development, and model such practices on a personal level. Being open to, and communicating, personal participation in ongoing learning and development goes a long way to showing support. When this is coupled with policies that provide time, resources and rewards for individual development it sends a powerful message.

Transition out of the organization has been a great unmentionable to be discussed in secret and often implemented abruptly. Being asked to hand over keys and then being escorted out by a security guard, after being with an organization many years, performing well, shows disrespect to the individual and is a visible sign to those remaining of the organization's values. Such behavior is not unusual. Transition, if handled well, lays the groundwork for a continued amicable relationship. This is an area of opportunity. Leaders and HR need to implement transitions in a manner that respects individuals, and provides support for people in bridging to other opportunities. Furthermore, the basis for the transition process needs to be communicated clearly when people join the organization so they understand the support they will receive on exit.

PRACTICAL STEPS

This brings us to a road map of the practical steps needed to effect organizational change to bridge to the organization and workforce of the future while building a greater sense of affiliation. Although the details of implementation will differ by organization, being influenced by organization size, the characteristics of the specific workforce, industry sector and organizational culture, the overall process outlined here is broadly applicable. It builds on the ideas developed in earlier chapters. Implementation involves the following five steps:

1. Define needed outcomes
2. Characterize the workforce
3. Understand employee issues
4. Implement solutions
5. Monitor and adjust as needed

1. Define needed outcomes. In building the relationship between the organization and the workforce, an important initial question is, what are the organizational driving forces and objectives? In a for-profit organization, economic value creation will be a primary outcome. In addition to overall short- and long-term financial measures, objectives will include progress against the organization's strategic drivers, for example the penetration of new geographic markets or customer sectors, or continued improvement in organizational efficiency as defined by revenue or profit per employee. They will also include some less tangible, but equally important aspects such as changing organizational culture. For example in one organization, which had been a regulated utility, a primary issue was becoming more commercially responsive as deregulation changed the competitive arena. In a nonprofit organization needed outcomes will address the ability of the organization to achieve its purpose. For example, reaching more broadly to communities the organization wishes to serve. Balanced scorecard techniques (Becker, Huselid and Ulrich 2001), extended further in time than the traditional one year, are a useful tool for establishing outcomes in either the for-profit or nonprofit arenas.

2. *Characterize the workforce.* Having defined outcomes, the next step is to characterize the workforce. The concepts, and some specific dimensions to explore, were introduced in Chapter 2. For example, the nature of the relationship with employees (transactional or extended) and the degree of individuality in the relationship (one-to-one vs. one-to-many) provide two dimensions that are important in characterizing the workforce. Defining key dimensions provides a framework for segmenting the workforce. From this process, policies and practices can be developed for each workforce segment. This leads directly to a conversation with existing and new employees about the nature of the employment relationship. It also provides a framework for highlighting key leadership competencies as they pertain to building a culture of affiliation. Processes such as coaching can then be used to enhance the development of such competencies.

3. *Understand employee issues.* Studies cited earlier in the chapter (Watson Wyatt 2000) showed how easily a gap can open between leadership perspectives and employee views about critical issues and concerns. If such a gap remains it can cause leaders to intervene in ways that either are irrelevant or detract from the relationship with employees. For example, employees sometimes express concerns in exit interviews about the recognition trinkets they receive when leaders are awarding themselves large financial bonuses. To avoid such disconnects diagnostic systems are needed that measure the what and why of attrition and the ongoing concerns of employees. Such systems include the attrition demographic analyses and interviews described in Chapters 4 and 6. Both components guide decisions about the appropriate nature and focus of solutions. Along with face-to-face contact by leaders, diagnostic systems help surface the needs and concerns of the employee population.

4. Implement solutions. Having defined the nature of the concerns and issues it is then possible to tailor solutions appropriately. Of the many potential solutions, only a few will be relevant to each segment of the workforce. They need to be sought, developed in depth, applied consistently, linked to leaders' rewards, and communicated to the organization. One example of potential actions at an overall level is summarized in Figure 9-1.

The actions are categorized by those focused on the individual, the leader and the organization. They are also categorized by stage in employee engagement from selection through development. In all cases the actions are within the control of leadership. A detailed definition of actions that address prioritized concerns people express in interviews can expand this further.

5. Monitor and adjust as needed. The final step in the process is to monitor the impact of the solutions and adjust accordingly. Monitoring can utilize the same tools described earlier to understand the issues, namely attrition demographic analysis and interviews. This provides a basis for reassessing the effectiveness of the solutions and making adjustments as needed.

Leaders and HR are central to the success of such a process. It requires an ongoing acknowledgment that the employee population is the primary engine of value creation in the organization. This means elevating development of the workforce to a major strategic issue, for it is only in that light that it will receive the needed priority. Some years ago I visited two fiber-producing facilities, both making the same complex material, both about the same size, one an industry leader in Italy, the other an industry follower in the United States. In the case of the industry leader, the CEO of the organization led a tour of the facility, stopping to talk with each person operating the equipment, knowing and using his or her first name. The warmth in these exchanges was clear. The facility was immaculate, reflecting the pride of ownership that all felt. The CEO's depth of knowledge of the business and concern for the employees shone through this operation. In contrast for the industry follower, the host was from a marketing area and unfamiliar with the operational practices. There was little warmth in any exchange and there was little attention to housekeeping. In this facility employees were merely a factor of production.

These cases are examples of the direct link between business success and the organization's relationship with each employee. This relationship is defined by leaders. HR must help leaders understand the implications of their behaviors, ensure that workforce issues remain central to the

Figure 9-1
Potential Actions to Enhance Affiliation

	EMPLOYEE	LEADER	ORGANIZATION
SELECTION	Build processes to engage employees in selection	Provide selection interview training	Communicate purpose and values to potential recruits
INTEGRATION	Build strong orientation processes	Support leaders in defining their role in the integration process	Strengthen effectiveness of systems to provide employees with resources immediately when hired
DEVELOPMENT	Institute Career Development Processes Virtual -Individual -Group	Examine leadership development practices Institute rewards linked to affiliation Provide affiliation training and practices	Implement comprehensive Human Resource Information System Build metrics to track the impact of development on affiliation and performance Remove barriers to internal transfers
GENERAL	Provide forums for listening to employee concerns and issues	Establish a framework for coaching in interpersonal skills	Explore implications of organizational structures

strategic agenda and create and advocate for processes that strengthen the workforce, knowing the nuances of different segments.

What benefits accrue from such an approach? This can be examined from the perspective of:

- Organizational leaders
- Employees
- HR
- The organization
- The community

Organizational leaders use a broad skill set to make informed choices on a range of issues related to resource allocation, balancing short- and long-term needs and risk profiles to secure the survival and prosperity of the organization. This is not easy, and it takes place in an unforgiving arena. Effective leaders need access to timely and accurate information and to a continuing stream of innovative ideas that are the cornerstone of growth and prosperity. A workforce of strongly affiliated and committed partners/employees is the source of such ideas and information. They become part of a self-creating system that grows in strength, valuing the contribution from each member. Creating this strength in the workforce allows leaders to direct much of their energy to the outside world, dramatically increasing their effectiveness.

From the *employee* perspective, a secure growing organization provides an environment in which to fully express capabilities, reaching for a sense of fulfillment and calling. The members of the most effective team in which I worked acknowledged their strengths and weaknesses, supported each other, picked up the pieces that others may have dropped, and never lost their sense of enthusiasm and commitment to each other. It is this kind of environment that replenishes and refreshes, in which the beauty and majesty of the human spirit can excel.

HR has the difficult challenge of reconciling the needs of the organization with the needs of the individual; simultaneously having to advocate for both. An environment in which leadership questions HR's business judgment and employees wonder about HR's advocacy compounds this challenge. A process to mitigate this tension and help bridge from the individual to the organization is of great value to HR. The process described in this chapter is one component of such a bridge linking individual and organizational interests and clarifying expectations.

The organization is represented by a complex mix of stakeholders that extend from employees and leaders to shareholders (in a for-profit entity), suppliers and customers. Employee satisfaction and customer satisfaction are tightly linked and connected in turn to business success and therefore shareholder satisfaction. Likewise suppliers benefit from the continued prosperity of the organization. A process that builds workforce strength consequently benefits all stakeholders of the organization, rather than one group at the expense of another.

The community can be considered a vastly expanded organization with a wide array of stakeholders. The vibrancy of a community is dependent on the economic health of its constituent organizations and the physical and emotional health of its members. Processes that strengthen affiliation of individuals to organizations address each of these elements. Affiliation then impacts at many levels from the individual to the community. Much of the responsibility for nurturing this process of affiliation rests on the shoulders of leaders and HR.

The focus of this chapter has been primarily on the internal dynamics within a given organization in relation to affiliation and workforce value creation. Organizations exist in external economic and social systems that offer both support and competition. The focus of the next chapter is on partnerships as a means to build the support component.

— 10 —

Partnerships for a Better Future

There were two of us in the lodge that cold and snowy night. I was there to give a workshop the next day on workforce affiliation for a leadership team. Kermit the falcon lived in the lodge. Kermit's owner explained some of the intricacies of falconry the next day. What it takes to build a relationship with the falcon so it is free to soar away, and yet returns to its owner and partner. An intense six months of training, two to four hours each day, leads to a strong bond of partnership between man or woman and bird. A partnership in which each complements the other and each respects the other. This partnership is not built lightly and it requires commitment to create and sustain it. The benefit is an enduring relationship in which the falcon is free to soar on the wind and chooses to return. These ideas translate to the world of workforce partnerships. This chapter will explore the definitions and driving forces for workforce partnerships, their rationale and benefits, examples from other areas, types of partnership, criteria for success, their characterization and implementation.

DEFINITION AND DRIVING FORCES

What is meant by partnership in the context of the workforce? The formal definition of a partnership is a relationship between two or more parties usually involving close cooperation, with each party having specified and joint rights and responsibilities. The operative words are cooperation and joint rights and responsibilities. Up to now partnerships typically addressed business or social aspects rather than the workforce. It is unusual for two organizations to collaborate around workforce recruiting, growth, development and transition other than acknowledging nonproprietary practices. It is in partnering in the more strategic areas that there is much future opportunity. The philosophy at the heart of a successful partnership is the recognition that it must benefit all parties to be sustainable. While it takes at least two parties to form a partnership, it only takes one to end it. That happens when a partnership is inequitable. The partnership between falcon and human continues because both benefit from the relationship. The falcon is guided to food and the human experiences the pleasure of close connection with nature. This mutual reciprocity is a different philosophy from that which has pervaded many workforce-related initiatives at an organizational level in the past. For example, the relationship between organized labor and organizational leadership has often been contentious. This is partly due to the perspective that there is a fixed pool of resources and the struggle is about who can capture the greater share. Interestingly, affiliation of individuals with organizations is an area where there is a natural convergence of organized labor and management interests. For the organization there is the prospect of greater productivity, for organized labor there is the prospect of greater employment stability. No longer is the pie a fixed size; instead, through the vehicle of partnership it is possible to enlarge the size of the pie so that all benefit.

Three evolving factors affect the dynamics of workforce partnerships. The first is the changing balance of power with respect to individuals and organizations. As employee scarcity increases, due to the changing workforce demographics we reviewed earlier, so decision-making power shifts. It will no longer be only a buyers' (organizations) market in the employment arena. The seller, the individual, will command greater negotiating strength. This will drive organizations to provide more effective platforms for individual development. Partnership with other organizations is one means to create a platform for such development. It can expand the range of options open to individuals.

The second factor is the changing perspective on work held by generations now entering the workforce. In workshops I will often pose the question "What does work mean to you?" separately of people from different generations. Those born before 1964 (the baby boomers and silent generation) are more likely to respond with references to duty and obligation. Those born after 1964 (generations X and Y) will more often refer to meeting their individual aspirations, frequently in the context of a greater purpose. This is sometimes mistakenly interpreted as a sense of entitlement. In fact it is recognition that we are stewards of our own lives (Palmer 2000). In that role we have a responsibility to fully express ourselves in the work we do. So again we see a driving force for organizations to recognize individual aspirations. Partnerships help enable this connection to occur.

The third factor is the emergence of a global marketplace for employees. This trend is well advanced in some traditional sectors such as textiles, where much of the source of production has moved to regions with low-cost labor, such as China. As we move forward the opportunity to rebalance labor availability in sectors of the information and service-based economy will arise also. It exists now with a movement of software development to India. In a similar vein another workforce balancing approach from the past and present, which may intensify in the future, is the organizationally supported movement of people to jobs. For example, nurses from various parts of the world are being sought by U.S. organizations to address a chronic nursing shortage. Partnerships extend the ability to access a workforce from areas with underemployment. In doing this there is an opportunity to increase organizational productivity by lowering costs, to provide employment for people that would otherwise not have access to work, and to strengthen distant communities through their economies. This will likely require the provision of education to upgrade the skills of individuals in areas of underemployment. Enhanced educational opportunities also directly benefit the local community. This introduces the prospect of much broader movement of work to people in addition to the reverse. New communication tools make this a practical reality today. Global workforce partnerships can increase the size of the pie, thus reducing the tendency to fight over who can capture the largest piece.

These three factors are creating an environment conducive to the formation of workforce partnerships that benefit the individual, the organization and the community. However, this is a radical departure from past practices and it will require a bold initiative on the part of organizational leaders and HR. Taking this step means building clarity about why engaging in partnerships is beneficial to the organization.

RATIONALE AND BENEFITS

Why engage in partnerships? As organizations focus increasingly on a core set of competencies to deliver superior value to customers, peripheral functions continue to be outsourced. This has been a trend in HR for a number of years, beginning with transactional activities such as payroll and benefits and moving to areas such as staffing and training. While a slowing economy can cause organizations to draw some functions, such as training, back in house, the longer-term trend of focusing on core capabilities holds. In the United States in recent years outsourcing is estimated to have grown at four times the rate of the general economy (Outsourcing Institute 2000). In terms of functional areas for outsourcing, the same study shows HR moving up from fifth highest to equal third, behind only Information Technology and Administration. Given this focus, there are fewer opportunities for individual development internally. From a workforce development perspective, partnerships are a means to expand the universe of opportunities for individuals while maintaining the business focus of the organization.

This is mirrored in the evolving relationship of employees with organizations where partner is a more appropriate term than employee. A partner is defined as one that shares. And this is the essence of the new, new deal, which is one of sharing. Sharing of expertise, of skills, of resources for mutual benefit. So partnership at an organizational level is a natural extension of partnership at an individual level. Partnerships need nurturing so that the perceived benefits exceed potential costs, just as we saw with the falcon. If a bird of prey, which by its nature is a loner, can engage in a relationship of mutual trust, then how much more effective we can be in such a relationship.

Engaging in workforce partnerships at the organizational level will require a change in organizational and leadership behavior. This is a change from viewing other organizations primarily as competitors to be outflanked for employees, to organizations who can participate in creating a stronger bond with employee/partners. As somebody once said, we want missionaries not mercenaries as our partner/employees. This is very different from framing this as a war for talent (Michaels et al. 2001) where Enron was cited as an organization to emulate. Enron's subsequent collapse points to the shortcomings of this approach. Instead the opportunity is to create a path to partnership. This means fundamental, organizational behavior change led from the top, reinforced and supported on a long-term basis throughout the organization.

What are the benefits of building partnerships? There are several. From an organizational perspective there is enhanced organizational learning. Interfacing with others bringing complementary skills and knowledge creates a natural forum for the exchange of ideas and the strengthening of institutional knowledge. Indeed a requirement of a successful partnership is that it provides enhanced organizational learning. This learning can take the form of content knowledge, learning about business processes and practices or learning about customer and market opportunities. These fundamentals address both the revenue and cost sides of the profit and loss statement. They not only enhance short-term performance but also strengthen long-term capabilities. Furthermore, on an organizational level partnerships provide for an expanded resource base. This increases the likelihood of meeting broad customer expectations. It also increases the likelihood of generating new business ideas from the interface of a wider range of perspectives and capabilities.

On an individual level, partnerships provide more options from which to create fulfilling, individual development paths. Changing priorities throughout our lives speak to the need for a rich and varied range of opportunities. The availability of more options increases the likelihood of matching individual aspirations to organizational needs, which in turn means greater individual fulfillment and organizational productivity.

On a community level, workforce partnerships can foster a more efficient labor market. This eases the entry of disadvantaged groups into the workforce and it increases the likelihood of continued participation. It also facilitates movement at all levels in organizations, again maximizing individual fulfillment and organizational productivity. A good example of a partnership at the community level is in a shopping mall in Nashville, Tennessee. As part of the process of creating this new retail mall, a local career resource center, the Opry Mills Learning Center was created (Nashville Career Advancement Center: www.career advancement.org). This learning center allows retailers to publicize job openings and readily access potential recruits. It supports employees in assessing their own direction and provides information on, and a means of access to, opportunities. It includes training resources for individuals and managers. The partnership that formed the center includes the Mills Corporation, government and local employment and resource agencies and national foundations and philanthropic institutions. It is particularly oriented to supporting members of disadvantaged groups facing hurdles to securing employment and subsequent development. This represents an innovative partnership of private and public agencies serving individuals, local organizations and the community.

Partnerships in the workforce area are a natural extension of the benefits that accrue to a single organization operating multiple business units with varied skill sets. In the case of the multi-business unit organization, individual transfers can occur across business units, introducing new learning and providing greater individual development opportunities. As with external partnerships, organizational vigilance is required to avoid the erection of parochial barriers to movement and development. There is a natural extension from an organization with multiple business units to external partnerships.

EXAMPLES FROM OTHER AREAS

Since forming workforce partnerships is a new endeavor we can explore whether there are examples from other fields that could inform the development of partnerships in the workforce arena. Some examples from other areas are as follows:

- Business
  - Joint ventures
  - Customer-supplier relationships
- Social
- Educational
- Military

Formation of joint ventures has been a cornerstone of some organizations' approaches to growth and development. A good example of this is Corning. At Corning the creation of partnerships was a basic component of the organization's growth strategy, for example with Dow in ceramic materials and with Asahi in panel glass. Partnerships are common when organizations enter new geographic areas; for example they were instrumental in Amoco's penetration of world markets with the new chemical technology to make polyester raw material that was reviewed in Chapter 8. In this case the local partner brought knowledge and understanding of the local environment, Amoco brought technical manufacturing capability. Partnerships help navigate new terrain as they provide a confluence of different perspectives that support innovation. Organizational innovation flourishes at the juncture of varied perspectives and such a benefit is a likely outcome of workforce partnerships.

This leads to the second example of partnerships, namely customer-supplier relationships. While the customer-supplier boundary can be a fertile source of new ideas it is also a source of cost saving and productivity enhancement through the supply chain. An example of such a partnership is in the supply of industrial gases for semiconductor fabrication. Open sharing of information allows both the customer and the supplier to optimize inventory and so lower carrying costs. Instrumental to the success of such partnerships is the open sharing of information that is the basis for identifying productivity enhancement opportunities. Such open information sharing about workforce practices will also be important in workforce partnerships.

Social partnerships involve the collaboration of agencies and individuals dedicated to supporting community development needs. An example here is the CASA (Court Appointed Special Advocates) organization. This organization includes full-time staff and volunteers who advocate for the best interests of abused and neglected children. It succeeds by addressing an important social need, namely helping secure safe, nurturing homes for children at risk. It does this by working at a local community level. There are more than 900 programs and 52,000 volunteers associated with this program (CASA: www.nationalcasa.org). It engages with a range of agencies including the juvenile court system, foundations and corporations. This illustrates the power of grass-roots activism coupled with institutional resources, an approach that can transfer to workforce partnerships.

One purpose of educational institutions is to prepare individuals to function effectively in the workforce. Success means understanding and bridging from the needs of individuals to the needs of organizations and the community. Partnerships can take many forms, for example companies providing resources directly, or through their foundations, to sponsor educational services in a discipline that is in short supply. This is often managed by individual educational institutions but sometimes it is coordinated at a community level. For example, Joint Venture Silicon Valley is an organization in Silicon Valley, California that focuses on building and strengthening a sustainable local community (Joint Venture: Silicon Valley Network: www.jointventure.org). It is a partnership of business, labor, government, education and community representatives. One aspect of this group's work addressed education, focusing on helping businesses, community agencies and educators to work together to change and reform schools.

A particularly relevant example from the educational area is that of the business incubator. In classical form (National Business Incubator Association: www.nbia.org) this consists of providing management assistance, access to financing, and access to technical and business support infrastructure to new businesses. A variant of this is a virtual incubator (Massachusetts Institute of Technology: http://web.mit.edu/) that is focused on a licensing model and connecting innovators to resources, rather than providing the bricks and mortar of a classical incubator. Using this approach more than 850 business agreements were completed by the

Massachusetts Institute of Technology incubator between 1980 and 1999, with revenues from resulting businesses exceeding $3 billion. Experiences in the educational sector demonstrate the value of providing multiple related resources to committed individuals. It is this combination of individual initiative and institutional resources that drive the process to success. Likewise workforce partnerships can provide access to multiple organizational resources for individuals.

The fourth area with examples of partnerships is that of the military. Traditional military partnerships include the joint disposition of forces in military campaigns, for example the United States and Britain in Afghanistan. However, other approaches include joint activities with businesses, as in managing cargo ships in the United States (Tauscher: http://www.house.gov/tauscher) or with nonprofit organizations to address the needs of children and youth in military families (Military Children & Youth: http://military-childrenandyouth.calib.com). Nontraditional linkages provide valuable partnership opportunities, a learning that can be transferred to the workforce partnership arena.

In summary then, key learnings from other partnership arenas are as follows:

• Seek to create a juncture of varied perspectives from the partners
• Drive for open sharing of information
• Couple grass-roots activism with institutional resources
• Couple individual initiative with institutional resources
• Explore nontraditional linkages.

TYPES OF PARTNERSHIP

With this in mind we can explore several types of workforce partnership as follows:

• Workforce sharing
• Workforce development
• Sequential employment
• Economic
• Philanthropic
• Educational

Workforce sharing formalizes a process that occurs implicitly with the contractor segment of the contingent workforce. Many people engaged in contractual relationships with organizations build connections with multiple organizations in addition to building private practices. Examples are in the therapeutic, training or educational fields where individuals may contract with several organizations to provide needed skills. This is a particularly effective model where demand for services is subject to cyclicality or seasonality that precludes the use of full-time staff. One approach to address seasonal needs has been the growth of organizations such as Manpower that act as brokers linking temporary needs in organizations to those seeking temporary work. Missing from this approach is extended affiliation of individuals with a given organization other than with the service broker.

A natural extension of this is for organizations to form direct workforce partnerships with each other where skill needs are similar and flexibility needs are complementary. Such an approach would require the creation of pooled benefit provisions. The advantage it offers the organizations and individuals involved is increased stability and the potential for increased tenure. It also fosters productivity growth over time and a better match of individual aspirations with organizational needs. Organizations can benefit from the infusion of a broader range of ideas than otherwise might be accessible. A related example internal to an organization is that of employees whose time is divided among different business units with costs allocated accordingly. Workforce sharing places an additional burden on management to make operational adjustments that readily accommodate changing organizational needs. It is rewarded by greater workforce flexibility, infusion of new ideas and greater individual fulfillment.

Workforce development is a related partnership concept built on the premise that adult development is most effective when addressing an immediate need, reinforced in a real-life setting that draws on direct work experience. This builds on the classical taxonomy of educational objectives proposed by Benjamin Bloom (Lowman 1995):

1. Knowledge recall and recognition
   ○ Commit to memory facts, theories or principles
2. Comprehension
   ○ Understand and explain concepts
3. Application
   ○ Apply learning to real situations
4. Analysis
   ○ Break down learning into constituent parts

5. Synthesis
   ○ Combine learning into a unified whole
6. Critical evaluation
   ○ Reference against values and judge importance

It is more difficult and more valuable to assess the effectiveness of learning at higher levels. Workforce development is the process of pooling learning and development across organizations so that a wider array of development opportunities is available to any individual in a real-life setting. By defining the level sought in the Bloom taxonomy it is possible for organizations to partner on specific developmental opportunities. An example is at the supplier-customer interface where providing development for individuals on the subject of supply chain management benefits all parties. Pooled development experiences also extend to interpersonal skills training where involvement of participants from a broad range of organizations can enhance the experience.

Sequential employment combines aspects of both workforce sharing and development. It occurs when a person works and develops in one organization then transfers to another in a coordinated process. An example is a publishing company that was examining how to extend the tenure of its packers. This position had high turnover partly because it offered little in the way of individual development. Leaders in the organization recognized that it offered limited opportunities to use more advanced skill sets. However, other organizations locally were short of employees with these more advanced skill sets so sequential employment was a possibility. By investing in the development of its employees, the publishing organization could prolong their tenure, which enhanced their contribution and productivity. These employees in turn would be better equipped to compete in due course for higher-level positions with other local employers.

Economic workforce partnerships are about outsourcing with an implied longevity and depth, and comprehensive sharing of information. An example is an employee group whose skills are maintained current by a supplying organization but who are dedicated to another organization to deliver services. The Sun case study in Chapter 7 illustrates this, where career counseling expertise was developed and maintained by a nonprofit organization whose counselors delivered the services at Sun sites.

Another form of workforce partnership is *Philanthropic*. In this case the partnership is formed around the concept of one organization providing employees with given skill sets as a donation to meet another organizational or community need. An example is the provision of diversity training developed in a for-profit environment, provided at no cost to a nonprofit organization as a community benefit. Employees in the for-profit organization had the skill to deliver the training. They were loaned to the nonprofit to conduct the training.

The final workforce partnership example is in the *Educational* area. Ongoing education is a basic requirement in the emerging work world for individuals to remain employable. It is also a basic requirement for increasing organizational productivity. One organizational responsibility is to provide ongoing educational opportunities. While much of this can occur through direct work experience, provision of academic learning opportunities—either in a virtual, classroom or individual setting—is an important adjunct. Partnerships between organizations and educational institutions can play a key role here. The organization contributes knowledge of specific workforce needs driven by market demands. It can also contribute financial and content resources. The educational institution contributes knowledge of the latest thinking in a given discipline and effective methods to enable adult learning to occur. Examples include functional and leadership training provided to intact teams in organizations by business faculty. Future partnerships could include deeper and more extended forms of such relationships.

CRITERIA FOR SUCCESS

Having outlined the benefits of partnerships, looked at examples from other areas and explored different types of partnerships we can now examine what is needed to form successful partnerships. This means defining criteria to assess the merits of a given partnership. The following criteria provide a solid foundation for such an assessment:

- High benefit-to-cost ratio
- Address complementary workforce needs
- Based on consistent partner objectives
- Include culturally compatible partners
- Incorporate a variety of perspectives

A fundamental requirement for a successful partnership is that the benefits outweigh the costs of engagement. Enterprise relationships that are successful demand commitment of time and resources. Such investments create the interfaces through which information flows and through which coordination occurs. These costs can be quantified. For example, for the workforce development form of partnership, each organization can clearly identify its development needs and resources. Together they can define interface resources and total costs.

From the use of the shared resources the partnering organizations will extract a benefit for their respective workforces. This benefit accrues in the future in terms of enhanced organizational growth (increased revenue in a for-profit, greater ability to execute against a purpose in a nonprofit) or increased productivity (driven for example by reduced attrition) or a combination of the two. There will also be intangible benefits and intangible costs. Examples of the former are increased levels of employee satisfaction or broader reach into the community; the latter may involve commitment of leadership time to maintain the partnership. These intangibles are also important in assessing the benefit/cost trade-offs. Having estimated benefits and costs, the partners can define a targeted benefit-to-cost ratio and monitor progress toward this goal.

The second criterion, which directly relates to benefits and costs, is the importance of each party having complementary workforce needs. These needs may be directly evident, as in the cases of workforce sharing, development and sequential employment partnerships. They may be more subtle, as in the case of economic, philanthropic and educational partnerships. For example in the case of a workforce sharing situation, the greater the commonality of needed skills and in some cases logistical needs such as proximity of location, the more readily workforce sharing can be implemented. A precursor to assessing complementary workforce needs is segmentation of the workforce and analysis of desired characteristics of each segment, as described in Chapter 2. As in the case of hiring individuals, so also with workforce partnerships, it is important to build clarity around needs and expectations prior to engaging. Defining the desired workforce characteristics provides a foundation to determine the form of partnership that may be most appropriate for each segment of the workforce.

Building this degree of clarity provides a basis for the next important criterion, namely consistency of objectives. For example, if one organization's primary focus is on expanding in a particular geographic region and a potential partner has different geographic aspirations such as remaining close to home, it will be difficult to forge a partnership that confers substantial benefits on both parties. On the other hand, for a situation where each party is focused on growing in a particular geographic region and each is seeking related skills, there is a high likelihood of identifying benefits from a partnership. An example would be a healthcare institution and a manufacturing organization, each seeking to strengthen the depth and capability of its financial analyst population in the same geographic area. Neither organization has financial analysis as a key business deliverable to external customers. Consequently the financial analysis function may be seen as peripheral within each organization, not warranting resources. It may therefore be less attractive to potential new recruits being perceived as lacking in development opportunities. By pooling their resources, knowledge and search capability the two organizations together can build an environment that is more conducive to development than either could create separately, and at lower cost. As a result both organizations can strengthen affiliation with their financial analysts, increase their job fulfillment, lower attrition rates which will enhance productivity, and increase ease of recruiting to support growth.

Beyond common objectives, another key component for a successful partnership is cultural compatibility. This is intimately interwoven with organizational values. There are many dimensions to corporate culture, some of which mirror the leadership dimensions examined in Chapter 1. For example in decision making, whether it is more participative or more directive. Other organizational culture dimensions include openness to different perspectives, willingness to accept risk, eagerness to adopt technical innovation, balance between short-term and long-term focus, and the balance between internal cooperation and competition. The greater the degree of compatibility in culture and values the more likely the relationship will endure and prosper. For example in the case of a workforce sharing partnership, if each participating organization is practicing decision making based on a high degree of individual autonomy then employees can move more readily from one organization to the other. This will be much more difficult if practices in this area differ substantially.

The final criterion, which builds on that of cultural compatibility, is the extent to which workforce partners bring varying perspectives. There is a natural tension between this criterion and that of cultural compatibility. The convergence of different perspectives provides fertile ground for innovation to flourish, which enhances the potential value-creating benefit to each partner.

PARTNERSHIP CHARACTERIZATION

Chapter 4 and Chapter 6 showed how leadership's ability to create a sense of inspiring purpose and fulfillment for individuals in an organization is a key determinant of people's anticipated tenure with the organization. There is a discontinuous sudden increase in anticipated tenure as the sense of inspiring purpose and fulfillment moves through a critical range. With the concept of workforce partnership, leadership now has the opportunity to expand the elements that can create this sense of inspiring purpose and fulfillment. The following factors contribute to this sense of inspiring purpose and fulfillment:

- The organization's products or services address significant individual or community needs.
- The organization's products or services are transformative in the lives of individuals.
- There is a direct and recognized connection between the contribution of employees and the organization's offerings.
- The organization operates with integrity in its dealings internally and externally.
- The organization values the communities with which it interfaces and demonstrates that in tangible ways.

It would be easy to dismiss these statements as irrelevant to many organizations. How is it possible to ascribe an inspiring purpose to apparently mundane products and services? Great leaders in great organizations do exactly that. I have seen it in the world of textile fibers, in the world of publishing, in the nonprofit world and in the realm of human resources. Great leaders find that sense of calling and provide a bridge to it. In creating partnerships the opportunity to build that bridge is magnified. Just as a network increases in strength with the number of connecting points, so does the value of a partnership. It enhances the richness and diversity of available opportunities and the likelihood of better matching individual aspirations with workforce needs. This leads directly to enhanced organizational value.

Partnerships can also be examined in the context of workforce characterization introduced in Chapter 2. The approach that was developed for individuals can be extended to partnerships. A good example is to take the perspective of the two initial dimensions for individuals, namely transactional vs. extended and one-to-many vs. one-to-one relationships. Using this framework, four quadrants were defined for the workforce segments as follows:

- Sweatshop
- Bureaucracy

- Contractual

- Entrepreneurial

What are the preferred attributes of potential partners in each segment? The case of the Sweatshop raises fundamental ethical and moral questions, and I suggest that it has no place in organizations moving forward. It conflicts with values at the core of the philosophy linking individuals to organizations and it insults our basic humanity. Perhaps the most important aspect of this quadrant is in helping to identify potential partners operating here so that we can avoid forming such partnerships.

The second quadrant, which was characterized as Bureaucracy, would include potential partner organizations that are operating with a traditional mindset concerning employees, based on extensive and standard operating policies. For potential partners from this quadrant, it is likely that the negotiation process will be extensive, that the terms of the agreement will be defined in great detail and difficult to change. Clarity rather than flexibility will characterize such a partnership. Some segments of the workforce may need to operate here due to the need for stability or customer contractual commitments. As long as expectations are clear to all parties then such a partnership relationship can be attractive. An example would be a government agency as a partner.

The third quadrant was defined as Contractual. In seeking partners in this area the emphasis is on organizations that effectively manage short-term relationships with employees. This implies a high degree of flexibility in the nature of the individual relationship and likely also in the partnership. Since the relationship with individuals is shorter term, it will be important that investments in individual development yield short-term results and that both partners share a common mindset in this area. It is likely that these partnerships will be the easiest to form and dissolve.

The fourth and final quadrant was defined as Entrepreneurial. Here the relationship with individuals is extended and one-to-one. It seeks to maximize value creation based on a balance of flexibility and depth. The greatest potential for value creation resides here, and also the greatest risk, due to the depth and extent of the relationship. In this area, above all others, it is essential to have close alignment of values and an extended commitment to work in partnership. Here lies the potential to develop the strengths that will propel the organization into the future. Workforce partnerships in this area will likely evolve from other forms of business partnership as they provide a foundation for the relationship.

IMPLEMENTATION

Recommended stages of implementation for workforce partnerships are as follows:

- Define outcomes
- Define preferred relationships
- Identify partnership opportunities
- Negotiate agreements
- Measure success.

A basic requirement in forming successful partnerships is creating a clear definition of the outcomes sought from the relationship. Outcomes will vary according to the driving force and could include for example: strengthened employee affiliation to reduce attrition, provision of more development opportunities to enhance ease of hiring, and strengthened flow of potential recruits by increasing the extent and effectiveness of local educational resources. The desired outcomes shape the nature of the partnership, whether it is primarily focused on internal workforce development issues, external workforce supply issues or some combination of the two. Outcomes can be defined in terms of both activity, for example the transfer of a certain number of people in a sequential employment situation, and financial impact in a for-profit organization.

Having defined outcomes then, it is possible to specify the types of partnership that would be most effective, using concepts of workforce characterization. For example a partnership in the entrepreneurial quadrant would likely build on existing or projected business ties whereas a partnership in the contractual quadrant may seek to address cyclical or seasonal workforce needs.

Having laid the groundwork for the nature of the partnership by defining outcomes and preferred relationships, it is then appropriate to identify specific partnership opportunities. They can be referenced against the criteria outlined earlier. Up to this point in the implementation process much of the analysis is focused internally. It now switches primarily to an external focus. This stage of identifying specific opportunities involves pooling of information about potential partnership candidates. This requires communication internally and externally about an interest in forming partnerships, the criteria used to assess partnership opportunities and the rationale. Having identified a range of potential partnership opportunities the screening criteria can be used to prioritize the opportunities and determine those to pursue.

This leads to the stage of negotiating agreements. As before, the nature of the agreement depends on the nature of the relationship, from fast and flexible to deep and extended. In negotiating agreements it is important to consider each stage of the partnership relationship, from initial engagement through development to a basis for separation. It is unusual for business partnerships to remain in place in perpetuity; workforce partnerships are no different in that objectives of the partners may diverge over time. With that in mind, clarity about the basis for separation should be established at the beginning, not the end, of the relationship. The negotiating process should be approached from the perspective of mutual gain with a view to increasing the total size of the opportunity. Time spent before partnership discussions begin on clarifying outcomes and criteria strengthens the entire negotiation process. It is in this negotiation stage that cultural compatibility or distance will become clear.

This leads to the final stage, which is that of measuring success on a continuing basis. Sustaining a successful partnership means investing time and resources in its growth and development. This may mean commitments at many levels in the organization. There will be barriers to the creation and continued existence of partnerships. I witnessed the resistance to forming a partnership of two nonprofit organizations due to many of the political issues highlighted in Chapter 9. Both nonprofits would have benefited from greater critical mass. While some initial partnership steps were taken, failure to execute a more substantive workforce relationship contributed to the demise of one nonprofit and the eclipse of the other. Limited spheres of identification, in Morison's terms, were major contributors. One approach that can help overcome such barriers is to establish clear measures of success and then regularly revisit the contribution of the partnership to these measures for all parties involved. These measures should include both tangible financial aspects as well as intangibles. They should address factors at both the organizational and the individual level. Examples would be enhanced revenue, lowered recruiting costs, reduced attrition, increased employee satisfaction with development, and increased employee identification with the organization's purpose.

Workforce partnerships are new tools to consider to strengthen the connection between the individual and the organization. They can benefit the individual, the organization and the community and repay many times over the investment of time and resources needed to sustain them. They complement and extend decisions about the internal workforce and offer a valuable, additional approach for leaders and HR to implement effective workforce strategies.

— 11 —

Awakening the Music

He met his spiritual icon and it was a surprise. A colleague of mine, Dick Snowden, had wanted to meet a well-known spiritual leader for many years when finally it happened. Through a mutual friend he was able to arrange an appointment while traveling. There was one problem. The appointment was only for five minutes. With months of advance preparation my colleague thought how he could best use this glint of time. He thought of all the profound questions he could ask and stored these away. Finally, the day came and my colleague left for the meeting with rising expectations. He was ushered reverently into the spiritual leader's presence acutely aware that he only had five minutes and determined to use it well. The scene was as he expected with the spiritual leader looking scholarly and thoughtful while seated cross-legged in an elevated part of the room. My colleague was not sure how to start the conversation when to his surprise the spiritual leader said, "How are you doing?" The conversation continued in this vein for about four minutes and my colleague despaired that his chance to touch profound thinking was evaporating. And then it was almost over, a bell rang and his time was up. He rose to leave but as he was about to open the door, the spiritual leader looked up and said to him: "I have one question for you to take with you. Who are you that they are who they are?" Then it was over and my colleague took leave.

He began to think about this question and repeated it to me. At first it seemed meaningless. Then the depth of this question slowly dawned on me. It is a question that all leaders of organizations should ask of themselves. Who are you that they are who they are? What is it in your behavior that causes people in your organization to think and act in the way they do? What is it about your behavior that either energizes or limits those around you? This resurfaces the central dilemma of Chapter 1, which is, how to integrate the needs of individuals with the needs of the organization? How to integrate the need for individuation with the need for community? From a leadership perspective, what is needed to awaken the music of those in the organization such that they and the organization are direct beneficiaries?

ADDRESSING THE CENTRAL DILEMMA

Central to addressing these questions is the creation of an environment where people can understand who they are and where they can make their best contribution. Dustin Hoffman the actor, speaking about his early life and formative experiences (Hoffman 1999), mentioned that he was not a particularly good student and that academic studies did not ignite much passion in him. When he was young he had been playing jazz piano and even went so far as to play in a band, but did not like it. Then he attended an acting class at a local community college in Los Angeles when he was about 18 or 19. His comment: "The ten hours of this class seemed like ten minutes and I knew what I wanted to do for the rest of my life." This was an epiphany for Dustin Hoffman. Most of us are not as fortunate in seeing so clearly the expression of our work lives. But it is there for all of us.

Does this mean that it was simple for Dustin Hoffman from this point on? Not at all. He spent ten years waiting at tables and trying to break into acting. Then Mike Nichols picked him for *The Graduate* and his acting career was launched. This is a vivid expression of a sense of calling. Those of us who have seen Dustin Hoffman in one of his many movies or stage plays have been blessed by his calling. I heard a similar description from a world-renowned cellist who described her early baptism in music. She was forced to play a range of instruments early in her life, none of which appealed to her. And then she discovered the cello, recognizing immediately the passion she felt for playing this instrument. Those who supported her learning of the cello gave her a gift that comes to all who hear her beautiful playing. Here is the moment of awakening for the poet Pablo Neruda as quoted by Whyte (1996): "I didn't know what to say, my mouth could not speak, my eyes could not see and something ignited in my soul, fever on unremembered wings and I went my own way deciphering that burning fire and I wrote the first bare line, bare without substance, pure foolishness, pure wisdom, of one who knows nothing and suddenly I saw the heavens unfastened and open." It can be this way in organizations, as each person realizes their sense of calling, awakens their music, the music of the whole organization stirs.

These stories illustrate the essence of the quest of leaders and HR wrestling with creating a relationship with the workforce. That relationship and its impact on organizations occurs one person at a time. Each single relationship can become one of meaning and personal expression. Leaders and HR must create an environment in which each of these single relationships connect, multiply and expand. In the words of Robert Kennedy: where each person "sends forth a tiny ripple of hope . . . and crossing each other from a million different centers of energy and daring those ripples build a current that can sweep down the mightiest walls of . . . resistance" (Peter 1979). The quest is to energize the workforce by awakening a sense of meaning in each person and a reason for each person to affiliate with the organization.

This is a good time to reflect on the meaning of changes in the nature of work. For as Winston Churchill said: "The farther backward you can look, the farther forward you are likely to see." (Brainy Quote: www. brainyquote.com). In the early 1900s the now-developed nations were emerging from an agrarian economy into a manufacturing economy. In making the shift from agriculture to manufacturing much was gained at an organization and individual level in terms of increased economic prosperity and reduced dependency on climate and related external factors. However, much was also lost. In many cases individual aspirations were subordinated to organizations relentlessly pursuing production efficiencies. People were viewed as merely a factor to be exploited to increase efficiency. Time and motion concepts were based on the analogy of people as machines. The structure of the economy led to a growing imbalance in the decision-making power between individuals and organizations.

Parsons' (1909) introduction of the Trait and Factor approach was an alternative that recognized individual needs in the context of organizational benefits. Over the past 100 years there has been a gradual equalizing in the balance of power between the individual and the organization. The formation of organized labor contributed much to this equalization trying, as it did, to address basic needs of individuals and to counter organizational excesses in the first half of the twentieth century. I still remember seeing an interview with a hard-boiled auto worker, who was moved to tears as he recalled the violent behavior of company-sponsored thugs fifty years earlier attacking his colleagues. It is good that such exploitation is receding. However, collective bargaining brought with it another set of constraints that limit individual freedom and enforce conformity to a different set of requirements.

Another major transition is emerging in this century. This time developed economies are moving from a manufacturing to an information and service base where intellectual capital and service are now the core components. While the drive in the manufacturing economy was for efficiency of production, the drive in the information and service-based economy is for effective utilization of human ingenuity. Effectiveness now comes from a combination of knowledge, capability, commitment, strategic focus and impact building over time as described in Chapter 6. The sense of affiliation that individuals feel for organizations is central to that effectiveness.

Strengthening this sense of affiliation means supporting each person in making deep, personal decisions about the changing course of their work lives. This, in turn, means supporting each person to develop a sense of self-knowledge and knowledge of opportunities. Self-knowledge includes understanding personality preferences and their meaning for potentially satisfying work environments and work content. It includes understanding innate interests and their implications for fulfilling work. It includes understanding personal values and the implications for organizational cultures that fit well, and motivated skills that energize rather than cause burnout. Leaders and HR can provide the support systems and instruments that help people refine the alignment of who they are with their work.

Regarding the external search process, in many cases employment opportunities exist within a given organization or could exist within an extended community built through workforce partnerships. However, they may not be readily accessible. Leaders and HR are responsible for providing a framework that gives ready access to such opportunities. This means making the internal job market more efficient than the external job market.

I am reminded of my decision to enter the field of career counseling. On the surface it is not obvious how or why a chemical engineer would become a career counselor. Some stages were serendipitous as opportunities to gather experience in business planning or business unit management arose. Others were intentional supported by reflection and self-assessment. Whyte (1996) and Palmer (2000) both invoke Dante's *Inferno* to describe the sense of loss and isolation "in dark woods" that precedes finding a path forward. I am grateful for guidance in finding a right path out of those dark woods. The path has led me to work that provides an emotional connection as well as intellectual stimulation. Career counseling is like wearing a comfortable pair of familiar shoes on a journey to a place of peace, full of new discoveries. Finding such a fit is a gift I would wish each person in our organizations. Sinetar wrote a book some years ago called *Do What You Love, The Money Will Follow: Discovering Your Right Livelihood* (1989), which contained many valuable insights. However, I suggest that finding our right livelihood is not a quest for money, for it may not follow. It is a quest for a sense of meaning and purpose that transcends the financial.

Further elevating the importance of our personal work quest is the intertwining of work and personal life. This is a departure from the traditional organizational mindset. Technology has made it possible to stay in constant communication with work. Furthermore, the needs of our complex family structures mean that it is not possible to leave personal responsibilities at home. They are part of our work lives. It becomes increasingly important to find shoes that fit at work as they are worn for many hours during the day, many days during the year, and many years of our lives.

Another responsibility rests with leaders and HR when stepping into the work arena. That is to maintain, in the organization, the ethical principles that guide personal lives. That means respecting the needs of others and conducting business recognizing that it impacts many people. Just as we would not throw a guest out of our home at a moment's notice, nor should we treat employees as disposable, to be jettisoned on a Wall Street whim. This, for both ethical and practical reasons, for such conduct will generate a response in kind. This leads to the question, what is the purpose of organizations?

THE PURPOSE OF ORGANIZATIONS

What is success for an organization, the question that was raised in Chapter 1? The perspective of value creation explored in earlier chapters included models that quantify financial aspects linked to the workforce. On one level an answer to this question is that success is a tangible increase in organizational value, which is reflected in shareholder value. However, shareholder value does not address the purpose of nonprofit organizations and there are other aspects in a for-profit organization that need to be included. Considering the organization as part of a broad social network, impacting the lives of employees, the communities in which it operates, and the destinies of partner, customer and supplier organizations, it is reasonable to conclude that factors other than short-term shareholder value are also critically important. One pre-eminent factor is the social contribution of the organization. This means the extent to which the organization enhances the quality of life for those in its constituent communities. Indeed this social impact is the essence of the long-term contribution of the organization. Value creation in financial terms, particularly related to shareholder value, is simply a subset of this larger contribution. The organization makes this larger contribution by being a key link in the chain between individuals and the broader con-stituent communities in which it operates. We come full circle to the questions raised at the end of Chapter 1. They are as follows:

- What is the nature of the relationship that should be built with people in the organization? Is it based on growing capabilities and accomplishments over time, or is it based on short-term transactions?
- How can an environment be crafted that enables each person to reach his or her full potential?
- How is the creation of value in the organization maximized while respecting the needs of each person in it?
- What is the appropriate role of the organization in supporting community well-being?
- How is success measured both individually and for the organization?
- How can we ensure that our own life is an expression of who we are?

What is the nature of the relationship that should be built with people in the organization? Is it based on growing capabilities and accomplishments over time, or is it based on short-term transactions? The process of workforce characterization described earlier provides a basis for iden-tifying different segments of the workforce and defining the form of relationship sought for each segment. For example, a segment where organizational and individual needs are best met by an extended rela-tionship based on continued development, or a segment where the em-phasis is on meeting contractual commitments maximizing flexibility and possibly providing support for movement to another organization for further development. The workforce characterization process is an im-portant precursor to setting mutually acceptable expectations on the part of the individual and the organization. It leads to multiple forms of re-lationship for a given organization that can cover a broad spectrum from in-depth, extended relationships to short-term engagements. In all cases it is incumbent on the organization's leaders to support individual development so people maintain their employability, enthusiasm and productivity.

How can an environment be crafted that enables each person to reach his or her full potential? Leaders must begin by identifying, nurturing and communicating an inspiring purpose for the organization that causes people to affiliate. Then providing a framework and tools that enable each person to strengthen their self-knowledge, building clarity about the path that will be personally most fulfilling. This is coupled with a focus on creating an open environment that provides information about, and access to, opportunities. It means building an efficient internal job market and links to opportunities in organizations that are workforce partners.

How is the creation of value in the organization maximized while respecting the needs of each person in it? The direct link between individual fulfillment and organizational value was demonstrated in Chapter 6. Leaders' responsibility is to create an environment that enables each person to understand who they are, where they can be most effective and fulfilled, and systems that allow people to align their work with their preferences. This does not mean installing complex bureaucratic processes. Instead it means equipping people with the wherewithal to take initiative for their own development and providing incentives for them to do so. It also means structuring rewards for managers to encourage development of individuals in their areas of responsibility, so avoiding the pitfalls of limited identification that lead to parochial behavior.

What is the appropriate role of the organization in supporting community well-being? The organization plays a pivotal role in bridging from the needs of individuals to those of constituent communities. Demonstration of contribution to social good is a fundamental purpose of all organizations, with shareholder value creation a subset of this. With that in mind leaders must continually reassess the contribution of their organizations to a broad range of constituents. This means developing a balanced scorecard that extends well beyond the traditional internal boundaries.

How is success measured both individually and for the organization? There is a need to build clarity about personal values and clearly articulate organizational values. From that appropriate measures can be built. The modeling techniques reviewed in Chapter 6 provide approaches to linking organizational value to individual fulfillment. They are examples of approaches that provide for predictive and prescriptive steps.

How can we ensure that our own life is an expression of who we are? This crucial question is at the heart of the responsibility of leaders and

HR. For it is from understanding ourselves that we are able to reach out to others and create the needed environments in organizations. It is from this sense of becoming ourselves that we can show behaviors that honor and respect those around us. Our responsibility to ourselves is to understand the essence of who we are and to live it. That means leaders and HR taking time to build self-knowledge and align themselves with organizational and community needs.

Answering these questions provides a basis for leaders to guide organizations in making the needed contributions to their respective constituencies. At the core of this process is the relationship of the organization with its employees and the extent to which this is built on a sense of connection rather than a sense of separation. This can be explored further by examining different forms of relationship that leaders and HR can create with people in the organization.

ALTERNATIVE FORMS OF RELATIONSHIP

Leadership behaviors and their impact on the sense of connection or separation were identified in Chapter 1. These leadership behaviors can drive to the following forms of relationship between individuals and organizations:

- Cooperative
- Competitive
- Exploitive
- Divisive
- Regenerative
- Inclusive

These relationships are not mutually exclusive; indeed some such as regenerative and inclusive are natural complements and others such as divisive and exploitive are natural consequences of each other.

A *cooperative* relationship is built on the premise that identifying and working jointly toward common interests will provide maximum benefit to each party. It is akin to the win/win concept of negotiating and it is based on open communication and the expectation that all parties are operating in good faith, respecting the needs of the other. To succeed it requires that the parties listen to each other, and that each be prepared to accommodate the needs of the other. The cooperative relationship is successful when the sum of the parts is greater than each individual component. Successful organizations remain together precisely because this is true.

A *competitive* relationship, on the other hand, is built on the premise that through competition individuals will exert maximum effort and make the greatest contribution. In this case the underlying assumption is that competition is needed to catalyze the effort needed to achieve excellence. Organizational structure and formation are needed only to the extent they foster an arena for competition. This represents a Darwinian approach to organizational development. It can be successful if individual initiative rather than cooperative endeavor is the primary engine driving organizational capability. Organizations practicing this approach need to provide regular, immediate rewards to their employees. Punishment for lack of success is likely quick and innovation will struggle in this culture that continually seeks a scapegoat.

An *exploitive* relationship can occur when the balance of power is far from equally distributed between the individual and the organization. Such an imbalance can lead to one party ignoring the needs of the other and exclusively pursuing its own interests. This occurred in the early years of the twentieth century with some organizations. Such exploitation extends beyond the financial to the repression of ideas by religious institutions (Sobel 1999). The exploitive form of relationship, aside from major ethical shortcomings, is inherently unstable and will ultimately dissolve.

A *divisive* relationship is rarely sought but sometimes created, for example as a consequence of an exploitive relationship. In highly political organizational cultures where progress of one person comes at the expense of others, management approaches that emphasize division to limit power may flourish. Such approaches lead to information being closely held, or worse misrepresented. In this relationship the sum of the parts is less than the individual components. This is a recipe for long-term organizational extinction. This approach destroys the sense of affiliation.

The *regenerative* relationship is focused on a continuing cycle of renewal. In this case both the organization and the individual recognize the need to evolve. While the timing of the cycles for each may differ, typically being longer for the organization, the relationship recognizes the need for the ongoing change and development of each party. An underlying premise of this relationship is the knowledge that innovation and exploration are essential to maintaining the vitality of the relationship. This form of relationship requires deliberate, constant challenge to the current state of equilibrium. It has the potential for great longevity, drawing as it does on an ever-renewing cycle of re-creation.

The *inclusive* relationship is one that values differences. It embraces varied perspectives, wide-ranging viewpoints and practices. On an individual level this means openness to new ideas, on an organization level this means openness to people with different backgrounds and to a breadth of partnership and community relationships. The inclusive relationship is likely to ignite the spark of innovation, bringing, as it does, varied perspectives together. It is inherently regenerative due to the infusion of new ideas that are implicit in this approach. Clear purpose and vision are needed to unite the wide-ranging viewpoints that are central to this relationship.

INCLUSION AS A KEY DIFFERENTIATOR

This leads to the concept of inclusion as a key differentiator for organizations. There are four forms of organizational inclusion:

• Internal inclusion, namely workforce diversity
• External inclusion, namely partnerships
• Community inclusion, namely philanthropy
• Global inclusion, namely pursuit of a greater good

Each form of inclusion provides an opportunity to build organizational strength and differentiation. Given a rapidly changing external environment, organizational flexibility was identified earlier as a key determinant of survival and success. This flexibility is enabled by breadth of inclusion. Internal inclusion means welcoming diverse ideas, perspectives and backgrounds into the workforce. While diversity has traditionally been associated with ethnicity, and this is an important component, the concept of diversity is much broader. It includes different generational perspectives and gender perspectives; it includes perspectives fashioned from various organizational, educational and experience backgrounds. Internal inclusion occurs when managers are supported in valuing a broad range of perspectives, and the complex exchanges that arise. Internal inclusion is a natural outgrowth of considering the organization one person at a time. It may seem that there is some tension with the need to recruit people whose values align with those of the organization. This is not the case as the goal is to seek diversity of perspective but alignment of values.

External inclusion means building partnerships with other organizations that complement and expand the capabilities of the organization.

The benefits of such an approach were explored in Chapter 10. External inclusion seeks to expand the capabilities and horizons of the internal workforce by forging partnerships with other organizations that bring complementary workforce needs and capabilities. This strengthens the organization and enhances the sense of affiliation that people feel for it.

Community inclusion is important because organizational purpose extends beyond immediate shareholder return, to address other constituencies served by the organization. Organizations are tasked with improving the lot of all the constituencies they serve, recognizing that the impact varies by constituency. The impact is high for employees and shareholders and less for the general community. Community inclusion contributes to the long-term health of the organization and active engagement in the community enhances the degree of employee affiliation. Community support can take many forms: it may mean supporting educational institutions, it may mean supporting employment of disadvantaged groups, or it may mean supporting the local community infrastructure. It can involve financial support, or more importantly direct involvement of employees in community service. This leads to a bond between the individual and the community with the organization acting as a bridge.

The fourth form of inclusion is that of global inclusion, which addresses a greater good. This continues to be a world of great disparity, with many people operating in survival mode on the Maslow Hierarchy. This is in spite of abundant material wealth and excess of basic support needs such as food, in developed countries. This presents major ethical problems and it has practical negative consequences for organizations. It places limits on the purchasing capability of potentially large consumer populations and the ability to access an extended workforce in many parts of the world. In other words it places both resource supply and product and service demand limits on organizations. While no single organization can redress these inequities, each organization can take steps to address these issues. For example, by supporting the provision of educational resources and providing employment in disadvantaged areas, organizations both increase the purchasing power of local residents, and increase their ability to support themselves and function independently. Ultimately this opens a path that allows people to discover and express who they are, rather than simply surviving.

These four components of inclusion can be integrated into the core of the organization, leading to a transcending purpose that is ennobling for everyone in it. This builds a deep sense of affiliation. These are complex and weighty issues for leaders and HR that do not vanish with the latest quarterly earnings report. Rather they serve as a reminder to focus on the importance of reaching for a greater sense of purpose. What does this mean for leadership behavior?

These are factors to consider:

- Gather strength from isolation
- Live with authenticity
- Create and nurture a sense of purpose
- Create an environment in which people flourish
- Live the principles of inclusion.

One of the challenges of leadership is that with it comes a sense of isolation and a degree of loneliness. Everyone in an organization carries much leadership responsibility, and the more effective the organization, the more this is distributed throughout the organization. However, some in the organization are charged more directly with igniting and sustaining the flame of organizational purpose. The members of this group in particular can suffer from a sense of isolation, as there are social and political barriers that can inhibit open communication. While it is a key responsibility of leaders to minimize these barriers, some isolation is also a natural part of the role. Leaders need to gather strength from the greater isolation that comes from their role. This means taking and using reflective time. Indeed one observer identified this self-reflection as a key distinguishing characteristic of leaders.

Developing a clear sense of self-knowledge and living with authenticity begins with self-understanding, or listening to ourselves, and continues with understanding others, which means listening to them. Discerning our right livelihood, as Sinetar (1989) expressed it, is one of the most crucial challenges for leaders in today's world. There are many pressures to stray from this path, pressures from others within the organization and from external constituencies. These pressures may come from the financial community demanding actions to enhance short-term performance that are detrimental to long-term capability. They may come from within the organization to distribute disproportionate rewards. They may come from other organizations or from customers seeking unreasonable, preferential treatment. The courage to resist such pressures and to hold true to a purpose of deeper meaning and transcending value is a measure of true leadership.

This is the basis for creating and nurturing a sense of purpose that ennobles others and builds strength and affiliation in the organization.

This sense of purpose will light the way for the organization and all those in it. It will be a beacon standing firm in the community, forming a rallying point for other organizations and creating a movement that can extend far. It will be a beacon that can unite across generations, unite across backgrounds and overcome the irritations and concerns of our daily lives. It will be a beacon that continues to shine and grow in our changing world. It will be a beacon that helps create an environment in which people flourish. Leaders have the opportunity to build organizations that ignite and nurture this spark in each person. In doing this they are closing the gap between our reality and our potential. It is this responsibility of leadership that transcends the petty vanities of everyday life.

Interwoven with this responsibility is the importance of living the principles of inclusion on a daily basis. I have been fortunate to see such principles expressed by many of those people with whom I have shared my life. It has been expressed as an acceptance of others whose views are different and sometimes conflicting, an acceptance of others who are less or more fortunate in their material possessions, an acceptance of others who struggle to uphold their principles succeeding sometimes but not always. This sense of inclusion is a powerful uniting and inspiring force in organizations.

This leads to some final thoughts on awakening the music. The great gift that we have been given is the opportunity to cause and to experience such an awakening in ourselves and in others. Awakening the music in us may not come as an epiphany, but it will certainly transform lives over time. This is an opportunity to reach out and move closer to the expression of who we are. Creating organizations that foster alignment of individual and organizational needs, rather than elevating one at the expense of the other, strengthens the contribution that people make and the sense of affiliation they feel. The lack of opportunity for people to do their best work is a primary reason for their looking outside an organization. It is in closing the gap between current fulfillment and aspirations that productivity and innovation can flourish. This is our equivalent of continuous-aim firing. As with continuous-aim firing the steps that are needed to close the gap are deceptively simple. They include providing resources to help people understand who they are and where they can do their best work, providing mechanisms to ensure that opportunities are known and readily accessible, and opening the organization to external constituencies. But just as with continuous-aim firing, parochial considerations can create internal barriers that limit both individual and organization potential.

It falls to leadership and HR to take a stand and to have the courage to overcome these barriers. To create the island that nourishes and prospers building on the strengths of all inhabitants. It falls to leadership and HR to step out and define the relationships the organization needs with each segment of the workforce and to create approaches that honor and strengthen such relationships. It falls to leadership and HR to look not only at the needs of today but also at the needs of tomorrow so that the legacy left by the organization is a legacy for generations to come. It falls to leadership and HR to know and respect the various constituencies that are part of the extended organizational family. To have the courage to balance equitably the needs of these constituencies, knowing that in so doing some will find fault. It falls to leadership and HR to stand tall in creating our new, brave organizational world in which each person is respected, in which partnerships are built and in which local and global communities are strengthened.

These may seem lofty ideals, beyond our reach. They are not. Our growing communication and information capabilities are freeing us from the tyranny of the production line, just as it in turn freed us from dependency on the soil. In moving into this new, brave world, leaders and HR are at the forefront of a movement that has lasting impact on individuals, organizations and the community. That begins as a small eddy and becomes a giant river. That begins as a single note and becomes a magnificent symphony.

Appendix: Questionnaire to Gather Input across Organizations

This questionnaire was used to gather input at a series of briefings, on participants' perspectives about their work lives and organizations. It was constructed as follows:

Please complete the following by entering the requested information or circling the appropriate item:

Today's date: _____ Location of this briefing: _____

1. Number of employees in your organization: _____

2. Primary business or functional area for your organization (e.g., healthcare, education, communications): _____

3. Number of years you have been with your current organization: _____

4. Number of organizations for which you have been employed on a full-time basis since completing your first degree or leaving high school:
1 2 3 4 5 6 7 8 9 10 or more

5. On a scale of 1 to 7 with 1 not important and 7 very important, how would you rate the importance of retaining employees as an issue for your organization today:

Not Important   Very Important
        1 2 3 4 5 6 7

6. What was the attrition rate for employees voluntarily leaving your organization in the last fiscal year (100 × number of employees leaving voluntarily during last fiscal year/total number of employees at mid-year): _____ %

7. On a scale of 1 to 7 with 1 being strongly disagree and 7 being strongly agree, please respond to the following statements:

a. I can articulate the primary purpose of my organization.

Strongly Disagree   Strongly Agree

       1 2 3 4 5 6 7

b. I am clear about my own career aspirations.

Strongly Disagree   Strongly Agree

       1 2 3 4 5 6 7

c. My aspirations are aligned with my organization's purpose.

Strongly Disagree   Strongly Agree

       1 2 3 4 5 6 7

d. My organization's purpose is inspiring to me.

Strongly Disagree   Strongly Agree

       1 2 3 4 5 6 7

e. I feel a strong sense of affiliation with my organization.

Strongly Disagree   Strongly Agree

       1 2 3 4 5 6 7

8. At this time, I anticipate remaining with my organization for:

a. Less than 1 year

b. 1–2 years

c. 2–3 years

d. 3–4 years

e. 4–5 years

f. 5–10 years

g. More than 10 years

If you are comfortable providing this information, please indicate:

Your name: _____

Your organization: _____

Your tel. no.: _____

Your e-mail address: _____

Thank you very much for your input!

Nomenclature

a	Attrition rate (% per year)
b	Slope of line linking attrition rate to HR spending
c_1	Constant
c_2	Constant
c_3	Constant
c_4	Constant
c_5	Constant
d	Constant
d_h	Constant in line linking attrition rate to HR spending
e	Individual expertise
f	Fulfillment
h	HR expenditures per employee
i	Net income per employee
j	Number of reporting levels in an organization
j_k	Constant $(= c_3{}^*c_1)$
k	Constant
k_b	Constant
k_d	Constant
k_i	Constant

NOMENCLATURE

k_l	Constant
k_s	Constant
k_u	Constant
k_0	Constant $(= n*p*k*100)$
k_1	Constant $(= o*k*100)$
k_2	Constant $(= A_E*k_3/100)$
k_3	Constant
n	Knowledge/time
o	Obsolescence/time
p	Capability
q	Constant $(= c_4*c_1)$
r	Discount rate (%)
s	Span of control (number of people reporting to a manager)
s_a	Average salary
t	Time
t_t	Tenure (time with the organization)
t_{tm}	Tenure at optimum value creation
u	Utility
v	Value created per person
v_m	Optimum value created per person
w	Number of people in the organization at any time
x	Investment in the individual by the organization
A_E	Cost of attrition per person
A_i	Aspirations
A_v	Annual cost of attrition as % of company value
A_{vT}	Cost of attrition as a % of company value in perpetuity
B	Benefit from reduced attrition due to investing in HR
B_i	$\exp(-A_i*k_b)$
C_a	Annual cost of attrition
C_i	$k_s - k_d*x$
C_{aT}	Total cost of attrition in perpetuity
C_0	Annual cost of attrition with no investment in HR
D_i	Constant $(= -(k_0 - k_1)/100)$
E	Total number of employees in an organization
E_i	Constant $(= k_2/100)$

Nomenclature

F	Cost added due to investing in HR
G_i	Constant $(= D_i/v_m)$
H_i	Constant $(= E_i/v_m)$
L_i	Constant $(= C_i/v_m)$
N	Number of organizations
R^2	Coefficient of determination
V	Organizational value (net present value of future earnings)
V_a	Net value from investing in HR
ΔGDPC	% change in Real GDP per capita (based on the workforce)
ΔUR	% change in unemployment rate

References

Accel-Team. http://www.accel-team.com/motivation/hawthorne_02.html.

Adler, Paul and Seok-Woo Kwon. 2002. "Social Capital: Prospects for a New Concept." *The Academy of Management Review* 27(1) (January): 17–40.

Ahr, Paul and Thomas Ahr. 2000. *Overturn Turnover*. St. Louis, MO: Causeway Publishing Company.

Alexander, Christopher, Sara Ishikawa and Murray Silverstein. 1977. *A Pattern Language*. New York: Oxford University Press.

Anders, George. 2001. "John Chambers, After the Deluge." *Fast Company* (July): 100–111.

Becker, Brian, Mark Huselid and Dave Ulrich. 2001. *The HR Scorecard*. Boston: Harvard Business School Press.

Benhamou, Eric. 1998. "Building a New Kind of Company for the New Economy." Keynote address at the Career Action Center's 16th annual Pinnacle luncheon.

Beveridge, William. 1957. *The Art of Scientific Investigation*. New York: Vintage Books.

Bliss & Associates, Inc. 2000. *Business Costs and Impact of Turnover*. Wayne, NJ: Bliss & Associates.

Bolton, Robert. 1986. *People Skills*. New York: Simon and Schuster.

Box, George, William Hunter and Stuart Hunter. 1978. *Statistics for Experimenters*. New York: John Wiley and Sons.

Brainy Quote. http://www.brainyquote.com/quotes/quotes/s/q136790.html.

Brandt, Richard. 1998. "On the Future of Communication and the Failure of

Deregulation: President and CEO of Cisco Systems Inc. John Chambers." *Upside* (October): 123–133.

Brewer, Betsy. 1996. "Vocational Souljourn Paradigm." Presentation to John F. Kennedy University Summer Institute, Walnut Creek, California (July).

Brewi, Janice and Anne Brennan. 1989. *Mid-Life Psychological and Spiritual Perspectives*. New York: The Crossroad Publishing Company.

Buckingham, Marcus and Curt Coffman. 1999. *First Break All the Rules: What the World's Greatest Managers Do Differently*. New York: Simon & Schuster.

Bureau of Economic Analysis. U.S. Department of Commerce. http://www.bea. doc.gov/bea/dn/nipaweb/TableViewFixed.asp?SelectedTable=4&First Year=2000&LastYear=2001&Freq=Qtr.

Bureau of Labor Statistics. U.S. Department of Labor. ftp://ftp.bls.gov/pub/special.requests/lf/aat1.txt.

Business Wire. 1998. "Employees Speak Out: New Study Links Employee Satisfaction and Retention to Job Training" (September 7).

Caple, John. 1991. *The Ultimate Interview*. New York: Main Street Books.

CASA. http://www.nationalcasa.org/casa/about.htm.

Daniels, William and John Mathers. 1997. *Change-ABLE Organization*. Mill Valley, CA: ACT Publishing.

Delery, John and Harold Doty. 1996. "Modes of Theorizing in Strategic Human Resource Management: Tests of Universalistic, Contingency, and Configurational Performance Predictions." *Academy of Management Journal* 39(4): 802–835.

DePree, Max. 1992. *Leadership Jazz*. New York: Dell Publishing.

Dilbert Zone. http://www.unitedmedia.com/comics/dilbert/scott/birth/birth15. html.

Dobson, Terry. 1994. "A Kind Word Turneth Away Wrath." In *The Awakened Warrior*, ed. Rick Fields (pp. 153–156). New York: G.P. Putnam's Sons.

Donlon, J. 1998. "The Fourth Comes Forth." *Chief Executive (U.S.)* 138 (October): 26.

Drizin, Mark. 2000. "Commitment to the Workplace—The 2000 Global Employee Relationship Report Benchmark." Hudson Institute/Walker Information. Presentation.

Elsdon, Ron. 2002. "Career Counseling in the Future World of Work." *CCDA News* XVII(1) (January): 2, 11.

Elsdon, Ron and Seema Iyer. 1999. "Creating Value and Enhancing Retention Through Employee Development: The Sun Microsystems Experience." *Human Resource Planning*. 22(2): 39–47.

———. 2000. "Measuring the Impact of Career Development on an Organization, Sun Microsystems Inc." Case Study in *In Action Performance Analysis and Consulting*, ed. Jack J. Phillips (pp. 53–66). Alexandria, VA: ASTD.

Elsdon, Ron and Deborah Warner. 1998. "Measuring the Impact of Career and

References

Human Resource Services on Organizations." Project in Career Development M.A. Orinda, CA: John F. Kennedy University.

Fast Company. 2001a. "Peoplepalooza." (January): 86, 97, 108, 122.

————. 2001b. www.fastcompany.com/keyword/email45.

Fortune. 2001a. http://www.fortune.com/lists/F500/index.html.

————. 2001b. http://www.fortune.com/fortune/bestcompanies.

Foster, Richard. 1986. *Innovation: The Attacker's Advantage*. New York: Summit Books.

Fullerton, Howard Jr. 1999. "Labor force participation: 75 years of change, 1950–98 and 1998–2025." *Monthly Labor Review* (December): 3–12.

Great Quotations. http://www.cyber-nation.com/victory/quotations/authors/quotes_graham_martha.html.

Halstead, Ted. 1999. "A Politics for Generation X." *The Atlantic online*. (August). http://www.theatlantic.com/issues/99aug/9908genx.htm.

Hamel, Gary. 2000. *Leading the Revolution*. Boston: Harvard Business School Press.

Hoffman, Dustin. 1999. Interview on *Fresh Air* (National Public Radio). November 5.

Horace. 1997. "Ode Book ii–Number 10, to Licinius." In *The Odes of Horace*, trans. David Ferry. New York: Farrar, Straus, and Giroux.

Humax. http://www.humaxnetworks.com/.

Inscape Publishing. 2002. Innovate with C.A.R.E. Profile. Minneapolis.

International Survey Research. 2000. *The American Workforce—Past, Present, and Future*. (May). Chicago: International Survey Research.

Izzo, John and Pam Withers. 2000. *Values Shift*. Vancouver: FairWinds Press.

Janz, Tom, Lowell Hellervik and David Gilmore. 1986. *Behavior Prescription Interviewing*. Boston: Allyn and Bacon, Inc.

Johnson, Carla. 2001. "Hit the Floor Running, Start the Cart . . . and Other Neat Ways to Train New Employees." November 28. http://www.shrm.org/emt/articles/default.asp?page=01wintercov.htm.

Joint Venture: Silicon Valley Network: http://www.nationalcasa.org/casa/about.htm.

Jung, Carl. 1976. *Modern Man in Search Of A Soul*. Orlando, FL: Harcourt.

Kirkpatrick, Donald. 1998. "Great Ideas Revisited." In *Another Look at Evaluating Training Programs*, comp. D. Kirkpatrick (pp. 3–8). Alexandria, VA: ASTD.

Levine, Rick, Christopher Locke, Doc Searls and David Weinberger. 2000. *The Cluetrain Manifesto*. Cambridge, MA: Perseus Books.

Levinson, Daniel. 1978. *The Seasons of a Man's Life*. New York: Ballantine Books.

Lowman, Joseph. 1995. *Mastering the Techniques of Teaching*. San Francisco: Jossey-Bass Inc.

Massachusetts Institute of Technology: http://web.mit.edu/tlo/www/startups Wasada1299.pdf.

REFERENCES

Michaels, Ed, Helen Handfield-Jones and Beth Axelrod. 2001. *The War for Talent*. Boston: Harvard Business School Press.

Military Children & Youth: http://military-childrenandyouth.calib.com/net_show.htm.

Mitchell, Terence, Brooks Holton, Thomas Lee, Chris Sabylnski and Miriam Erez. 2001. "Why People Stay: Using Job Embeddedness to Predict Voluntary Turnover." *Academy of Management Journal* 44(6): 1102–1121.

Morison, Elting. 1966. *Men, Machines and Modern Times*. Cambridge, MA: The M.I.T. Press.

Moyers, Bill. 1995. *The Language of Life*. New York: Bantam Doubleday Dell Audio Publishing.

Myers, Isabel Briggs and Peter Myers. 1995. *Gifts Differing*. Palo Alto, CA: Davies-Black Publishing.

Nashville Career Advancement Center: www.careeradvancement.org/oprymills/default.asp.

National Business Incubator Association: http://www.nbia.org/whatis.html.

Niehaus, Richard and Paul Swiercz. 1996. "Do HR Systems Affect the Bottom Line. We Have the Answer." *Human Resource Planning* 19(4): 3.

O'Malley, Michael. 2000. *Creating Commitment*. New York: John Wiley & Sons, Inc.

Outsourcing Institute. 2000. *Outsourcing Index 2000*. Jericho: The Outsourcing Institute.

Palmer, Parker. 2000. *Let Your Life Speak*. San Francisco: Jossey-Bass Inc.

Parsons, Frank. 1909. *Choosing a Vocation*. New York: Houghton Mifflin.

Peter, Laurence. 1979. *Peter's Quotations*. New York: Bantam Books.

Peters, Thomas and Robert Waterman Jr. 1982. *In Search of Excellence*. New York: Harper and Row.

Phillips, Jack. 1997. *Return on Investment*. Houston: Gulf Publishing Company.

Reichheld, Frederick. 1996. *The Loyalty Effect*. Boston: Harvard Business School Press.

Rhodes, Lynn. 1999. Presentation to San Ramon Valley United Methodist Church, November 7.

Rifkin, Jeremy. 1995. *The End of Work*. New York: G.P. Putnam's Sons.

Rogers, Carl. 1942. *Counseling and Psychotherapy*. New York: Houghton Mifflin.

———. 1995. *On Becoming a Person*. New York: Houghton Mifflin.

Rosenfeld, Jill. 2001. "Free Agents in the Olde World." *Fast Company* (May): 136–140.

Rubin, Harriet. 2001. "Roger Cass The Last Optimist." *Fast Company* (July): 88–98.

Sharf, Richard. 1992. *Applying Career Development Theory to Counseling*. Pacific Grove, CA: Brooks/Cole.

Sheridan, John. 1985. "A Catastrophe Model of Employee Withdrawal Leading to Low Job Performance, High Absenteeism, and Job Turnover During

References

the First Year of Employment." *Academy of Management Journal* 28(1): 88–109.

Sheridan, John and Michael Abelson. 1983. "Cusp Catastrophe Model of Employee Turnover." *Academy of Management Journal* 26(3): 418–436.

Sinetar, Marsha. 1989. *Do What You Love, The Money Will Follow: Discovering Your Right Livelihood*. New York: Dell Publishing Company, Incorporated.

Sobel, Dava. 1999. *Galileo's Daughter*. New York: Penguin Books.

Society for Human Resource Management (SHRM). 2001. "The New Workforce: Generation Y." *Workplace Visions* (2): 2–8.

Sorensen, Theodore. 1988. *Let The Word Go Forth. The Speeches, Statements, and Writings of John F. Kennedy 1947 to 1963*. New York: Delacorte Press.

Tapscott, Don, Alex Lowy and David Ticoll (eds.). 1998. *Blueprint to the Digital Economy*. New York: McGraw-Hill.

Tauscher, Ellen: http://www.house.gov/tauscher/press/05-02-00.htm.

Tushman, Michael. 1993. "Managing Strategic Innovation and Change." Executive Program Graduate School of Business Columbia University. (May).

Uhl, V. and A. Hawkins. 1971. *Technical Economics for Engineers*. AIChE Continuing Education Series. New York: American Institute of Chemical Engineers.

U.S. Census Bureau. *http://www.census.gov/population/www/projections/natchart .html*.

Varian, Hal. 1979. "Catastrophe Theory and the Business Cycle." *Economic Inquiry* XVII: 14–28.

Ward, Dan, Thomas Bechet and Robert Tripp (editors). 1994. *Human Resource Forecasting and Modeling*. New York: The Human Resource Planning Society.

Watson Wyatt. 2000. Strategic Rewards 1999/2000 Supplemental Study of Top Performing Employees. Washington, DC: Watson Wyatt.

Whyte, David. 1996. *The Heart Aroused*. New York: Bantam Books.

Williamson, Edmund. 1939. *How to Counsel Students: A Manual of Techniques for Clinical Counselors*. New York: McGraw-Hill.

Wright, Patrick, Gary McMahan and Abagail McWilliams. 1994. "Human Resources and Sustained Competitive Advantage: A Resource-Based Perspective." *International Journal of Human Resource Management* 5(2): 301–326.

Zemke, Ron. 2001. "Generations at Work." *Executive Update online!* (February). http://www.gwsae.org/executiveupdate/2001/february/generations. htm.

Zunker, Vernon. 1998. *Career Counseling Applied Concepts of Life Planning*. Pacific Grove, CA: Brooks/Cole.

Index

About the Author

RON ELSDON specializes in the workforce development and career fields through organizational consulting, individual coaching, career counseling, and lecturing. He is a Principal in New Beginnings Career and College Guidance. As Director of Retention Services for DBM, and in prior leadership roles, he has worked extensively with U.S. and international organizations.